The A-Z of School Improvement

Also available from Bloomsbury Education:

Creating Tomorrow's School Today
Richard Gerver

Inspirations: A collection of commentaries and quotations to promote school improvement
Tim Brighouse and David Woods

The Literacy Leader's Toolkit
Graham Tyrer and Patrick Taylor

What Makes a Good School Now?
Tim Brighouse and David Woods

Why Are You Shouting At Us? The dos and don'ts of behaviour management
Phil Beadle and John Murphy

The A-Z of School Improvement

Principles and Practice

Tim Brighouse and David Woods

B L O O M S B U R Y
LONDON • NEW DELHI • NEW YORK • SYDNEY

Published 2013 by Bloomsbury Education
Bloomsbury Publishing plc
50 Bedford Square, London, WC1B 3DP

www.bloomsbury.com

9781441135667

10 9 8 7 6 5 4 3 2

Typeset by Fakenham Prepress Solutions, Fakenham, Norfolk, NR21 8NN
Printed and bound by CPI Group (UK) Ltd, Croydon, CR0 4YY

This book is produced using paper that is made from wood grown in managed, sustainable forests. It is natural, renewable and recyclable. The logging and manufacturing processes conform to the environmental regulations of the country of origin.

All efforts have been made to seek permission for copyright material, but in the event of omissions the publisher would be pleased to hear from the copyright holders and to amend acknowledgements in subsequent editions.

Thank you to the following for the use of their material:

FIGURES: p.19 'Managing complex change', adapted by Tim Brighouse from Knoster T (1991) presentation at TASH conference, Washington DC. (Adapted by Knoster from Enterprise Group Ltd); p.87 'A framework for leadership' from *Leading in a Culture of Change* by Michael Fullan, Jossey Bass, 2007, p.4; p.139 'Toolkit to improve learning: summary overview' The Sutton Trust, 2011, www. educationendowmentfoundation.org.uk

LONG QUOTES: p.xiii Gabriela Mistral; p.32 Pablo Casals, from *Sorrows and Reflections*; p.81 H.G. Ginott from *Teacher and Child*; p.116 Evidence submitted to the 'National Commissioning of Teaching and America's Future', 1996; p.175 Robert Fried from *The Passionate Teacher*; p.178 'The Average Child' by Ed Buscemi.

THE GREATEST DANGER IS NOT THAT OUR AIM IS
TOO HIGH AND WE MISS IT...

BUT THAT IT IS TOO LOW AND WE REACH IT.

Michelangelo

CONTENTS

ACKNOWLEDGEMENTS

There are too many people to thank. All the good bits in the book are taken from colleagues with whom we have worked. Inevitably most of those are in schools.

So thanks to all the heads and teachers we have met in so many places, but especially those in London and Birmingham and earlier in Solihull and Oxfordshire. Thanks too however, to the heads, teachers and support staff we have met on our travels most recently in Burton on Trent, Barrow, Cumbria, Shropshire, Bucks, York, Redcar and Cleveland, Leeds, Sheffield, and especially West Sussex and Suffolk. Special thanks are owed to Teresa Tunnadine at The Compton School, Rachel Macfarlane at Isaac Newton Academy, Sue John at Lampton School, George Berwick at Ravens Wood School, Chris Owen at Bartley Green School, Delia Smith at the Ark Academy, Jackie Valin at Southfields Community College, Sue Barrett at Bournville Junior, Sarah Rutty at Bankside Primary, Pete White at Brunswick Park Primary School, Chris Taylor at Steyning Grammar School, Niall McWilliams at Carterton Community School, Jill Hudson at Pegasus Primary School, David Lewin at Woodfarm Primary School and the heads and staff of the two schools where we are separately governors in Oxford and Telford. All the above have either provided ideas or given critical feedback on some aspect or another: indeed some have gone far further and suggested sins of omission and commission to our advantage.

Others beyond the school itself have helped too. So thanks to Andy Powell and Susan Piers-Mantell and their friends in Somerset for allowing us to glimpse their extraordinary Learning to Lead programme. Kit Tavinor offered ideas on design and Gina Henderson was, as always, a tower of strength in putting everything together often at short notice.

John Hill deserves recognition for the pioneering work on data which he pioneered twenty years ago in Birmingham and which led to the adoption of Families of Schools both there and later in London and more widely. Indeed his exemplary work perhaps shamed the DfEE – as it was at the time – to get to grips with sharing data with schools and LEAs when they existed.

Finally our thanks to Holly Gardner whose sharp eyes and honest comments have made us reconsider our very rough first draft.

In truth we could have written a book of the thousands of people in and out of schools who have extended our thinking and to whom we owe so much.

The faults of course are ours.

Tim Brighouse and David Woods

INTRODUCTION

We began teaching in secondary schools in the 1960s – we both taught history in schools which were in the same part of the world, on the Derbyshire/Cheshire border. We didn't meet then and we have each travelled a long journey in education practice and leadership since, including in Tim's case being a Director of Education in both Oxfordshire and Birmingham as well as the First Commissioner of London's Schools. For David this time has included leading the Government's Education Department team of advisers and being the Chief Adviser for both Birmingham and London Schools. We both had short periods working in higher education where we acquired a respect for research and for those who have thought long and hard about educational theory and philosophy.

We met in Birmingham where we first worked together and became fascinated with school improvement in practice. It was very unusual for a local authority then to be as focused as Birmingham was on school improvement. We had a theory, namely that if we could establish a shared map and language of school improvement, focus publicly on what was good while dealing expeditiously and quietly with what was not good enough, talk endlessly about 'improving on previous best' and use data to measure our progress, we could multiply the number of schools that improved. This was, as we say, an unusual approach then. We think that the evidence from Birmingham and London where we worked together later, suggests the approach can be successful if you are lucky enough to have sufficiently talented people who work flat out and share more or less the same conviction.

We can both look back individually therefore on almost 50 years of educational service from when school effectiveness and school improvement were hardly researched and discussed at all, to a period over the last 20 years or so which has seen many radical changes and initiatives designed to improve schools. These have included a national curriculum, a national assessment system with published data, OfSTED inspections, Excellence in Cities, the National Strategies, various National Challenges and the creation of a National College of School Leadership.

We have charted the impact of some of these changes and the response of schools generally to the challenges of school improvement through previous publications including *What Makes a Good School?* (1991), *How to Improve Your School* (1999), *Inspirations: A collection of commentaries and quotations to promote school improvement* (2006) and *What Makes A Good School Now?* (2008). We have also edited several collections of ideas from Birmingham and London schools that we have called 'butterflies' to stimulate school improvement, and written many articles and think pieces in various education journals. As well as this Tim Brighouse has written two very influential pamphlets on *Essential Pieces: The Jigsaw of a Successful School* (2006) and *How Successful*

Headteachers Survive and Thrive (2007). Through all these publications, speaking at numerous education conferences throughout the country, and most crucially visiting thousands of schools and many more classrooms to observe and discuss practice, we have gathered the information and ideas to produce this *A–Z of School Improvement*. There are 138 entries; often these are very short summaries of key aspects of school improvement, others have further references for the interested reader. The book is illustrated by quotations, 'butterflies' and extended pieces of prose and poetry that have given us inspiration.

We really like butterflies partly because they derive from chaos theory which on a bad day should resonate with any school leadership team. The chaos theory was that if sufficient butterflies whirr their wings in the Amazonian rainforests then they can create a climate change which might lead to a tornado in North America; in other words some very small actions can have a disproportionate effect. If therefore we could identify practices in schools which have a large impact, they would be worth focusing on, not least because schools are places where lots of energy is expended. David Hargreaves calls them 'low effort' and 'high impact' interventions: in short they have high leverage.

We began collecting such butterflies in our visits to Birmingham schools in the 1990s and carried on in the next decade in London. We have scattered a few throughout this book showing how they can have an impact on any aspect of school life, from some small organizational practices to everyday life in the classroom.

Of course, like the original concept, our butterflies are context affected. So to work they depend on the people who take them up and the context in which they deploy them. Moreover what can be a 'butterfly' for one person might, as we used to joke with heads, turn into a 'hornet' for another.

It is for the individual to decide whether any particular one butterfly is right for them, but we are convinced that there will be some out there that will make a big difference and have a significant impact. Indeed we know schools which have made their own collections because they are committed to school improvement.

This is not a book about the school system as a whole or how governments can and do help or hinder school improvement. Nor is it a book to be read as a whole. It is a book specifically about school improvement, which can be defined as 'a systematic and sustained effort aimed at making changes that accomplish educational goals more effectively and enhance student outcomes, as well as continuing to strengthen the school's capacity to make and sustain further improvements'. School improvement is a journey whose path is always under construction. As a guiding compass and map we have spent many years championing a framework of school processes which, if we learn ever more about each of them, is likely to help any school to get better. They are as follows:

- *Leading at every level* – while recognizing the need for different styles in different circumstances and at different times.

- *Managing* – again at different levels, ensuring that everybody plays their part in getting the detail right.
- *Learning, teaching and assessing* – as part of a broad and balanced curriculum; the bread, butter and jam of schooling at the forefront of everybody's efforts.
- *Developing staff* – not just teachers but all staff, by making good appointments, providing thorough inductions and extensive continued professional development, which combines individual and collective need.
- *Creating a fit environment and climate* – visually, aurally, behaviourally and in a way that encourages and stimulates aspiration and learning and embeds ambition.
- *Developing partnerships* – with parents, the community and other schools and networks so that the public place that is the school is accessible to all who might benefit and contribute.
- *Self-evaluating and critically reviewing* – an activity that prompts gradual or great change accepting the challenge of continuous improvement.

To those we would now add an eighth which we think we have not emphasized enough, namely:

- *The involvement of pupils.*

Under 'S is for Student voice' we have outlined what we mean by this. It is accordingly a longer entry and we very much hope that the book will provoke thought and action by school leaders on this aspect – indeed on any aspect which will take our understanding of school improvement further.

In very broad terms there are two main approaches to school improvement. The first can be termed as the pragmatic and rational approach in a system of increasing accountability. This approach stresses the need to set a range of targets and to monitor progress rigorously. Gaps between performance and requirements are identified and the steps to close these gaps are set out in action plans. Success is then measured in terms of the achievement of these targets. The danger with over-reliance on this approach is that a set of targets can be achieved, but it's possible that no real and lasting changes take place. The second approach can be termed as creative, stressing ownership and personal motivation. This places attitudes, feelings and ways of working collaboratively at the heart of any improvement process. Changes are collectively endorsed and the individual's contribution to school improvement is encouraged and developed. The danger of relying on this strategy alone is that there may be little change in terms of students' attainment and achievement, but only a generalized sense of feeling better, with a tenuous link to school improvement.

The challenge for schools is to use both of these approaches and to find a judicious balance that fits the situation of the school. Which brings us to the most important message of all: 'the situation of the school'. In writing this book we are deeply conscious of the importance of context – urban and rural schools, small and large schools, schools that serve a particular phase or type of education and schools at different points on their improvement journey. What may work well in one school at a certain time doesn't necessarily work at another time and in a different place.

Nevertheless we believe that much in this book is relevant and challenging to all schools in their constant endeavours to improve on their previous best performance. We are also conscious that by writing it we will be defined by what we include and prioritise and by what we leave out. We have unashamedly made our own collection and expressed our own views about school improvement. The reader will notice that we have strong views, beliefs and values about the moral purpose and culture of schools based on equity, social justice and unshakeable principles, and about the importance of a common language and a shared ethos. We stress throughout, the crucial importance of developing an optimistic, energising learning environment, embedding ambition and success for all.

We recognize that there will be different audiences for the book. We hope of course that the 'professional' audience of senior school leaders, teachers and support staff will find it very useful as a source of reference and that various entries will stimulate discussion and debate and help schools refine and change their practice to accelerate their journey of improvement. As governors of various schools ourselves, we hope that the book will also help governing bodies in their central task of both supporting and challenging their schools to improve further. We also hope that parents will find it a helpful resource as it explains some of the 'jargon' of educational practice guiding them so they are better able to support their children. Therefore there are some entries that are simple explanations which will seem obvious and unnecessary to experienced school leaders and governors. They can skip those entries. In any case this is not a book to be read as a whole. It is rather one, we hope, that the above groups of people will enjoy dipping into and will regard it as a collection that will encourage and stimulate them to continue to help all our schools achieve ever greater success.

We think that the Gabriela Mistral quotation below is the best justification for tireless attention to school improvement.

Mankind owes to children the best it has to give.
Their life is fragile.
If they are to have a tomorrow
Their needs must be met today.
Many things can wait, but not the children.
Now is the time that their bones are being formed.
Their blood composed, and their senses developed.
We cannot answer their 'tomorrow'.
Their name is 'today'.

Gabriela Mistral

Tim Brighouse and David Woods

Acronyms

In education generally, and in school improvement specifically, there are a lot of acronyms that are used often to the bewilderment of parents and even governors; indeed some school staff are not always sure what all these stand for. We suggest that all schools take the trouble to produce a list of all the acronyms they use and place these on the school's website, spell out any acronyms in communications to parents and in the prospectus, and also have a reference list for governors with full explanations. For the record we have set out here all the acronyms in this book although we have also spelt them out in the main text.

Acronym	Meaning
AfL	Assessment for Learning
AST	Advanced Skills Teacher
CPD	Continuing Professional Development
DFE (in previous incarnations DCSF, DfES, DfEE, DES)	Department for Education
FFT (also FFT (D): the level many schools set as their internal benchmark)	Fischer Family Trust
HMCI	Her Majesty's Chief Inspector
GCSE	General Certificate of Secondary Education
GTP	Graduate Teacher Programme
IEB	Interim Executive Board
INSET	In-Service Education and Training
ISV	In-School Variation
ITT	Initial Teacher Training
LLE	Local Leader of Education
NCSL	National College of School Leadership
NLE	National Leader of Education
NQT	Newly Qualified Teacher
NSS	National Support School
OfSTED	Office for Standards in Education
RAG	Red, Amber, Green (a system for tracking progress, based on traffic lights)
RAP	Raising Attainment Plan
RMG	RAP Management Group
RWCM	Reading, Writing, Communication and Mathematics
SDP or SIP	School Development Plan or School Improvement Plan

Acronym	Meaning
SEN or SEND	Special Educational Needs or Special Educational Needs and Disability
SLE	Specialist Leader of Education
SLT	Senior Leadership Team
SMSC	Spiritual, Moral, Social and Cultural education
TA	Teaching Assistant
TDA	Training and Development Agency for Schools
TES	Times Educational Supplement
VLE	Virtual Learning Environment

An alphabet soup of school improvement

The diagram below gathers together some mnemonics of school improvement related to qualities and characteristics grouped under commandments, drivers, learning, 'e factors' and the 'magnificent seven' for progress.

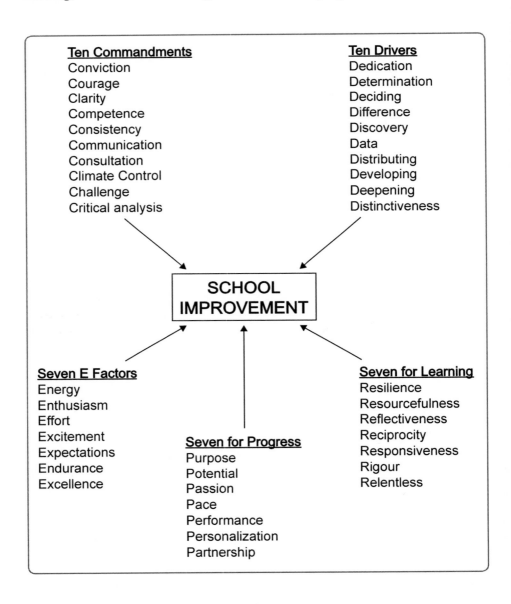

Ten Commandments
Conviction
Courage
Clarity
Competence
Consistency
Communication
Consultation
Climate Control
Challenge
Critical analysis

Ten Drivers
Dedication
Determination
Deciding
Difference
Discovery
Data
Distributing
Developing
Deepening
Distinctiveness

SCHOOL IMPROVEMENT

Seven E Factors
Energy
Enthusiasm
Effort
Excitement
Expectations
Endurance
Excellence

Seven for Progress
Purpose
Potential
Passion
Pace
Performance
Personalization
Partnership

Seven for Learning
Resilience
Resourcefulness
Reflectiveness
Reciprocity
Responsiveness
Rigour
Relentless

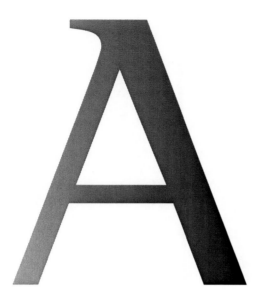

A
B
C
D
E
F
G
H
I
J
K
L
M
N
O
P
Q
R
S
T
U
V
W
X
Y
Z

A is for Action research

 In a research-engaged school research and enquiry would permeate all aspects of its life, including teaching and learning, professional development, school planning and decision-making.
Graham Handscombe

This is still a term that can mystify teachers when all it really means is that teachers systematically record and analyze their practice and seek to make improvements. Teachers are natural researchers in the sense that all teaching is based on enquiry, and the response of the pupils provides ready evidence as to the effectiveness of various teaching and learning approaches. Most teachers, while in the act of teaching, mentally check whether the planned activities are appropriate and how learners are responding. Such pieces of action research, commissioned around collective issues of teaching and learning in the particular context of the school, add immensely to the school's knowledge of what worked and didn't work and provide evidence to make adjustments to policies and practices.

Some examples of action research in schools:

- lesson study

A
B
C
D
E
F
G
H
I
J
K
L
M
N
O
P
Q
R
S
T
U
V
W
X
Y
Z

- partnership teaching
- learning styles
- accelerated learning
- questioning techniques
- attitude to learning
- Assessment for Learning
- peer learning
- classroom layout
- use of learning technologies.

It is a mark of an effective teaching culture for a school to have an expectation that teachers and indeed other staff carry out action research. This can be done either individually or collectively but findings need to be written up as short 'Learning narratives' (see L is for Learning narratives) and disseminated so that learning can be shared and practice monitored and improved. Some schools use their learning platform and their 'Teaching and learning rooms' for easy staff access to action research outcomes.

As part of a culture of self-evaluation it is important to identify from formative and summative assessment groups of pupils not experiencing success in their learning. The engagement of everybody in action research could be applied to these groups and to 'closing the gap', as well as raising standards. Sometimes there is significant in-school variation of performance. What can action research tell us about successful practice which can be applied elsewhere?

Some schools are now at the point where they can describe themselves as a research-engaged school. The Essex Forum for Learning and Research Enquiry (FLARE) has identified four dimensions of the research-engaged school:

- it has a research rich pedagogy
- it has a research orientation
- it promotes research communities
- it puts research at the heart of the school policy and practice.

In such schools all staff are engaged to a greater or lesser extent on a research topic, often in learning pairs or larger groups such as a subject department or year group staff. Some have formalised this into action learning sets with a 'learning leader' appointed to run each set giving staff the choice of joining these at different points throughout the year. The aims of these sets are to embed the notion of the learning centred school, ensure all members of the community are engaged in learning, that all teachers have learning targets in terms of performance management, and provide opportunities for staff growth and to continue to raise the standards of teaching and learning.

In a sense these are 'communities of practice' maximising the potential for learning. There is a level of engagement and a shared repertoire of approaches, techniques and skills that can be developed over a period of time. Essentially the school is providing high quality CPD led by professionals for professionals to improve the quality of teaching and learning for children and young people. This shared process of collective investigation and review builds stimulus and energy in terms of analyzing evidence and planning future developments. All this helps to guarantee the successful implementation of change. Such schools routinely publish and/or put their action research online either in the form of short, learning narratives or longer case studies thereby enriching their culture of self-evaluation. Once schools have done this they are in a position to share the dialogue of school improvement with other schools and organizations such as universities. Some organize an annual learning conference for schools and educationalists in general to share findings and debate key issues of school improvement. In a school led improvement system, action research is an essential part of professional reflection and should be the norm rather than the exception.

Further reading

For those wanting to pursue ideas further, there are many higher education weblinks including www. collegeofteachers.ac.uk. Also, see L is for Learning narratives and, R is for Research.

A is for Acts of unexpected kindness

One of the most overlooked aspects of successful leadership involves what might be called the 'personal touch' – not just remembering people's personal concerns, but in acts of unexpected kindness. Before examining these in particular, it's perhaps worth making one fundamental point. Unless you know people, you are lost. This is why it's much more difficult to be a successful headteacher in your early days, when you don't know anyone. It's also why those destined to be successful heads spend the months before taking up the appointment pouring over photos and the personal files of staff, so that when they arrive at school they have a flying start. I know one head who took this to the lengths of looking at photos and memorising the names of Year 7 and Year 9 pupils 'since they are the ones who, when I arrive, are going to make the most difference to how my early influence on the school is perceived'. One may disagree with her selection or even her motivation, but it is hard to fault her reasoning, intentions or commitment.

Feeling special

This last and most important element of 'expenditure of time' derives from a head's commitment to people and realising that everyone needs to feel special. So a good head will remember staff birthdays and cater for emergencies in their private lives. They will respect privacy and use handwritten notes, or a word in the corridor to express thanks for some small contribution made by a member of staff, and this will provide the energy which sustains collective spirit. One head told me she keeps a collection of cards for birthdays and other events and

A
B
C
D
E
F
G
H
I
J
K
L
M
N
O
P
Q
R
S
T
U
V
W
X
Y
Z

doesn't leave her desk each Friday without sitting down and reviewing the week ahead. Even a thoughtful email will sometimes do! Most successful heads confess to practice like this and most will say that, however spontaneous it may and must seem to recipients, it requires a system – not least in order to avoid the impression that there are 'favourites' and 'outcasts'.

A is for Advanced Skills Teacher (AST)

Advanced Skills Teacher (AST) status is a nationally assessed recognition of excellence based on the following standards:

- excellent outcomes with pupils showing considerable progress in relation to prior and expected attainment
- excellent specialist/subject knowledge – able to advise on the best knowledge and practice and lead innovation
- excellent ability to plan both operationally and strategically to ensure successful learning
- excellent ability to access and evaluate
- excellent ability to advise and support other teachers, including coaching and training both in their own school and in other settings.

Great teachers who want to stay in the classroom have chosen to become ASTs, which can also provide a financially viable alternative to taking the promotion route into leadership and management. The main duty of an AST is to be an excellent teacher and coach other teachers, sharing their good practice supporting professional development not only in their own schools but in the local area.

Although only 1% of teachers in England are ASTs their impact has been considerable both in their own schools but also across the school system. Headteachers who employ them refer particularly to their key roles in managing knowledge and stimulating innovation and the best professional development, as coaches and mentors to other teachers, while promoting collective responsibility for school improvement. Perhaps most important of all, they are the role models for a school in developing the best policies and practice in teaching and learning. They often lead teaching and learning forums, action research and professional development programmes. In terms of their 'outreach' work much depends on the effectiveness of their deployment – whether through local authorities, chains of schools, as part of a National Support School led by a National Leader of Education, and now increasingly as part of a teaching school and its alliances. In some of the best practice we have seen groups of primary schools having access to ASTs specialising in literacy and numeracy or specialist subject ASTs in secondary schools working very effectively with underperforming subject departments.

The White Paper *The Importance of Teaching* (2010) commits the government to re-examine the range of designations for outstanding teachers, including ASTs, to create a single simple designation. We both think that the AST is representative of the need in school improvement to focus on teaching and learning and the role enables teachers to learn from each other.

A is for Appreciative enquiry

 A learning organization is an organization that is continually expanding its capacity to create its future.

Peter Senge

In essence, appreciative enquiry is a major tool to drive forward school improvement and expand the capacity to create an even better future.

It is a way of managing change that originated from business psychology but it now increasingly implemented by education leaders. The starting point is the assumption that organizations have many strengths which they can harness to meet any number of challenges, rather than a deficit model which is always looking at the gap between what the organization needs to do to meet a new challenge and the organizational capacity they see themselves as having.

Thus rather than simply identifying a problem, analyzing the causes, mind mapping the solutions and deciding on a plan of action, the process of appreciative enquiry is as follows:

- appreciate the best of what is in terms of current strengths
- ask what it could be like if you could only have more of the good things identified
- discuss in order to find out what it should be like – a vision of a preferred future
- decide what it will be like and plan accordingly.

This model is particularly attractive since it builds on existing strengths, whereas an over-reliance on problem solving might be always seen as a deficit model and one, therefore, which saps energy rather than creates it. Appreciative enquiry promotes creativity, questioning and dialogue and a collective mentality of growth. Typically, elements of appreciative enquiry will be manifest in teachers and school leaders who frequently exclaim on and celebrate good practice, drawing it to the attention of a wider learning community, and thus encourage speculation about emulating what has been identified. This model aligns well with the best practice of performance management, collective review and self-evaluation.

A
B
C
D
E
F
G
H
I
J
K
L
M
N
O
P
Q
R
S
T
U
V
W
X
Y
Z

> **By appreciating, we make excellence in others our own property.**
> Voltaire

A is for Assessment for Learning (AfL)

> **The process of seeking and interpreting evidence for use by learners and their teachers to decide where the learners are in their learning, where they need to be, and how best to get there.**
> Assessment Reform Group

Assessment for Learning (AfL) is not new, but as richer data has become available, it has become a more important and sharper tool, aided by developments in the technology of pupil tracking. The emphasis here is assessment for learning rather than assessment of learning, so that pupils can improve on their achievements and make progress. There are different ways of achieving this, but the rationale is always the same: you need clear evidence about how to drive up individual attainment and clear feedback for and from pupils on what they need to improve and how best they can do so. Learning intentions need to be shared and criteria for success understood. It is also necessary to involve pupils in the ownership of their learning, through self-assessment and peer-assessment. Good teachers recognize that this is not an occasional activity at the end of a unit or work but an ongoing joint activity between teacher and pupil. Teachers gain information that helps them adjust their practice, while pupils increase their understanding of their progress and of the standard expected.

Although most teachers are familiar with many of the elements of AfL – and respond flexibly to their pupils' needs; unless this is a whole-school priority, supported by effective professional development, and effective systems for tracking pupil progress, the overall impact will be limited.

Good schools make AfL a central core of their teaching and learning, planning and assessment, so that both learner and teacher obtain and use information about progress towards learning goals and how further progress should also be planned. They recognize that AfL is central to everyday classroom practice involving teacher and learners in tasks, questions, reflections, dialogue and decision making. As a key professional skill, AfL is constantly practised and developed through professional development opportunities such as teacher observation. Emphasis is always placed on constructive feedback and guidance about how the pupil should improve but it is worth noting at this point that the same process can be applied to the teacher on their overall performance – how can they move from satisfactory to good or good to outstanding? Good schools also recognize the full range of improvements of all learners and use AfL to enhance all learners' opportunities to achieve their best and to have their efforts recognized.

> **All assessment is a perpetual work in progress.**
> Linda Suskie

Further Reading
One of the best websites for practical ideas for development is http://www.tes.co.uk/teaching-resources/ and for Northern Ireland readers www.nicurriculum.org.uk. See also Paul Black, *Assessment for Learning: Putting it into Practice.*

A is for Attention to detail

> **I take my stand on detail.**
> Edward Thring (Victorian headteacher)

Great schools can sometimes be described in words which summon up such a clear and bold picture of strategic decision making that it can obscure the daily grind of 'getting things right'. Choosing the right things to do and to emphasize is of course crucial but so too is doing things right. Some would say it is the difference between leadership and management but we think that what Edward Thring was getting at here is what we would describe as administrative clarity. So for example, when a school decides to change its school uniform policy and practice it must make sure the suppliers know and that parents are consulted and informed. However, if its website is badly organized it may fail to make the changes explicit, leaving the anxious parents uncertain about the details. The advent of an electronic handbook would make getting the details right easier, especially where consequential changes in school organizational practice are required. This can be communicated in email and postings and underlined at departmental and other staff meetings and briefings.

As one head wisely remarked, 'It is when you change some aspect of school life that you are most at risk of not seeing through consequential change. You can be so easily caught out on changes in exams by exam boards or not anticipating the changes in detailed practices that some change in the OfSTED framework may require'.

Homework and marking, simply because they are such disputed but vital areas of school life, are obvious areas where paying attention to detail can pay dividends. One leader we know likens her practice on paying attention to detail to 'tunnelling right to the bottom of an issue in school life' from time to time just to see what happens at different layers of the organisation.

We know that successful schools have someone tasked with exactly that purpose. One head remarked to us that they have an 'expediter' whose task is to closely examine all aspects of school life to suggest any possible conflicts between everyday school practice and the stated purpose of the school so that very minor but crucial adjustments can be sorted out.

A
B
C
D
E
F
G
H
I
J
K
L
M
N
O
P
Q
R
S
T
U
V
W
X
Y
Z

B is for Backward (or forward) looking organizations

All schools have a dilemma. They have to emphasize the legacy and yet avoid complacency, however great their previous achievements, by pointing to the future. If they rest on their laurels they are in immediate danger of decline. So they need to balance being a future-orientated organization with a justifiable sense of pride in the past. It is a tightrope from which they dare not fall.

Many years ago The Industrial Society issued a placemat for their members which had on one side this image:

A Backward Looking Organization

- Opinion
- Reasons
- Explanations
- Being right
- Looking good

 Leaders are historians who are guardians of the legacy.

On the flip side was another image:

A Forward Looking Organization

- Results
- Action
- Opportunities
- Possibilities
- Relationships

 Leaders are futurologists who are full of hope and optimism.

We have added the comments underneath to reflect on the connection between leadership behaviour and whether a school is backward looking as well as forward looking.

The Industrial Society's placemat however, was meant to be a warning not to be in the first category which was characterized by 'Looking good' being the bottom line, justified because you are right and if challenged further reinforced by 'explanations' and 'reasons' for 'it always being like this' and finally falling back on 'opinion'. The Industrial Society was warning its members to realize that in a fast changing world the successful business would perish if they failed to be 'forward looking'.

The other side of the placemat emphasizes 'relationships' as the bottom line. How that must resonate with school leaders. The first thing you must do when you arrive in a school is to build up relationships with all your key stakeholders especially staff – and particularly if the school or department has been through a difficult patch. After that, conversations will turn to 'possibilities' often with the regretful comment from a particularly keen member of staff that 'if only something were possible and resources available' the particular change being discussed would make such a difference. Of course, the canny leader then makes resources available so the 'opportunity' can be realized with a clear 'action' plan and ultimately 'results'. So for most schools there must be a heavy emphasis on the future, where of course their pupils are going to live.

To maintain balance however, as school leaders we have to also honour the past. The successful school leader has to remind the school community of the past achievements of all those connected with the school. One of our butterflies is the creation over time of an achievement wall where pictures illustrate the deeds of former pupils and members of the school community. One head we know makes sure he and the deputy give an intensive set of presentations to Year 7 classes about the great 'legacy' of the school and the ways in which he is sure the present generation will add to it.

So we are not averse to history – how could we be as we are both originally historians – but we do see the need for schools to keep a good balance and never be so preoccupied by the past that they ever think the school 'has arrived' at its destination, for if they ever do they are surely going down hill!

B is for Balance of skills in the leadership team

'It's all very well to look at Belbin and Myers Briggs,' a colleague remarked ominously one day, 'but I think the infant teacher could teach us a thing or two about what to look for in a leadership team'. After all she assesses her charges' progress in 'listening', 'speaking', 'reading' and 'writing' and while they are doing it, she looks to see whether they are thinking and learning. If we could get that right in our team, she concluded with a smile, 'we would be doing all right.'

She was referring to our practice of putting every new member of staff through the Myers Briggs profile of preferred leadership operational styles, and then inviting an external coach to talk to us about ways in which we could improve our collective efforts. Nothing too unusual in that: most school leadership teams in larger schools do something similar. They use coaches, assess the profile of preferred operational styles of leadership and work on the gaps. They rotate chairing of meetings and encourage departments to do the same. It's standard practice. But we never quite forgot our colleague's remarks. The more we thought about them, the more sense they made and we realized how easy it was to neglect one or the other of the four activities of 'listening', 'speaking', 'reading' and 'writing'. It certainly provides a very useful compass in looking at how successful head teachers spend that precious commodity: time.

Further reading
See K is for Key expenditures of time and T is for Time management.

B is for Breakfast clubs

There are very few schools in challenging areas which would go back on the decision to have pre-school breakfast clubs. Indeed more than one school has declared its intention to earmark part of their 'pupil premium' for the purpose of sustaining the breakfast clubs. Run well, the breakfast club presents a myriad of opportunities including access for pupils and staff to morning papers. Usually, of course, the chosen place for breakfast is the school dining room. One primary school we heard about has a big plasma screen with a real-time connection to an African watering hole where animals can be seen gathering jostling and drinking in the wild – all to the accompaniment of appropriate calming music. Another bedecks its dining room walls with achievements of past pupils. For many schools – primary and secondary – breakfast clubs have become much more than an add-on. These schools see it as a chance to use 'before school' as a time for peer group mentoring, one-to-one coaching and targeted parental consultation in a conducive atmosphere. 'We have seen it as a chance to have an extra planned period in the day' is how one head put it.

Further reading
For those wishing to get started we suggest visiting www.continyou.org.uk who have collaborated with Kelloggs on the issues involved.

B is for Buildings and the environment

The importance of the physical appearance of a school was brought home to us recently, in a rerun of the *Guardian*'s famous 'The school that I'd like' competition, which inspired Edward Blishen's equally famous book of the same title around 30 years earlier. This time the judges sifted the final shortlist of 40 or so from the thousands of school pupil entries the competition had inspired. It was a salutary experience: one of the most vivid was from three Year 8 pupils, all boys. Their school was a 1960s system–built steel-framed cluster of boxed and connected buildings in a sea of tarmac, with a moat of a drive through a small windswept muddy field. The video film left little to your imagination, as the viewers could see the usual squalid lavatories, the desolate flaking corridors and doors and the litter-strewn playgrounds. It was sustained for its ten minutes by a humorous commentary from the 13 year-olds, who had put the film together. The viewers met only one adult, the motherly librarian, working in an environment which contrasted with the rest of the barren school; a welcoming adult in a beautiful oasis of calm. The film ended with a 'zoom out', incorporating all the glass and rotting wooden clad and panelled building with the words, 'In our ideal school, all of this would be the library'.

There isn't much a school can do about the buildings bequeathed to them, although one of our butterflies (see Q is for Quotations) illustrates what one determined headteacher did manage to do something. Moreover, we know of other schools which through judicious planting of Virginia creeper and Wisteria have managed over time to improve the external appearance of their buildings and have regarded the outside tarmac area as a challenge to solve with seats and play opportunities. So it falls also to schools from time to time to have the chance, through small and large capital projects, to affect the general layout and juxtaposition of faculties, libraries and so on. We don't want to lay down any hard and fast propositions about the ideal arrangements on layout beyond arguing for spaces that are large enough for purpose and are a suitable mix of large plenary and smaller break out spaces all suitably linked to e-learning possibilities. Above all, those schools which make the most of these opportunities visit other schools which have interesting features and quiz them about things they would have done differently before making the final decisions.

Further reading
For years the Learning Through Landscapes Trust (www.ltl.org.uk) has provided expertise which has been invaluable to many schools seeking to transform their external environment.

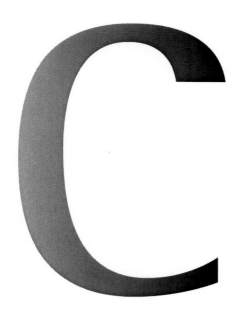

C is for Capability

A dreaded phrase, but just sometimes it cannot be avoided. As one head told us, 'You have tried everything and in the end you have to ask yourself whether it is fair on the pupils to allow things to carry on in the way they are. Of course it applies to all staff but it is especially true for teachers since their impact is so great.'

So you have what Steve Munby, the former Chief Executive of the National College, describes as 'courageous' conversations. When we both heard him use that phrase, we thought guiltily of the number of occasions when we had failed to have such conversations. It is incredibly hard in any case but especially so if the person concerned is decent and committed, but just not competent in their job; not capable. It is doubly difficult for heads because schools are very collegiate places and even though staff may privately think that a head grasping the nettle of a fellow professional's incompetence is doing the right thing, they will keep their thoughts to themselves and be supportive to a colleague in distress.

We think the following sequence may be useful to the head who decides that the courageous conversation has to get more explicit.

- Make sure that you have good systems in place from the start for professional review.

A
B
C
D
E
F
G
H
I
J
K
L
M
N
O
P
Q
R
S
T
U
V
W
X
Y
Z

- Start record keeping early and informally.
- Build an evidence base.
- Give support, but be clear about timescales.
- Choose an advisor and seek advice early.
- Learn the procedures.
- **Check the possibility of informal links with the professional association.**
- Be meticulous in recording.
- Think about the range of evidence.
- Use your team.
- Take formal action when you are secure about the outcome.

We have emboldened one because the reaction of the professional association is crucial.

C is for Case studies

 Make sure you catch people doing something well.

Charles Handy

Schools are constantly managing change and developing best practice. Such is the pace of school life that groups of staff often plan and put into place excellent practice on a variety of topics, but they tend to spend little time on evaluation and very often fail to write up what they have done as a continuous review of implementing successful change.

Some schools, as previously mentioned, have tried to systematize their approach through action research groups of practitioners reporting back either orally at staff conferences or through short, written accounts. A few schools have gone further and committed themselves to annual publications of case studies where they can 'show and tell' about their practice not only for themselves but to other schools. Other schools have joined specific programmes such as 'Going for Great', a London Leadership programme, whereby all the participants have to write a case study of great practice to share which are then all published as a book.

Case studies vary but the most effective are usually structured as follows:

- title and focus area
- aims and rationale
- background / context
- the story: action, events, who was involved, timescale, methods used
- results, outcomes and impact
- reflections and evaluation
- next steps.

Where individual schools have made this a regular practice they tend to publish annually around six case studies in one collection with each case study being around 3,000 words. The case studies are usually whole-school topics such as partnership links, developing literacy, improving attendance, outstanding teaching practice in a particular area or phase, exceptional pupil progress, closing gaps, creativity in the curriculum, and developing inspirational leaders.

Collections of case studies are good evidence of self-evaluation in practice and demonstrate the school's reflective intelligence. They also increase the store of intellectual activity amongst the staff, releasing energy and creating a buzz of excitement around the best practice that makes a real difference to school improvement.

Further reading
See C is for Continuous Professional Development, S is for Staff development, I is for INSET (or Occasional days) and L is for Learning narratives.
Rachel Macfarlane and David Woods (Eds.) *Three collections of case studies from outstanding schools in London: Going for Great, Glimpses of Greatness, Growing Greatness.*

C is for Chains

'Chains' is a word that would not have been in the vocabulary of school improvement ten years ago. It arose from thinking in Tony Blair's Number 10 policy unit. The idea was that the future lay in groups of schools – not through the work of traditional local education authorities (LEAs) – but in groups of semi-autonomous schools led by either the private or charitable or not-for profit sectors. Inevitably, early comparisons were made with chains of shops. The thinking was also based on existing chains of schools whose allegiance was to livery companies or charitable foundations often linked to the church, such as Haberdasher Aske's, Mercers, Woodward, or the King Edward Foundation. More recently the creation of the City Technology Schools in the early 1990s and the Academy movement has created other chains such as Ark, Harris, Ormiston, Oasis, U.L.T, the Emmanuel Trust and the Priory Federation. Many of these are limited in their ambitions to expand to one area of the country. The prospect of more schools becoming academies has spawned others such as EACT and CET. Meanwhile other bodies, for example CfBT which is a not-for-profit company with a relatively long history of providing advisory services to schools, have expanded their roles to become sponsors of academies.

There is also the prospect of church schools becoming academies as the various diocesan authorities consider changing aided school and controlled status for their schools.

One of the most popular and fast growing 'Trust' chains is run by the Co-operative movement. The reason it is popular is that its values most clearly accord with the moral purpose of most schools.

A
B
C
D
E
F
G
H
I
J
K
L
M
N
O
P
Q
R
S
T
U
V
W
X
Y
Z

Those schools which already belong to one of these chains will know how important it is to be comfortable with the values promoted by their parent body. Those contemplating joining chains – and under the changes implemented under the 2011 Education Act it isn't necessarily the case that a school will have any choice in the matter and will be 'forced' to join a chain as an academy because of their previous record of results – also need to be comfortable with the overhead costs charged by the chain and be sure that they are not stepping into a situation where the parent chain will restrict their freedom unduly.

At their best, chains exhibit the qualities of the very best LEAs while at their worst they run the danger of being more controlling than the old style LEA. In 2012 the National College commissioned research which led to a report from Robert Hill who lucidly outlined the pluses and minuses of various approaches by chains. Put simply: the danger of belonging to a large national chain is that you may lose freedom and pay high overheads; conversely the advantage is belonging to a group of schools prepared to share school improvement practice.

Further reading
See F is for Federations and P is for Partnerships.

C is for Challenge

 The best challenge is the best support.
David Woods

There are various definitions of the word 'challenge' ranging from 'to make demands on'; 'to invite or summon someone to do something'; 'to call something into question'; 'to engage in a fight, argument or contest', and to 'stimulate and excite'.

In terms of school improvement the term 'challenge' has been used both as a collective noun and a verb. The collective noun has been prominent in the last ten years or so and describes a collective invitation and aspiration to tackle the status quo and make rapid progress. For example, in 2002 the London Challenge was created initially to bring about a step change in the success of London's secondary schools. The ambition was to develop a system that was not merely good, but excellent – matching the best anywhere. To do that it was necessary to harness the dynamism and innovation already in the system to meet the scale of the challenge and to devise a programme of radical reform. The key elements of the Challenge programme – strong shared values, system leadership and partnership working, school-to-school support, benchmarked data within Families of Schools, 'Keys to Success schools', bespoke school improvement programmes, the teaching and learning syllabus and expert advisers able to broker and commission support – were extended to the City Challenge Programme as a whole, encompassing all schools in Greater Manchester and the

Black Country and subsequently to the National Challenge for secondary schools across England who were struggling to meet floor target attainment standards. The key learning for school improvement from these various Challenge programmes has been forensic attention to data and pupil tracking systems, the importance of Raising Attainment Plans and RAP Management Groups (see R), a relentless focus on teaching and learning, building sustained capacity for change through both school and system leadership enhanced through school-to-school support programmes, and honest, sharp self-evaluation moderated by an external adviser.

In terms of everyday schooling, where challenge is used as a verb and an invitation to do something, there is in improving schools an enhanced understanding of its use as an accelerator of school improvement. To challenge is not necessarily to confront, unless the brutal facts reveal unacceptable performance, but to be robust and rigorous about where progress needs to be made. This may apply to specific areas within the school or the performance management of individuals. The best support systems in schools are based on a disciplined culture of responsibility and accountability. Data is understood by everybody and regularly scrutinised leading, to smart interventions where necessary. The staff are comfortable with the exercise of professional challenge, recognizing that it will bring support where necessary and often the celebration of success. The 'engine' of improvement within the school is clearly understood and success criteria are explicit.

Further reading

See *Evaluation of the City Challenge Programme*, Hutchings et al. London Metropolitan University (DfE). Also, the OfSTED report on London Challenge.

C is for Change

Change is the sum of a thousand acts of re-perception and behaviour at every level of the organization.
John J. Kao

Change is an ever present feature of life in the 21st century. It has prompted numerous books in many disciplines. The most important one from our viewpoint is Michael Fullan's *The Meaning of Educational Change*, together with his many shorter books directed at school improvement. It is that sort of change on which we focus, for as those in schools know only too well change has penetrated the walls of every school on a frequent and continuing basis. Handling it is one of the key issues for teachers, governors and headteachers and their senior leadership teams. Of course it has always been a feature for students as they grapple with the need to learn and demonstrate their learning of new skills, knowledge and their ability to interact in school life as an individual and as a member of a team or community.

...nge affects both the individual and the organization

As an individual there is the need to keep abreast of changes in what is to be taught and how it might best be taught and learned. Continuing Professional Development (CPD) is crucial to this. Nowadays the changes in the immediate availability of knowledge via the internet means that school staff can access a wealth of sites which are very helpful to their task in respect of personal professional learning. Our opening quotation will prompt the teachers among the school staff to look in particular at the implications for pupil or student involvement as the teachers can no longer, if they ever should or could, pose themselves as the arbiters of what is 'the true position' on a particular issue. Students will access the same internet as the teachers! Relevant sections of this book are therefore L is for Library (staff), I is for Induction and C is for CPD.

There are two sorts of change as it affects the school organizationally; minor and complex and each have at least two dimensions: that is whether it is internally or externally imposed. Of these two dimensions the internal is best generated from staff working groups and as a natural outcome of self-evaluation processes. If it is minor, it reflects usually an uncontroversial need to change, which is really learning and change at their best. If it is major and complex change, it will be contested and should be introduced with a promise of review so that any glitches can be ironed out and any strategic changes in direction undertaken. The same is true, of course, for externally imposed or available change. The dangers here are that such change can challenge the principles and values on which the school is apparently united; 'going Academy' can be represented as such a 'value threatening' change. If imposed from the outside it almost always involves a change of leadership and considerable turbulence. If chosen, the wise school leadership team seeks to work with those who are most resistant, involving them in planning some of the detailed implications.

One of the visual representations of complex change we set out on the next page, in the figure entitled 'Managing Complex Change'. It seems to us to be a powerful reminder of the factors those engaging in change need to bear in mind.

Further reading

For those wanting to learn more, we suggest any of the works of Michael Fullan but especially *Leading in a Culture of Change* and we can't resist ending with the excellent Hoffer quotation:

In an age of change, it is the learners who inherit the future while the learned are beautifully equipped to deal with a world which no longer exists.

Eric Hoffer

Managing Complex Change

| Vision | + | Skills | + | Incentives | + | Resources | + | Action Plan | = Change |

| | | Skills | + | Incentives | + | Resources | + | Action Plan | = Confusion |

| Vision | + | | | Incentives | + | Resources | + | Action Plan | = Anxiety |

| Vision | + | Skills | + | | | Resources | + | Action Plan | = Resistance |

| Vision | + | Skills | + | Incentives | + | | | Action Plan | = Frustration |

| Vision | + | Skills | + | Incentives | + | Resources | | | = Treadmill |

Adapted by Tim Brighouse from Knoster T (1991) Presentation at TASH Conference, Washington DC (Adapted by Knoster from Enterprise Group Ltd).

C is for Classroom interventions

 By teaching we are learning.

Seneca

We discuss elsewhere whole-school interventions for school improvement, but at the micro level of teaching and learning teachers are constantly adjusting their practices in terms of what works best for particular classes and groups of children. In this sense they are detectives and researchers balancing such things as teacher led and pupil focused activities, independent learning and collaborative learning, levels of challenge and match of tasks, questioning techniques and feedback to pupils. All the while they are calculating whether learning objectives have been met, what outcomes have been achieved, and how they are making an impact on general attitudes to learning.

In 2008, Professor John Hattie published his book on *Visible Learning*: a synthesis of over 800 meta-analyses relating to successful practice hailed then as the 'holy grail' of teaching research. In 2011, he published an updated version, *Visible Learning for Teachers: Maximizing Impact on Learning*. This newly-updated league table of classroom interventions includes 150 factors and their impact on learning measured by 'effect sizes', which is roughly equivalent to advancing learners' achievement by one year or improving the rate of learning by 50%.

ten influences on educational outcomes were rated as follows:

reported grades. This is when pupils have a 'reasonably accurate erstanding' of their levels of achievement and chances of success based on their past experiences of learning.

2. *Piagetian programmes*. Programmes that aim to set pupils work that is one step ahead of their current level thereby stretching and challenging them.
3. *Responses to intervention*. Programmes and strategies for early intervention, and frequent progress measures for pupils in danger of being left behind.
4. *Teacher credibility*. Characteristics include trustworthiness, competence, dynamism and immediacy. (See T is for Teacher credibility.)
5. *Providing formative evaluation*. Continual evaluation of all aspects of a learning programme to improve implementation and outcomes.
6. *Micro teaching*. Lesson 'post-mortems' where a teacher reviews a video of the teaching to find out what has worked and what has improved or discussions with an observer.
7. *Classroom discussion*. (See P is for Peer learning.)
8. *Comprehensive interventions*. Particularly for learning disabled pupils.
9. *Teacher clarity*. The importance of learning objectives and clear understanding of the process of learning.
10. *Feedback*. A key part of the Assessment for Learning process so that pupils know exactly what they have to do to improve. (See A is for Assessment for Learning.)

Further reading
Phil Beadle's book, *How to Teach*, is also a valuable resource for classroom interventions.

C is for Closing the attainment gap

For most pupils school is a rich and rewarding experience, but it is an uncomfortable fact that at every ability level in the system, pupils from poor backgrounds achieve less well than their counterparts.

The Importance of Teaching, White Paper (2010)

It is absolutely crucial that closing the attainment gap is a fundamental part of the school's purpose and culture. Real school improvement has to be founded on the achievement of <u>all</u> pupils. We want a society where all children and young people achieve their full potential and where the momentum of success, enjoyment and learning continues into their adult lives. The ambition for all children and young people is that they can be helped to progress, achieve and be successful whatever their background and circumstances. However, an examination of the data over the last few years reveals that, despite an overall rise in standards, attainment gaps between groups of children are proving difficult to close in many schools.

In 2011, 78% of pupils in primary schools achieved at least a level 4 in both English and mathematics but only 58% of disadvantaged pupils did the same. Similarly, in terms of progress in English and mathematics, disadvantaged pupils did less well. In secondary schools at GCSE there is an attainment gap of some 27% between the performance of pupils on free school meals (FSM) and the rest, with working class white boys doing particularly badly with a gap of well over 30%.

The most stubborn gap is between the performance of pupils on FSM and the rest, although this varies hugely between schools, with some schools doing exceptionally well. About half of pupils entitled to FSM are to be found in the third of schools with the greatest concentration of disadvantage, and the other half are spread across the other two thirds of schools. In each year 600,000 children enter state education, of these the poorest 80,000 are eligible for FSM. These children do significantly worse than their peers at every stage of their education; they are half as likely to get good GCSEs as the average. More young people from some private schools go to Oxbridge than from the entire cohort of young people on FSM. Although there may be other reasons for this state of affairs, this does dramatically illustrate the issue. This is further compounded by gender differences: boys generally outnumber girls by three to two in terms of low achievement and white working class boys experience persistently poor educational achievement. Educational attainment is influenced by wider factors than just school: for example, what happens in a child's home, their family background, their overall health and well-being. In a number of communities there is a deeply embedded culture of low aspirations strongly tied to long term unemployment and generalized poverty. Other gaps in the system are related to the performance of particular ethnic minority groups (although this varies considerably across schools and the country), children with special needs and looked after children who nationwide have very poor education outcomes.

So what can be done about this? Schools do have a central role to play and we know through benchmarking data that particular schools in the same context can make dramatic differences. Their most effective strategies seem to be:

- Developing a culture of 'success for all' where education is seen as the key to realizing ambition within a climate of high expectations.
- Forensic data tracking of individuals and groups of pupils – regularly analyzed for trends and anomalies used to challenge existing practice and set ambitious targets with individual pupils and targets overall for the school.
- The formation of a vulnerable children's task group, coordinated by a senior leader meeting regularly and monitoring progress and well-being and to provide case studies of best practice.
- Prompt, smart interventions designed to make an immediate difference and prevent pupils from falling behind, such as one-to-one tuition and assertive mentoring.
- Parental engagement and family support in learning and regular consultations on progress.
- Systematic and targeted study support and opportunities before and after school and out of school.

A
B
C
D
E
F
G
H
I
J
K
L
M
N
O
P
Q
R
S
T
U
V
W
X
Y
Z

- The use of ICT to facilitate independent study and home learning.
- Developing pupils' social, emotional and behavioural skills to build character, self esteem and resilience.
- Senior leadership mentoring of particular students (particularly looked after pupils) with regular contact and feedback.
- Offering experiences and opportunities to broaden horizons and instil a sense of high, realistic aspirations.
- Developing effective rewards and incentives to maintain motivation and engagement.
- Having a clear audit trail on funding from the Pupil Premium in terms of value for money.

In 2011, the Education Endowment Foundation (EEF) was established, funded by a grant from the DfE together with other investments and fundraising income. EEF's vision is to break the link between family background and educational achievement, ensuring that pupils from all backgrounds have the opportunity to fulfil their aspirations and make the most of their talents. An EEF Toolkit has been provided, synthesising the considerable evidence that already exists so that practitioners have open access to the research on what works. This will be further developed through funded projects to raise the achievement of disadvantaged children in the country's most challenging schools. Those that are cost effective and replicable will be scaled up.

Further reading

See www.educationendowmentfund.org.uk and *The Extra Mile – How Schools Succeed in Raising Aspirations in Deprived Communities (DCSF)*. Also DCSF, *Breaking the Link between Disadvantage and Low Attainment*, Everyone's Business.

C is for Coaching

 Good schools grow good teachers.

Andy Hargreaves

It is the personal and professional growth of teachers that will have the most impact on pupil development and performance. Teachers teach, but they also have to be advanced learners themselves in order to develop new skills and insights. To help 'grow' good and outstanding teachers, good schools have explicitly identified their own 'coaches' and given them a clear definition of their role. They are drawn from recognized outstanding practitioners who have great credibility in their institution. They may be ASTs, leading or excellent teachers, or specialist leaders of education. As well as being available for 'observation' they are expected to work with other teachers to specifically enhance skills in teaching and learning, particularly helping 'satisfactory' teachers to become 'good', and 'good' teachers to become 'outstanding'. It is recognized that not all outstanding practitioners are good coaches and some training is necessary for this role. Coaching has to get beyond teacher talk and the sharing of ideas to the specific enhancement of skills and practice.

There are four aspects of the teacher as learner which must be seen in combination and which coaches should develop:

- the improvement of specific skills
- the capacity to analyze and reflect upon practice
- the ability to investigate, explore and collect evidence
- the confidence to receive and give ideas and assistance.

A team of practising coaches adds considerably to the capacity of the school to make all of its teaching consistently good or better. They can analyze individual lessons, provide instant feedback and suggest practical strategies for improvement. Staff who are coaches who welcome responsibility, do not have to be chased or watched but take initiative. Coaches can also lead aspects of professional development and are a vital part of any professional development community. Furthermore they can develop action research and make sure that good practice is written up in the form of learning narratives or case studies.

Further reading

For those wishing to see a wider picture there is Sage, *The Complete Handbook of Coaching*. It is expensive in hardback, though cheaper in paperback but it is only worth adding to the staff library if it is something which a school wants to take as a major initiative. See C is for Continuous Professional Development.

 Coaching nurtures a frame of thinking.
Bill Lucas and Guy Claxton

C is for Common language

 Language is the armoury of the human mind and at once contains the trophies of its past and the weapons of its future conquests.
Samuel Taylor Coleridge

Language can make or break a school. Careless talk can sap a school's energy. More than one head we have known has recognized its importance in the story of their school's success: 'It isn't a question of political correctness, as it could reasonably be argued in everyday life, because we all recognize that the language we use in front of the pupils at assembly, in tutorials and lessons and when we take them on trips is an important consideration. So we discuss it as it affects every aspect of school life.'

A
B
C
D
E
F
G
H
I
J
K
L
M
N
O
P
Q
R
S
T
U
V
W
X
Y
Z

If the wrong language is used, at best it can unintentionally convey messages we don't want to send and at worst it subconsciously saps the energy and motivation of even the most optimistic and willing colleagues. So, using 'we' rather than 'I' and 'you' is important, not simply in the spoken word, but in written form too. You can use 'I' when taking the blame and 'you' rather than 'we' when giving praise and celebrating genuine success. It's here that the buzz word of a few years ago – 'personalization' – properly comes in. Letters home, supposedly individual and personal, which refer to 'your son/daughter' and fail to mention names, are impersonal. Of course, general messages of information are different; but here too presentation is important. More than one successful headteacher has told me that the most important job they do is to write the weekly newsletter home, and recognizes how important it is to find the right words and tone.

'Non-teaching' staff is as offensive as it would be to refer to 'non-white' staff or pupils: it betrays a subliminal message about a hierarchy of the value put upon certain tasks and certain people in a bygone age. Continuing to use 'general ability' descriptors to describe 'bands' or 'streams' or referring to the 'bottom set' in their presence (or for that matter at all?) is the modern equivalent to stamping 'remedial' on the inside cover of a book. It will encourage a misplaced notion of general ability, rather than the more generous multi-faceted form promoted by Howard Gardner, to which a school may be saying it subscribes. Using 'learning' instead of 'work' is also a plus rather than a minus: it's amazing what a difference it makes to refer to youngsters getting on with their learning rather than work.

The written language used in job descriptions, the school prospectus, job advertisements, marking, school reports and staff handbooks is as vitally important as the spoken word in assemblies, tutorials, lessons, the corridors and the playground. All meetings are redolent with implied messages in what is said and in the body language of participants.

In short, language is a topic worth having a knowledgeable outsider check from time to time. Or perhaps it's one for the School Improvement Group.

 One of the simplest and at the same time most profound ways in which we signal the degree of empathetic engagement is through the language we use.

Bill Lucas

C is for Continuing Professional Development (CPD)

 Continuous Learning for everyone is central to the notion of the intelligent school.

Barbara MacGilcrist, Jane Reed and Kate Myers.

We think that there are some essential preconditions for the establishment of the best Continuing Professional Development (CPD):

1. *That there is an agreed school policy about the practice of teaching and learning, which is subject to continuous review.* The policy emphasizes a shared philosophy and a shared language about learning and teaching. It covers the central issues of learning styles, teaching skills, assessment practices, inclusion, as well as resources for learning. The key messages of the overall policy are transmitted effectively into every area of the curriculum. Staff working in year groups, key stages or subject departments can base their planning on these overt principles, processes and practices, and monitor and evaluate accordingly. There is a consistency of educational practice across all staff in the school founded upon values and beliefs about the complexities of learning and the craft of teaching connected to high expectations and appropriate challenge.

2. *The school, and in particular those in leadership positions, continually emphasize the importance of the study of learning and teaching as the core business of the school.* There are some obvious manifestations of this such as a staffroom noticeboard dedicated to the practice of learning and teaching where everybody takes it in turns, either individually or as a department, to provide appropriate materials such as newspaper articles, book reviews and generic teaching resources. Further, there is a staffroom resource area where staff can gain easy access to information to help them develop their practice. The learning and teaching policy is displayed, along with the priorities outlined in the school development plan. There is an annual publication of case studies of the best practice in learning and teaching based on action research with an expectation that staff will wish to contribute. There are also collections of 'butterflies' on various themes such as starting lessons, plenaries, the best use of ICT and so on. Also available in hard copy and online is a collection of reports that staff have written after returning from courses, conferences or visits to other schools. These reports are written to an agreed format so as to easily inform everybody's practice. Perhaps most crucially no staff meeting ever takes place without the first item being devoted to some aspect of learning and teaching.

3. *Collaboration is supported and fostered. What makes a good school now is the crucial ingredient of collegiality among the staff, initiating, supporting and sustaining improved learning and teaching.* Good schools have the

organizational capacity to work productively both as groups and subgroups to ensure high quality learning for all pupils. Collaboration is not left to chance or even goodwill but structured through the development of teams and teamwork, study groups, reference groups and cooperative planning, teaching and assessment. The successful school will have a commitment to sharing and designing planning for learning and preparation and dissemination of learning materials. The more that staff work together in appropriate teams, the more a shared understanding emerges about the complexity of learning and teaching with the aim of impacting significantly on pupil achievement.

4. *As part of staff development in any successful school there will be well organized coaching and mentoring involving pairs or small groups of staff working together.* We are familiar with the role of mentor as applied to new or trainee staff, but less familiar with the concept as applied to other staff. We need to be clear here about the distinction between mentoring and coaching. Coaching goes beyond general advice and personal support to the specific enhancement of skills in learning and teaching (see C is for Coaching). Good schools have explicitly identified their coaches, commonly acknowledged as outstanding practitioners, specialist leaders of education or ASTs, and skillfully matched them to other staff with the explicit purpose of improving delivery and raising standards.

5. *Action research and professional reflection is the norm rather than the exception. In an effective learning and teaching culture there will be an expectation that staff, either individually or collectively, carry out action research and disseminate their findings so that practice is continuously evaluated and improved.* Teachers are natural researchers in the sense that all teaching is based upon enquiry, and the response of the pupils and the pupil voice generally provides ready evidence as to the effectiveness of various learning and teaching methods. The school could commission additional research from groups of staff and pupils to find out what works best in its particular context and thereby provide the evidence to make adjustments to policies and practices. Clearly, even good schools are not successful for all pupils, and it would be important to identify from formative and summative assessments those pupils and groups that are not experiencing success in their learning. For example, why are boys falling behind girls in particular learning activities and subjects? Does the school know exactly why this is? What is it doing to find out more? How can the school rectify this? Some of this action research could be done as part of a school/higher education link and it could contribute to a staff accreditation programme, where all teachers have to provide a 'professional reflection', a 'learning narrative' or it could take place on a smaller level as part of everyday practice.

6. *Performance management and CPD are integrated.* Performance management is crucial, particularly at assessment stages, especially as teachers have more responsibility for their own CPD. Within a culture of action planning and target setting CPD needs are recognized and shared. Whole-school CPD is then based on this to meet both whole-school requirements and the personal needs of individuals. The teaching standards provide areas to look towards, especially the way they are set out as a progression model. Using these standards alongside the future-based planning model through performance

management objectives, staff can plan for, and define, development needs. Where CPD personal development plans lead to an 'excellent' teacher, ASTs specialist leader of education and senior leadership posts in particular, staff are encouraged and supported to identify appropriate development needs and links to succession planning. Examples might include special expertise in curriculum development, experience of new school structures, expertise in the 'Inclusion' agenda and success in improving particular provision.

Further reading

There is a comprehensive literature on CPD but see Sara Bubb and Peter Earley, *Leading and Managing Continuous Professional Development* and *Helping Staff Develop in Schools.* Also Peter Earley and Vivienne Porritt, *Effective Practices in Continuous Professional Development – Lessons From Schools.* See C is for Coaching, I is for Induction (staff) and S is for Staff appointments.

 Great organizations create talented people.

Malcolm Gladwell

C is for Critical friendship

 He has the right to criticise who has the heart to help.

Abraham Lincoln

As well as developing robust self-evaluation processes to drive forward school improvement, schools will benefit from seeking the views of outsiders in either the monitoring or the speculating on evaluation of evidence collected. In this era of a school-led improvement system, where School Improvement Partners are no longer provided and local authorities' capacity to support is severely diminished, where increasing numbers of schools have opted to convert to Academy status, it is even more essential that schools make arrangements to secure external, critical friendships. This may come from a variety of sources: the retention of a respected School Improvement Partner, the appointment of a new education 'expert', a contract with a company providing education services, an Academy sponsor, a collaboration of schools practising peer review, or retained services from a local authority or diocese. Wherever it comes from it is vital that the school receives both challenge and support to assist in the process of self-evaluation and school improvement. We have previously defined in other publications 'critical friends' as falling into three broad categories:

- *The hostile witness*: someone who tends to focus on what is wrong with the school and has a bias towards negativity. Their preferred style is to judge and tell rather than listen and ask open questions.
- *The uncritical lover*: someone who tends to be besotted by what they perceive to be as the all-embracing success of the school and devalue the currency of praise because all their comments are undifferentiately positive.
- *The true critical friend*: someone who understands and is sympathetic to

A
B
C
D
E
F
G
H
I
J
K
L
M
N
O
P
Q
R
S
T
U
V
W
X
Y
Z

the purpose of the school and knows its circumstances very well. They are skilled in offering a second opinion, or sometimes a first opinion and balance appreciative enquiry with problem solving. Crucially, they recognize that challenge done well can be the best sort of support.

The best critical friends, like good teachers and leaders, are seemingly effortlessly skilled at asking questions. They bring to that questioning task a mastery of inflection and timing, so that questions are never damaging. They speculate aloud so that the development of their thinking is shared, as though with a third party, when they sift the evidence of a possible line of enquiry. When hard messages are necessary, they are often conveyed in the form of half-finished questions to preserve dignity. If presented in the form of statements, the liberal use of the first or third person, rarely the second person, punctuates their remarks.

A school may need a range of critical friends for different aspects of school life and they may of course call upon the leaders of other schools to perform the role. As they are now often paying for this service, they will need to commission appropriately so that the school is seen to improve as a result of the best support and challenge. There are now no self-evaluation forms to complete for OfTSED so schools will need at all times to have self-evaluation statements that reflect the best collective review systems. Critical friends can complement and challenge this process from an external perspective thereby ensuring that the school has compared itself to the most stretching of benchmarks.

C is for Culture of schools

 A whole school teaches in three ways:
By what it teaches
By how it teaches
By the kind of place it is.

Anon

We know that the culture in some schools inhibits school improvement and in others it is enhanced and sustained. Every school will claim to have explicit ideas and values but the test is how far this is shared by the whole school community. Culture is the glue that should hold everyone together and be a positive force for development. It manifests itself in customs, rituals, symbols, stories, language and norms of behaviour. Where a school has a positive culture, established norms of behaviour are taken for granted as unspoken rules and the ethos is implicit, embedded and shared by everyone. There is a compelling and inclusive moral purpose driving the school forward based on equity, social justice and unshakeable principles.

Clearly the context of the school will have an impact on its culture. Some schools will build on an established tradition, others will be newly established;

some will be selective or quasi-selective, others will be community schools open to all; some schools will be faith schools others will be secular; some schools will have a good social mix, others will be skewed towards a particular sector of society. Most schools represent only one stage in education (despite the growth of 'all through' schools) and some are extremely small or extremely large.

However, whatever the context, the school culture will be expressed through three inter-related generic dimensions:

- professional relationships between all members of staff and the way pupils relate to each other and work together
- organizational arrangements relating to structures, systems and processes
- opportunities for learning for both pupils and adults.

The school's culture and ethos will result from the application of its vision and values expressed through the ways the school community relates to each other and works together, the organization of the school's structures, systems and physical environment and the quality of learning for both pupils and adults. Leaders of the school at all levels will always act in a way that is consistent and models these ways of working.

Although school culture is a holistic concept most effective when it is shared by everybody, there may well be several cultures in some schools, some of them even competing – for example, distinct pupil and teacher cultures and possibly a separate leadership culture. Dangerously, a set of counter-cultures can develop with damaging 'us' and 'them' relationships. Sub-cultures, on the other hand, within the overall norms of the school, can be extremely positive with, for example, a pronounced student voice or a teacher culture sharing ideas and planning, with a passion for collective enquiry. In such a culture, passionate teachers can mobilize energy – from 'secret agents to agents of change' – and operate as a force for positive contagion.

In schools where there is an established and expanding improvement culture we would expect to see and experience:

- shared values and goals
- collegiality and joint work
- professional accountability and challenge
- focused support
- transparency and openness
- continuous improvement and risk taking
- generosity of spirit and mutual respect
- celebration and humour.

By contrast, one of the first tasks facing a school that is struggling is to begin a process of re-culturing by which we mean the process of developing new values, beliefs, norms, and mindsets.

Perhaps the key task for any institution is to encourage the growth of a growth mindset – when that kind of philosophy becomes embedded in the culture, the consequences can be dramatic.
Matthew Syed

Some questions to consider:

- Is there a dominant culture and ethos in your school and can you describe this in detail?
- Are there identifiable sub-cultures and how do they complement the whole?
- Is there a counter-culture and how is this dealt with?

Further reading

See V is for Values and V is for Vision and Vision Statements. See Tim Brighouse and David Woods, *What Makes a Good School Now?* and John West-Burnham and Helen O'Sullivan, *Leading and Managing Schools.*

C is for Curriculum

There are two ways of looking at the curriculum; the first from the perspective of the subject, the second in the round – that is to say everything a school does, not just within the timetable but including assemblies, what happens at break times and after school, as well as in residential trips and so on.

'Subject' of course is part of what attracts people into becoming teachers in the first place. That's why the professional subject associations for teachers exist. It is also why we like the secondary schools which pay the first year's subscription fee for all new teachers to belong to their subject association and ensure that they attend one of their meetings. It is also why the head of department exemplifying their love of the subject is so important to the well-being and success of his/ her department. Small wonder therefore that the original discussions of the National Curriculum in 1987-89 were dominated by subject associations vying with each other about 'how much time our subject needs'. So the curriculum debate at that time and since is dominated by discussion of subjects and the 'essential knowledge' each pupil needs to know. And this view is reinforced by the increasingly high stakes caused by examination and testing systems.

Moreover, in primary schools in recent years, the subject interest of teachers has come more to the fore, not merely in obvious areas like music, ICT and languages but also in large schools with specialist appointments. It is interesting to reflect that until the debate about the National Curriculum in the late 1980s it was not thought possible or desirable to define the curriculum in terms of subjects. Moreover, exactly what the curriculum should be was left to the schools themselves even though, as we have suggested above, the exam system exerted an influence on secondary schools.

Indeed in the 1970s and 1980s local education authorities, as they then were, looked for school leaders who demonstrated that they had thought about the curriculum. There was no National Curriculum and it was before the attention to school improvement. So we looked for people who had thoughts and were innovative about curricular matters. It was the same within schools. Applicants for heads of department in secondary schools would try to demonstrate that they were up to speed on the latest developments in their subject area and one of the two deputies would be termed Deputy (Curriculum) which was often more highly sought after than their running mate, Deputy (Pastoral). In primary schools it was the same; applicants had to demonstrate their philosophy about curricular matters if they were to be successful.

With the establishment of the National Curriculum after the 1988 Education Act all that changed. Curriculum thinking took a back seat as it was centrally prescribed.

In the last few years curriculum thinking at school level has made a come-back in the wake of three factors. First there has been a relaxation and multiple national changes to the curriculum. Secondly, the focus on basics – particularly English and mathematics – has made schools concerned that they should not lose sight of creativity and thirdly Academies and Free Schools are promised 'freedom' from the constraints of a National Curriculum.

So different approaches to Key Stage 3 in particular, have meant that schools have begun to think creatively about the curriculum. The RSA has led some of that thinking through its 'Opening Minds' project and all sorts of innovative approaches have followed in its wake. Moreover, the same approach has been tried in primary schools which themselves have started to break the shackles of centrally prescribed curricula.

The International Baccalaureate, best known for its alternative to A level post-16 approach has also stimulated curricular thinking and innovation in primary and the middle years.

As a simple practical observation we would say that how secondary schools, in particular, frame their interpretation of the national orthodoxies will have a powerful impact on how motivated their students are likely to be. We do not believe that one size fits all. Nor do we see successful schools doing that, though we are aware that schools can be equally successful when deploying different approaches to the curriculum which is once again a topic of serious discussion in the senior leadership team. We think that is likely to continue as politicians from all parties either tinker or effect major overhauls of the National Curriculum.

A successful school which motivates and energizes all its pupils needs to think of the wider definition of the curriculum which we outlined at the beginning.

Further reading

See www.thersa.org/newcurriculum, www.guardian.co.uk/teacher–network, www.ibo.org

A
B
C
D
E
F
G
H
I
J
K
L
M
N
O
P
Q
R
S
T
U
V
W
X
Y
Z

Sometimes I look around me with a feeling of complete dismay. In the confusion that afflicts the world today, I see disrespect for the very values of life. Beauty is all around us, but how many seem to see nothing. Each second we live is a new and unique moment of the universe; a moment that will never be again. And what do we teach our children? We teach them that 2+2 makes 4, and that Paris is the capital of France. When will we also teach them what they are?

We should say to each of them: do you know what you are? You are a marvel. You are unique. In the entire world there is no other child exactly like you. In the millions of years that have passed, there has never been another child like you. And look at your body – what a wonder it is. Your legs, your arms, your cunning fingers, and the way you move. You may become a Shakespeare, a Michelangelo, a Beethoven. And when you grow up, can you then harm another who is, like you, a marvel? You must cherish one another. You must work – we must all work – to make the world worthy of its children.

Pablo Casals
Sorrows and Reflections

D is for Data

Twenty years ago schools operated in the dark so far as data were concerned: we had very little. GCSE results weren't published in the local or national papers and SATs didn't exist. Attendance data and fixed and permanent exclusions were a hidden world. Now, so great is the proliferation of data that the truism of 'Being data rich but information poor' has never been more deserved than it is in the schooling system.

How data is presented is crucial. In different settings it will be presented differently. Politicians use the data for accountability purposes and although in the early days OfSTED assured schools they took no notice of data, they soon entered a phase of starting their visit with a 'working hypothesis' based on data, which it was for the school to wrestle with and challenge. Indeed, although they claim they have moved on from that phase, it still dominates. After all, we have experienced successive governments which have set differing 'floor targets' below which a school's status or very existence is openly threatened.

The most successful school leaders understand the uses and abuses of data. They use data sparingly – because there is still relatively little really useful available – for comparative purposes in finance. More can be expected on this front, since the basics are in place and the pressure will be on to make the best of diminished real terms resources.

So far as pupil performance data is concerned, school leaders are sufficiently familiar with the field to make sure that, for external accountability purposes, there are two occasions to be specially prepared for:

- The first is the annual publication of exam results which annoyingly seems to occur on two occasions. For secondary schools it happens in the local press very shortly after the results days in August and then later in the year when the DfE publishes the same set of final data. For primary schools, there are SAT results at seven and then at 11 not to mention the Early Years Foundation Stage data. Facing outwards to the community at these times, heads realize that they simultaneously need to be honest, confident, present the information in the best possible light and be restless for further improvement. Facing inwards at staff meetings and to governing bodies, is a different and in some respects more complex matter. There, weaknesses must be openly explored and possible uncomfortable implications faced.
- The second occasion where data are vital is the inspection by OfSTED. As this now is often at a moment's notice, it becomes imperative to be completely comfortable with a whole profile of data and what it is telling us, so far as school improvement and pupil progress are concerned. It is also important to have thought of angles that a less than friendly inspector might be persuaded to consider. Having the whole senior team *au fait* with what data tells us is both impressive to inspectors and a sign of a school being able to translate school level data to classroom practice.

The key, however, is to move beyond the 'accountability' use of data so that it becomes embedded in the daily life of the school. 'The secret', one head reflected at a meeting of fellow leaders, 'is to set out to use the data formatively even though its generation is from summative assessment data intended to be used informatively, comparatively and for accountability purposes. Just as the teacher in the classroom has to decide when and how to use assessment data to avoid complacency or despair in the individual pupil, so we have to use it in the school as a whole, both to inform classroom decisions by teachers and to help individual teachers and heads of department to improve'.

There's now a wealth of data to use for this formative purpose.

- The Fischer Family Trust (FFT) provides a wealth of useful comparative data and there are few schools aiming at less than FFTD (i.e. the top 25% of performing schools) although the clever ones will be aiming at FFTD plus one. (See F is for Fischer Family Trust.)
- The 'Family of Schools' is a data set invented in Birmingham and developed in London as part of the London Challenge. It can helpfully lead to inter-school visits and the formation of school improvement partnerships. (See F is for Family of schools.)
- RAISEonline. 21,500 schools are active users, with over 1,000,000 reports created each year. Usage peaks in November when new data become available. In November 2011, 170,000 reports were generated in the system. It is at this time of the year that school leadership teams and their governors use

RAISonline to ask themselves about the progress of the school as a whole and individual groups of pupils as revealed by the data.
- The three School Examination Boards (OCR, Edexel and AQA), not forgetting WJEC in Wales, are providing new services, made possible by the availability of candidate performance data at item and topic level. A survey showed that they are highly valued and represent a key tool for future improvement. The exam board portals are being used to help teachers identify topics they need to teach differently (53% of users), with 52% using them to identify areas for revision. Achieving the right balance by topic was a reported benefit for 42%. Given these solutions are still at an early stage, it is likely examination boards will be able to innovate further to provide richer support to schools, for example, through linking reports to learning or training content, providing exemplar responses, or creating data-rich school communities to foster best practice. This is true even though confidence in exam boards varies from time to time in the wake of their own mistakes.

Below is our advice for using data effectively to help underachieving students:

- Make sure all the senior leadership team (SLT) knows and understands the data and can talk to those they line-manage. If even one member of the SLT doesn't, the message is 'It's not important'.
- Don't flood staff with unnecessary data; just give them the important stuff relating to the youngsters they teach and encourage them to visit other schools doing worse and better.
- Have 'red', 'amber', 'green' for Year 11 students by subject-listing on staffroom wall after mocks. Do it by tutor group and get the SLT to share visits and discussions as follow-up.
- Have photos on staffroom wall of students 'at risk' of under achieving and discuss them with their tutors, head of year, subject teacher from time to time.
- Give extra lessons/one-to-one support to the 'at risk of underachieving' students and make sure the best teachers run them.
- Before Year 9 options are made, make a list of students most at risk of underachieving and make sure they don't get into courses where either they disrupt others or are at most risk of failing themselves.

D is for Delegation

The great gift of leadership is to bring about the gifts of followship in everybody else.

Michael Fullan

One of the key skills of leadership, delegation, often receives less attention than it deserves. This is especially unfortunate since delegation affects so powerfully staff development as well as staff energy both at school and departmental phase levels. Get it wrong and there is a huge frictional drag on a school's

A
B
C
D
E
F
G
H
I
J
K
L
M
N
O
P
Q
R
S
T
U
V
W
X
Y
Z

or department's capacity to improve. So anything which reduces mistakes in delegation is to be welcomed.

Many schools find the following hierarchy helpful to debate delegation:

1. Look into this problem. Give me all the facts. I will decide what to do.
2. Let me know the options available with the pros and cons of each. I will decide what to select.
3. Let me know the criteria for your recommendation, which alternatives you have identified and which one appears best to you with any risk identified. I will make the decision.
4. Recommend a course of action for my approval.
5. Let me know what you intend to do. Delay action until I approve.
6. Let me know what you intend to do. Do it unless I say not to.
7. Take action. Let me know what you did. Let me know how it turns out.
8. Take action. Communicate with me only if action is unsuccessful.
9. Take action. No further communication with me is necessary.

As you can see the list sets out possible positions when determining how and when to delegate. Taking first the individual: somebody just appointed will need to be nearer the top but as they grow in confidence reflecting your own view of their competence, you can move them down the scale. As for issues, the more important and complex they are, the more likely it is that the person making delegation decisions will edge back up the scale. Clearly, as we relax or revert to type we will all have our preferred position, which we should be aware of and guard against in a crisis.

Of course the surest way of creating chaos – and de-motivating staff in the process – is to tell them they are at number 7 on the scale but at the height of a subsequent crisis, regret it too late and tell them they were at number 5! So one head who was always losing staff would frequently ask a colleague to do something and then complain about the outcome. For example, he asked one keen young colleague to put up a display in the hall for a parents' evening but then complained he wasn't consulted about the detail when a parent complained that her child's work was not displayed. Small wonder his staff stayed only for so long as it took them to get another job.

D is for Differentiation

Differentiation is defined by Geoff Petty as:

 The process by which differences between learners are accommodated so that all students in a group have the best possible chance of learning.

Geoff Petty

The term differentiation has been referred to in a variety of ways from mixed-ability teaching to personalized learning. Indeed, mixed ability teaching was initially advocated and developed to enable pupils to follow individual learning programmes matched to their needs. This has rarely been translated into practice perhaps because managing and monitoring individually differential work with a large class, even with class groupings, requires a very high level of teacher skills and a wide range of differentiated resources. Of course much depends on the organization of learning generally within the school.

There are now generally three accepted categories of differentiation which teachers use in various combinations:

- *by task* – which includes setting different activities for pupils of different abilities
- *by support* – which gives more help to certain pupils within the group (the growth of the teaching assistant workforce has helped this)
- *by outcome* – which involves setting open-ended tasks and allowing pupils to regroup at different levels.

The problem of differentiation by task is that pupils may be treated differently in the classroom and that there can be low expectations of the weakest pupils. This can actually set back attempts to close achievement gaps. However, it is possible to use AfL in a positive way with high expectations and appropriate challenge through differentiation. Differentiation by outcome would be to set pupils the same tasks which they can all attempt and stretch the most able. In practice, a good teacher will probably use all three categories adopting teaching and learning styles to suit the whole class, groups or individuals. It is the teacher's task to create routes through learning that will allow all pupils to achieve and progress which is a complex undertaking. It is interesting to note that the OfSTED Framework (2012) does not specifically mention the term differentiation but rather 'the extent to which teacher's expectations, reflected in their teaching and planning are sufficiently high to extend the previous knowledge, skills and understanding of all pupils in a range of lessons and activities over time', and 'the extent to which teachers secure high quality learning by setting challenging tacks that are matched to pupil's specific learning needs'.

Further reading
See *Teaching Today – A Practical Guide*, Geoff Petty and *How to Teach*, Phil Beadle.

D is for Display

Things won are done, joy's soul lies in the doing.
William Shakespeare

Here, secondary schools still have much to learn from primary schools. It is one of the essential skills of an experienced primary teacher that they will have a critical eye on display. Pupils' work is beautifully mounted, with an eye to all pupils being represented in the display but with an equal concern for quality. Wall displays also include a reinforcement of language, scientific and mathematical thinking and speculation. Different parts of the circulation space are transformed into grottos, thinking areas, and quiet rooms with frequent reinforcement of the school's key messages about what the community stands for and how members of it behave one to another.

Nowadays there will be a whole-school approach to display in primary schools. So there will often be 'working walls' devoted to reinforce approaches to literacy and numeracy.

Since the introduction of PPA time and the demarcation of teachers' duties, a contrast has sharpened between primary and secondary practice on display and between the habits of outstanding teachers and those of the average teacher. First, primary practice which used to rely on teacher goodwill, has had to be formalized so that teachers' and teaching assistants' respective hours enable a cooperative and thorough approach to optimizing the use of display for learning both explicitly and subliminally. So there are local, national, and international themes but there is still room for the individual to exercise their creativity. As one head reflected 'I always loved doing display: it is now much better organized than it was when I started teaching when there might have been outstanding practice in some schools but others remained a desert'.

Secondary practice has always been different. Typically the school will be strong in the entrance foyer and less impressive in the corridors further away from the entrance and in the classrooms. The best schools have 'display' as an issue in departmental reviews and one we know has persuaded the art and design department to lead displays and has employed older pupils as 'display for learning advisers' (DLAs) in all departments and as volunteers to do something to improve all aspects of display in the school.

One of our butterflies refers to the use of staff and departmental meetings as a means of promoting discussion of display.

Further reading
See also B is for Buildings and the environment.

E is for Energy creators

 Everyone is full of 'E', in all its forms. The trick is to release that 'E' – the excitement as well as the effort, the enthusiasm as well as the energy.

Charles Handy

In an energetic, exciting and enterprising school every form of 'E' is encouraged and rewarded. The more the school as an organization can match these personal 'E' factors and bubble with them, the more successful they will be. We can all think of these characteristics related to children and young people and throw in effervescence on top and many schools do exceptionally well in drawing out these factors and putting them to good use. However, in order to develop a dynamic teaching and learning culture we need to apply this thinking to the energy status of the staff as a whole. To produce the right amount of energy to transform pupil achievement the school needs to have a high proportion of energy creators who:

- are always positive
- use critical thinking, creativity and imaginations
- stimulate and spark others
- practise leadership at all levels

- are able and willing to evaluate their practice and make it accessible to others
- wish to improve on their previous best.

Above all, energy creators are rich with ideas and creativity and through their unfailing cheerfulness and optimism, affect for the better the behaviour of the energy neutral staff who are:

- competent, sound practitioners
- good at 'maintenance'
- usually willing and cooperative
- sometimes uncomfortable accepting examination of their practice by others
- capable of improving on their previous best.

Sadly, there may be some energy consumers for whom every silver lining has many clouds and every glass is half empty. Such staff tend to:

- have a negative view of the world
- resent change and practise blocking strategies
- use other people's time excessively
- not feel good about themselves
- be unable and unwilling to critically examine their practice
- appear not to want to improve on their previous best.

The task of the school is to develop their teaching and learning culture so that everybody is an energy creator for at least part of the time and never less than neutral at other times. In doing so it will build its reciprocal relationships based on trust, and develop its social capital for the benefit of everybody.

E is for Engagement

A report from the Organization for Economic Cooperation and Development (OECD) claims that highly engaged students from poor backgrounds outperform disengaged students from wealthier backgrounds. Not surprising you may say. But when that is added to the finding that underperforming students from poor backgrounds and/or with poor prior attainment who then engage seriously with music, for example in a band, then go on to perform as well as students from wealthier backgrounds, perhaps one has a clue to interventions that work and make a difference to students whether poor or not.

Engagement is key and at the heart of successful teaching.

A 2012 short publication called *Learning Futures*, from the Paul Hamlyn Foundation and the Innovation Unit chronicles some intensive innovation and research into what works best so far as 'engagement' is concerned. We reproduce as follows a précis of their findings:

'....a simple mnemonic has emerged – the four ps of engaging activities:

- *Placed:* the activity is located either physically or virtually in a world that the student recognizes and is seeking to understand.
- *Purposeful:* the activity feels authentic; it absorbs the student in actions of practical and intellectual value and fosters a sense of agency.
- *Passion led:* the activity enlists the outside passions of both students and teachers, enhancing engagement by encouraging students to choose areas of interest which matter to them.
- *Pervasive:* the activity enables the student to continue learning outside the classroom, drawing on family members, peers, local experts and online references as sources of research and critique'.

Activities incorporating as many of these design features as possible have been seen to trigger high levels of student engagement. These four criteria have provided a useful checklist for teachers formulating their learning designs, but also suggest what a school seeks to offer to become more engaging in itself: a place based curriculum, purposeful projects, passion-led teaching and learning and pervasive opportunities for research and constructive challenge.

The case for changing the quality and focus of young people's experience of education is compelling. But we have learned that becoming an 'engaging school' cannot be seen as an isolated project – it demands a root and branch rethink, not just in pedagogy, but in every aspect of the way the school is organized, its structure, culture and the use of space, place and time.

Of course that might put you off! They are the words of pioneers and advocates but the document is worth reading because, despite this last sentence it explains how you can get started. We both believe that through a different approach to the timetable and by devising a set of experiences, a school will ensure all their students enjoy a framework which allows gradualism. If you do read their pamphlet you will learn more about:

- *project-based learning;* where students design, plan and carry out extended projects that produce a publicly-exhibited output such as a product, exhibition, publication or presentation. Here you will learn of 'multiple drafts' the 'use of peer (and expert) critique' and the subtleties of successful 'public presentation of projects'
- *extended learning relationships;* where the full gamut of relationships (peer-peer, student-teacher, involving parents or external mentors or businesses) are explored so that learning can happen at any time and in any place and the range of coaches mentors and experts is extended
- *school as base camp;* with the implication that school is no longer seen as the sole source of learning, a different view made the easier by the accessibility of the internet
- *school as learning commons;* transforming school into a place where all – students, teachers, support staff, parents and members of the wider community

A
B
C
D
E
F
G
H
I
J
K
L
M
N
O
P
Q
R
S
T
U
V
W
X
Y
Z

see school as a place to learn and share their own learning with others seeking to learn.

Further reading
See www.learningfutures.org where you will read of co-production and above all clearly written case studies of progress made by named schools you could visit.

E is for Essential tasks of successful leaders

There are at least six essential tasks for successful school leaders:

1. *Create energy.* A head's own example – what they say, how they behave, who they are – is one of indomitable will and a passion for success. They don't talk about staff. They ask 'what if' speculative questions. They are fussy about appointments, taking care not to fritter time with 'energy consumers'. Because they are full of hope they look for optimists – those who say 'how we could' rather than 'why we can't.' They show interest in every aspect of school life. They realize they are a role model all the time and express a faith, which brooks no denial, that all pupils 'can do'.
2. *Build capacity.* Heads set an example. They teach themselves and are observed by staff doing so; or they take over a class to let others observe somebody else's practice. They rotate the chairing of meetings to grow the skill of others. They ensure young staff members are involved in a school improvement group and act on their suggestions. They have a programme for staff development which considers the better future of individuals, as well as of the school. They know and cherish all the interests of all staff – especially those which the staff used to do in previous jobs or in the world beyond school. They use the collective first person pronoun 'we' rather than the singular 'I'. They take the blame when it's not their fault and they are generous with praise to others for collective success. They set an example of learning, for example, by adopting an annual learning plan. They read and share articles, and encourage others to do the same.
3. *Meet and minimise crisis.* At a time of genuine crisis, they find cause for optimism and hope, for points of learning. They stay calm. They acknowledge their own mistakes. They are 'pogo-stick' players: they can simultaneously be in the thick of things, yet still be seeing the wider picture. A present crisis is the source for vital learning and future improvement. They themselves show willing to be a 'utility player' – one who 'in extremis' will turn their hand to any task.
4. *Secure and enhance the environment.* They ensure classroom teaching and learning materials are well-organized and in plentiful supply. They make sure the management arrangements are seen by staff as 'fit for purpose' – right in detail and serving the needs of staff and pupils alike. For example, they

often review meetings to ensure that 'transactional' or 'business' meetings are minimised. The staff handbook – so often now in electronic form – is repeatedly updated. The computer system works and provides a useful database for staff, each of whom have laptops. Students and parents have access to lesson plans, homework tasks, reports and progress grades, both at school and remotely, by the internet. They improve the staffroom and the whole environment of school – visually and aurally.

5. *Seek and chart improvement.* Heads themselves use comparative benchmarking, comparing data from their own and other schools. They are keen on 'benchmarking', but they do it in a climate of encouraging risk – and striving for the 'El Dorado' of the 'best it can be'. They ensure there is a proper mix of 'appreciative enquiry' and 'problem solving'. Those who seek and put improvement at the heart of what they do, need to mark steps in the journey by celebrating success. Of course they know it must be genuine. For they know the best of 'genuine' is an improvement on past practice, either individual or collective. But they celebrate other social events too – creating the climate in which energy, capacity and ultimate success depend. So governors and staff meetings, awards ceremonies and briefings are crucial to that. They are, above all, good at 'collective' as opposed to 'individual' monitoring.

6. *Extend the vision of what's possible.* Clearly, this involves being both historian and futurologist. Any leader wishing to extend the vision of what's possible is deeply aware of this double requirement: the present dominates so much of school life. And if sometimes that present seems overwhelming, the energy levels drop. So telling stories which remind people of past success and keeping respected predecessors in the role honoured are both things wise leaders do. But they are also forecasters of the weather and describers of future possibilities: they confidently describe a path from the present to the future. They are good listeners and readers. They write 'future' pieces for their community. They ask 'why not' aloud and 'why' silently in their heads.

Further reading
See L is for Leadership.

E is for Ethos

 Ethos and culture is the emergent property of coherence between common experience, shared values / beliefs and community symbols / institutional processes. Together they form an intangible sense of 'the way things are around here'.
Teach First, Ethos and Culture in Schools in Challenging Circumstances

A school's ethos, which can be defined as its distinctive character, spirit and guiding beliefs, has a powerful effect on the quality of relationships and

A
B
C
D
E
F
G
H
I
J
K
L
M
N
O
P
Q
R
S
T
U
V
W
X
Y
Z

the effectiveness of teaching and learning within it. It is composed of many ingredients including high expectations, discipline for learning, personalized support, pride in achievement, and getting the best from everyone.

An ethos which is conducive to high morale and high expectations, affecting staff as well as students, is not a matter of accident but a product of good leadership at every level. Better outcomes are likely if there are agreed ways of doing things which are consistently applied throughout the school. School leaders have a crucial role in developing, communicating and applying the vision and values of the school. This is expressed through the ways a school community relates to each other and works together, the sense of shared purpose and mutual commitment. It is not easy to talk values: they need to be practised so that ethos goes hand in hand with education for character, for personal development and for citizenship. Some schools have developed their own 'ethos indicators' as a means of keeping this under review. They include: student morale, teacher morale, teacher student relationships, the learning context, the physical environment, discipline, equality, justice, extra-curricular activities, and leadership at all levels. They adjust these indicators through staff and student surveys and a programme of internal reviews.

For a school anxious to take a view on its pervasive ethos the following two questions may prompt more:

1. What would be your ethos indicators?
2. How would you evaluate these?

E is for Examinations

Secondary schools in particular are in no danger of underestimating the attention which needs to be given to exams! Increasingly, their very existence – and the security of tenure of the head and some members of staff – rests on the performance of their pupils in external exams at 16. So there are many considerations, the most important of which is making sure their pupils are showing their best in whatever form the exam takes.

The following covers at least some of the issues:

- *Getting the right person to be the Examinations Officer.* Many schools choose someone who is utterly reliable so far as getting the detail right. We can't help also noticing that this job is often their only task and the post may be held by someone recently retired who can and is happy to do it on a part-time basis.
- *Choosing the right exam and exam board.* Exam boards vary and it's important that a choice is made which optimises the chances of success. As one head said 'Just accepting that 'we have always used a particular exam board' isn't a good enough reason. We want to know relative success rates, feedback and

options that may suit particular pupils. I expect each faculty to justify their board preference in my annual discussions of results'.

- *Anticipating changes in exams.* As we write this book we know that substantial changes are expected in the rules for exams in the future. Indeed a complete change in GCSE even its abolition can't be ruled out. In the meatime, grammar, spelling and punctuation will attract or lose marks in other GCSE subjects as well as English and controlled assessments and modular accumulations will be less available. Both these changes will make examination success harder for those pupils who are academically weaker. Attending to literacy and numeracy earlier in secondary school life in Years 7 and 8 are already priorities for schools and seeing whether an extended Key Stage 4 starting in Year 9 with some mixed age groupings, offers at least some chance of accumulating GCSE or equivalent success, which can be banked for the 'Year of reckoning' (Year 11) which may of course eventually move to Year 13.
- *Making sure somebody in each faculty has 'examiner' experience.* Too many schools suffer because they are not sufficiently aware of the marking idiosyncrasies in particular subjects. Clearly, paying attention to the exam board reports and attending the meetings offered by boards to elaborate the features of the best and worst candidates are essential. Moreover, the better the teacher the more likely it is they can coach others in the faculty to help pupils show their best in the exams. Nevertheless, we think there is nothing better than having someone with present or very recent experience of being an external examiner with the board.
- *Having a list of ideas all designed to improve exam results.* See the box below for 25 tasters!

25 ideas for improving exam results

1. Don't run open revision courses. Target which students should attend which classes. Give them an individual timetable and inform their parents. Ensure revision classes are short and pupils get sweets or treats during them.
2. Get famous people to write to the students wishing them luck and put these on an 'Inspiration' wall.
3. At the beginning of Year 10 invite in an inspirational athlete who will motivate students with their own story and focus, discipline and determination to improve on previous best. Display these 'essential features of success' on tutor room walls.
4. Make sure you hold 'achievement days'/'parents evenings' in early autumn term Year 11 so parents and students together know what they are aiming for. Provide 'tips for revision' and best way for parents/carers to support their children.
5. Give parents examples of say '30 questions your youngster needs to be able to answer to get a grade C' – plus the answers!

A
B
C
D
E
F
G
H
I
J
K
L
M
N
O
P
Q
R
S
T
U
V
W
X
Y
Z

6. Use post-16 students as mentors for Year 11.
7. Put personalized messages for different pupils on the e-learning platform in Year 11.
8. In year 11, have separate assemblies for different groups – the A*/A; the C/D; the lazy; the vulnerable; the students who are doing their best at all levels.
9. Have an information evening at the beginning of Year 10 with key dates; especially dates for coursework completion leading up to GCSE. Also put these details on the e-learning platform.
10. Put revision tips on tutor room, library, dining room and entrance lobby walls.
11. Look for early exam entries and not necessarily just among the high achievers. Year 10 or November entry in e.g. mathematics and English literature/media studies allows a well informed second attempt; examiners' debrief on questions attempted.
12. If you have a faculty, e.g. art, which is willing to get GCSE or other level 2 exams completed in Year 10, don't hesitate to enter them. It gives more time to pick up another four.
13. Take the weakest students in Year 11 out of some lessons after the autumn half term and give them extra lessons taught by the best teachers in school; this gives them time to boost coursework and exam grades.
14. Encourage them to revise with appropriate background music; research suggests that baroque music aids thinking and concentration.
15. Have a serious debrief of 'mocks' after pupils have collected brown envelopes with grades, as they will in summer. Display pictures of successful students from the previous year collecting their envelopes.
16. Have a revision week away – outward bound mixed with revision.
17. Get faculties to publish past papers, mark schemes and examiners' reports on the e-learning platform so students can see what makes the difference between grades.
18. Make sure the head of year welcomes students to the exam room and starts the exam rather than an unfamiliar face. Have a member of the senior leadership team who is well-liked to say something as they enter too.
19. Get students in early to their first exam to have a half-hour motivational reminder of what they are going to do.
20. Provide breakfasts on exam days.
21. Provide water and wine-gums (no sweet papers please!) in all exams for all students.
22. If possible, run all exams from Year 9 onwards exactly like GCSEs so students become familiar with the format.
23. Make a list of students who will get grades but might not turn up. Phone/text them on the morning of the exam. Pick them up if necessary!
24. In revision near and during exam season, don't hesitate to use model answers as part of coaching where appropriate. Make sure pre-exam

revision groups are for different groups; don't mix A* candidates with Fs.
25. Set aside a budget for re-marks in the summer; focus on the key marginal candidates. Don't hesitate to get re-marks of a whole set.

Teams for success: Pupils competing together for exam success

Description

One school decided to reinforce the push to accelerate progress in Year 9 when youngsters all too often have a stall in their learning, by introducing a team approach as follows.

The five form entry school had 30 pupils in each Year five tutor group. All were mixed ability although they were taught mainly as setted groups; so the school decided to break each tutor group – still with one tutor – into two teams of similar ability. They then brought in sixth formers as 'managers' for each team, hence there were ten teams in the year group. The ten teams competed in attainment, attendance and participation in school life. Suitable points were devised for each of these with Key Stage 3 tests the obvious one for attainment.

Each manager negotiated expert coaching from members of the faculties for their team. At the end of the year there were prizes for the best team for each of the three aspects and league tables were published mid-year and at the end.

Comment on impact

It was obviously crucial to make sure each team had a fair cross-section of abilities and motivation. Although the school used Key Stage 3 tests which are now abandoned it would be possible to use internal school exam results to the same end – and in any year of the school. The approach could also be modified to embrace collective influence on good behaviour, so individual credits for good behaviour would be collected in a team competition with worthwhile rewards and a team reinforcement of desirable behaviour.

A
B
C
D
E
F
G
H
I
J
K
L
M
N
O
P
Q
R
S
T
U
V
W
X
Y
Z

E is for Experiences, enrichment and entitlements

Most schools value experiences that are beyond the metronomic rhythm of weekly or fortnightly timetabled lessons: so visits to places of local interest or field trips or other residential experiences are part of the valued ebb and flow of school life. Just because they are not reviewed as part of the OfSTED or other accountability systems, it is easy to overlook the part they play in school life especially for those pupils whose home circumstances restrict opportunities for enrichment.

We think there is a case for a school formally agreeing and then publishing widely to the local community a 'guaranteed' list of experiences that all pupils *should* enjoy and then, with their governors, involve the various agencies locally and the pupils' parents in making sure all pupils at the school have such experiences as an entitlement.

When we were in Birmingham we had long public debates about what those 'experiences' might be and in the process revealed a mismatch between what officers, advisers, heads and school staff knew they would provide in their own families as experiences for their own children and what the schools' most challenged families could or would provide. In setting out a minimum list, we were aware both that schools would add to it and convey to their own families what their particular list was and also that all schools could do was to act as a kind of check that all were getting their entitlement.

In the primary years we focused on five experiences which we collectively (those working in schools, parents, community groups) would guarantee all children would experience between the ages of five and 11:

- taking part in a public performance at least twice during their primary years
- by the age of seven to have an opportunity to have extra coaching in some aspect of the expressive arts in which they have appeared to have an interest in / passion for
- in a group creating a 'book / multi-media DVD' which would be suitable for another age group, present it and then collectively critique it
- take part in a residential experience during Key Stage 2
- in Year 6 take part in an environmental study relevant to their local community but chosen from a shortlist of themes established in the city. (We intended to have an exhibition of these).

Similar plans were agreed for the years between birth and five and for the teenage years. It seems increasingly that good and outstanding schools have debates with their local community and establish their own sets of 'experiences' or 'entitlements' and ensure that their reporting systems keep track from time to time of how each and every pupil is taking part.

F is for Failure (as an essential ingredient of success)

 Ever tried. Ever failed. No matter. Try again. Fail again. Fail better.

Samuel Beckett

There's a world of difference between 'failing to learn' and 'learning to fail'. It's one of the features of outstanding schools that they understand this truism almost as a matter of course. 'Failing to learn' is a part of the challenge of AfL or formative assessment and of improving teaching. It's a springboard for learning and success. Teachers quite often encourage pupils to take risks, in the full knowledge that they may fail. Of course they are then at hand to help the pupil reflect and learn from the experience.

'Learning to fail' is quite a different and more dangerous matter. It means simply that the pupil no longer believes they can succeed at anything You could make a list of factors that make youngsters more likely to be 'at risk' of 'learning to fail'.

A
B
C
D
E
F
G
H
I
J
K
L
M
N
O
P
Q
R
S
T
U
V
W
X
Y
Z

Based on research, theoretically the primary school considers the following: low birth weight; summer born; being a boy; coming from a violent home; having a mother and a father who left the home at or before the school leaving age; living in a neighbourhood with high levels of drugs and crime; developmental delay. But of course the primary school is far too wise to believe that even a combination of these necessarily produces an 'at risk' child. They also know of other children 'at risk of learning to fail' who satisfy none of these criteria but have sudden family or personal traumas or who move schools frequently and find themselves in lower setted groups within the classroom.

Secondary schools have more to go on: poor SAT scores, attendance records and fixed term exclusions, plus a view from the previous school. These will be moderated at the end of Year 7 with tutor lists of those they are worried about. We know a school which does just that. For them the next stage of the process has started – the need to build 'resilience'. They mind mapped interventions which might work, ranging from helping theses pupils into clubs at school and in their local area, one-to-one catch ups, giving them responsibility for Year 7 induction when in Year 8, going on a residential trip and many others. The one we were impressed by was allocating the 20 pupils in the category, without telling them, to 40 members of staff; they had two pupils each and the deal was that the member of staff would at least twice a week have a casual friendly conversation with their pupil in the corridor, playground or dining area. They claimed that it worked a treat and that by the end of Year 8 they were doing well.

Of course school organizational features can also affect the likelihood of children 'learning to fail'.

Tea with the head

Description

A primary school head decided that she wanted to encourage writing and get to know all her children. First of all she shared the idea with her staff and confirmed that they liked the idea. Then came the implementation of the idea. It involved her writing cards inviting three pupils to have tea and biscuits with her at break times on Tuesdays and Thursdays from September to Easter; that way she got through 120 pupils having 'tea and biscuits' with her. She followed up, as a result of skilful questioning and listening, with notes to the class teachers and a note home letting the parent or carer know of the occasion and how good it had been to talk with their child.

Comment on impact

It turned out to be an easy way to build parental confidence, trust and involvement. She said that since the class teacher knew in advance who was attending, it enabled them to have a discussion about each child so none were 'invisible'. She soon asked invitees to bring their best piece of work at the end of the day and to tell her quietly what they found most difficult so that she and the class teacher could help. It also helped with the problem of the 'invisible' or 'at risk of learning to fail' child and to model an interest in teaching and learning.

F is for Family of schools

The 'Family of Schools' initiatives, at first in Birmingham and then in London, Greater Manchester, the Black Country, Yorkshire and Humberside have been important because they have enabled schools to compare themselves, not anonymously as in RAISEonline, but in groups or families of named schools whose results they can see in detail.

The diagram below shows the format of how each family of schools is represented.

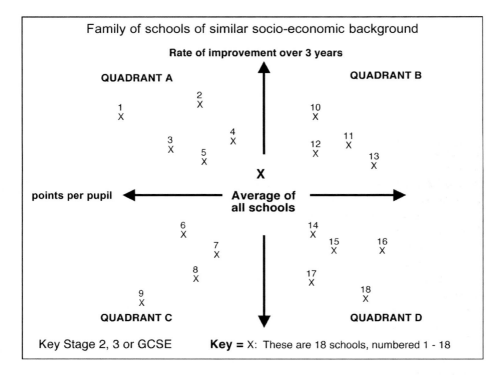

Quadrants

Clearly Quadrant C schools have low performance and are not improving as fast as other comparable schools, perhaps 'not waving but drowning'? Quadrant A schools are improving more quickly but have low points per pupil, perhaps 'heads above the water'?

Quadrant B consists of schools with high points per pupil and high rates of improvement, perhaps 'walking on water'?

Finally Quadrant D schools have high points per pupil but low rates of improvement, perhaps 'treading water'?

The point of the 'Family' is that schools have similar 'prior entry attainment' scores and similar numbers entitled to free school meals. So, schools do not need to waste time, instead they can visit and learn from schools they know to be broadly similar. When such data are added to the data from the Fischer Family Trust, there is the potential to learn from each other, subject by subject and with different groups of pupils. We think there is potential here, as yet unrealized, for the emerging chains to cooperate and for groups such as the Core Cities to produce Family of Schools sets to enable schools to learn from each other.

Further reading
See C is for Chains, L is for Learning Walks, I is for INSET (or Occasional days).

F is for Federations

The word federation crops up a great deal in discussions of school improvement. It used not to be the case. Politicians have become more interested in them, as some of the self standing autonomous schools which they have promoted, have experienced failure through a combination of poor leadership and undue insularity. Moreover in the first quarter of the 21st century it has become increasingly difficult to recruit sufficient high quality applicants for headship especially at the primary level where there are over 20,000 schools, many of which are very small. So the increasingly tough measures of accountability underlined by high stakes testing and successively tougher and narrower criteria frameworks for OfSTED inspection, have influenced the number of people who are ambitious to run their own schools when failure to succeed threatens dire consequences for the school leader.

These factors have resulted in the creation of what we call 'hard federations' – that is the running of more than one school by a chief executive or Principal with two, three or more constituent parts each with a head or associate head who runs each of the 'schools' on a day to day basis. There are variable governance arrangements within such federations but the overall purpose is to ensure that there are some of the efficiency advantages – financial, managerial but also educational – of size. We both know that success in small primary schools can disappear very quickly and noticed that this was less likely to happen in larger primary schools. Nor have we come across any one school that meets all of the needs of all of their pupils so if, through federations, it is possible to bring more expertise to bear on pupils' needs without losing the personal advantages of small size, then we can see strong arguments for federations.

Most federations are combinations devised locally for a variety of reasons including the head leaving and it proving difficult to recruit, or when the head has left and the school is at a low ebb. They are different from externally imposed solutions and chains, and have been strategically promoted by National College advice and an active local authority. They are likely, in future, to be seen as variants of chains of academies, even if regarded as small local chains.

Further reading
See also P for Partnerships and C for Chains.

F is for Fischer Family Trust (FFT)

The Fischer Family Trust (FFT) data have been used – and abused – by an overwhelming majority of schools over the last decade. They have given two examples of what they call 'dodgy' use as follows:

Example 1: A Year 9 student

A student in Year 9 emailed us, with the opening line of the email being 'your data is crap'. It seems that he was objecting because he had been given his Key Stage 3 targets (note: targets not estimates) – but thought that he could do better. Interestingly, the school was actually being quite ambitious – what they had given him were above FFT 'D' estimates and would have put him in the top 10% of pupils nationally (in terms of progress from Key Stage 2 to Key Stage 3) if he achieved them.

Would his reaction have been any different had the information been presented as 'here's what we think, what do you think you can achieve?' instead of 'these are your targets?'

Example 2: A Year 10 student

The student was given a printout with targets for GCSE grade, included 'C' as estimated grade for science. Student and parent felt that this was far too low, given that he had attained high level 7 in science at Key Stage 3. When they questioned the science teacher the response was 'this data is very accurate because it is based upon ...'! It turned out that the 'target' was based upon Key Stage 2 data – the student had made very good progress from Key Stage 2 to Key Stage 3 – and the Key Stage 3 data had been ignored.

Why did the 'system' (provision of data to departments by somebody responsible for data in the school) take precedence over other, more recent information? Why did the science teacher try to justify the (obviously incorrect) estimate?

We think that the FFT would be impressed by the following evidence from a headteacher we know: 'We decided that we were at sixes and sevens over the use of data relating to targets in the classroom. We were all using them in different ways. So we had a debate as a leadership team involving all heads of departments about trying to be more consistent in the use of 'estimates', 'predictions' and 'targets'. By 'estimates' we mean what the FFT would say, for example, that the top 25% of youngsters at any given level would proceed to in say one or two year's time. We set our expectations high deliberately. A 'prediction' is something different. It means what, given what we know of the particular student's current progress and attitude – and if nothing changes – we think they will reach. Then – the vital part – we shared these with the pupil to arrive at a 'target'. It always turned out to be higher than the prediction because handled correctly by good staff the pupil sees the sense of showing what they can do.' She went on to describe how these three: 'estimates', 'predictions' and 'targets' coupled with an 'effort' grade formed the basis of parental reports and discussion on achievement days. It forms a major part of the school's teaching, learning and assessment policy and practice and is on the school's e-learning platform too.

Further reading
See D is for Data.

F is for Forums for teaching and learning

> Good colleagues inspire and encourage each other...good colleagues compliment and complement each other...they keep themselves and they keep each other alive.
>
> Jonathan Smith

Schools that are deeply interested in teaching and learning have gone beyond policy and plans to establishing a forum for intellectually curious staff who want to meet every so often to discuss and debate pedagogy. They are appreciative enquirers with the disposition and attitude to try out new ideas to grow learning competences in their pupils, but also to make this fun. They recognize that learning can occur through multiple channels and through different styles – and that all children can learn successfully. Similarly, they believe that if they think about and share enough practice they can teach anyone to succeed.

Teaching and learning forums are voluntary and anti-hierarchical. They are about research and development and form a 'think tank' for other parts of the organization. It is, of course, important to structure meetings appropriately with a focus for discussion and to provide appropriate stimulation and input, but essentially these are forums to bring people together who are passionate about what they do and not constrained with formality and accountability. There may be different levels of expertise and experience in the forum: ASTs, teachers undertaking Master degrees, newly qualified teachers, Teach First teachers, teaching assistants and acknowledged expert practitioners. What matters is that the group grows personally and professionally together and is able to profoundly influence the practice of teaching and learning in the school as a whole.

Ideally, it is the forum that will suggest and produce learning narratives, particular suggestions for reading, and stimulate action research. They will also organize 'super learning' days, that will help to lead staff INSET and ultimately ensure that the excitement and energy and 'buzz' of teaching and learning is maintained and developed.

Further reading
See C is for Continuous Professional Development, A is for Action research and L is for Learning Narrative

F is for Four stages of headship

 Leadership and Learnership are indispensable one to another
John F. Kennedy

There are four stages to leadership of any sort that involves people. So what follows applies to senior posts of responsibility. The first stage is 'initiation'. It's when all your stakeholders – staff, pupils, parents, governors and the local community in the case of headteachers – are trying to match up 'what you say' and 'what you do' with 'who you are' – or not as the case may be. The better your homework about people before you arrive, the sooner you'll form a trusting rapport based on their certainty that you know about and remember their individuality. The more you put yourself about, the quicker the 'initiation' phase will be over. Until this stage is over it's difficult to make energetic progress based on shared commitment. During this phase it's best to avoid all mention of where you have worked before. Too much of that and colleagues will silently wish you were back where you came from.

A
B
C
D
E
F
G
H
I
J
K
L
M
N
O
P
Q
R
S
T
U
V
W
X
Y
Z

The second is the 'developmental' stage when, after listening to everyone's hopes, you are privileged to steer the school through the next chapter of its story. You'll find yourself using a few key defining phrases over and over again – sometimes so often you feel self-conscious about repetition. You need constantly to affirm and reinforce the vital essence, purpose and values of the shared enterprise with all members of the community: pupils, staff, parents and governors. You know you are winning when you hear others using the same language. Another key ingredient of this phase is to focus on staff development so staff members never run short of intellectual curiosity and energy. Usually the ambitions set out for the school are realized within seven, eight or nine years and a new defining chapter needs to be agreed.

The next is a dangerous period for leaders – a third 'plateau' stage which can so easily become a 'stall'. Can you summon the imagination and resolve for another sustained period of development? Or do your colleagues know you so well that they can be quietly effective in resisting any more ideas? Perhaps you are so exhausted by obligations to so many stakeholders that in that situation you can no longer lead? Should you leave for another school? Certainly taking a break after seven or so years is a good idea – ideally for half a term but even a month's study visit will recharge batteries. (Is this why, incidentally, that Peter Mortimore's research showed heads at their best between their third and seventh year? There are loads of exceptions to the rule, though we haven't met too many heads whose second ten years were better than their first!)

Most people emerge from the third stage with a new defining chapter or they leave. But of course there is no way of avoiding the fourth stage of headship – the 'decline' or end phase when you have decided to go. The school goes 'on hold' as people pay less attention to you and await your successor. So don't hang around and allow things to lose momentum. Don't keep saying you are going to retire and then postponing it 'for one more year'. Once the decision is made in your mind, stick to it and announce it with the minimal notice consistent with not leaving the school in a mess. In short make it an honourable 'exit' not a 'decline'.

Further reading
See L is for Leadership and E is for Essential tasks of leadership.

A
B
C
D
E
F
G
H
I
J
K
L
M
N
O
P
Q
R
S
T
U
V
W
X
Y
Z

G is for Good to great

 You don't have to be ill to get better.

Anon

Much of the general school improvement literature has concentrated on schools in difficulty – either in the OfSTED categories of 'Notice to improve' or 'Special measures' – or those deemed to be underperforming in terms of floor standards and progress measures. Latterly there has been some concentration on schools deemed by OfSTED to be 'satisfactory' which is now assumed to be 'unsatisfactory'. However, school improvement is the business of <u>all</u> schools whether currently judged to be 'good' or even 'outstanding'. Indeed, once a school assumes that it can't get any better it will inevitably become complacent and decline. In 2001, Jim Collins completed a study of companies in the US that had progressed from 'good' to 'great' and his first proposal was that 'good is the enemy of great – and that is one of the key reasons why we have so little that become great. We don't have great schools, principally because we have good schools'. He referred to 'the curse of competence and complacency'. Although writing from a business perspective Collins offers a prescription for moving from good to great. This includes the exercise of level 5 leadership by which he defines as a combination of fierce resolve and personal humility, confronting the brutal facts, getting the right people on the bus and in the right seats, the 'hedgehog' concept of striving to be the very best at the core business, a culture of disciplined action, and the idea of the flywheel with a pattern of build up, increased momentum and breakthrough. Since then many other educational publications have picked up on this theme – for example Andy Buck, *What Makes a Great School?* and the three studies done by Peter Matthews for OfSTED on *12 Outstanding Secondary Schools and 12 Outstanding Primary Schools* subtitled – *Excelling Against the Odds.* Also *12 Outstanding Special Schools – Excelling through Inclusion.* He concludes that 'great schools are more than the sum of their parts' and stresses the key characteristics as being:

- strong values and high expectations that are applied consistently and never relaxed
- outstanding and well distributed leadership
- sustained excellence
- highly inclusive cultures having complete regard for the educational progress, personal development and well-being of every student
- constantly evaluating performance and looking for ways to improve further.

Of course, schools that believe themselves to be 'good' overall will be aware through their monitoring and evaluating systems where they believe they are already outstanding and where they fall short of being outstanding. However, the trick is to put into place the strategies that will enable them to make the breakthrough. Schools can call on their 'critical friends' for assistance in this process and some may commission independent reviews. However, the best resource is other schools, particularly those who have been consistently outstanding for some time. Some local authorities, private providers, collaboratives and chains offer Good to Great programmes where schools can come together to discuss and debate their progress. A good example is the London Leadership Strategy which developed out of the London Challenge. Here there is both a Good to Outstanding programme and a Going for Great programme for those schools already outstanding. Schools meet half-termly to discuss and debate best practice often with visiting speakers and expert practitioners. Arrangements are made for inter-school visiting and learning walks in particular 'hubs', where schools can see practice first hand. In the Going for Great programme schools have to commit to producing a case study of great practice which is published at the end of the year as well as choosing an area for particular development. The message of both these programmes, which have now been running for several years, is that schools should never settle for what they currently provide and should constantly look for ways to improve. Further, in the new landscape of school improvement, the aim should be to create a school system which is more effectively self-improving, allowing the most effective practice to spread more quickly. To do this, schools need to support and challenge each other to be the best they can be.

G is for Governors

 Governors are most effective when they are fully involved in the school's self-evaluation and use the knowledge gained to challenge the school, understand its strengths and weaknesses and contribute to shaping its strategic direction.
OfSTED Report on School Governance (2011)

The relationship of the governing body with the whole school, including the head, other staff and parents is the most under researched part of school effectiveness and improvement. Unlike other stakeholders, governors represent not only themselves but also a constituted group such as parents, staff, the local authority or the community. They particularly need to work hard at being the 'critical friend' to the head and staff: this requires them to be known in the school, since otherwise their questions will lack authority.

Governing bodies have four main tasks:

1. To provide a strategic view of where the school is heading and help to decide the school's strategy for improvement so that its pupils learn most effectively and achieve the highest standards.
2. To monitor and evaluate educational standards and the quality of education provided, asking challenging questions and pressing for improvement.
3. To assume direct responsibility for oversight of financial management, the recruitment of senior staff and some disciplinary matters.
4. To act as a critical friend to the school, providing the headteacher and staff with support, advice and information, drawing on all governors' knowledge and experience.

In carrying out these tasks there needs to be a clear understanding by governors and head of the difference between management and governance. In practice, most governing bodies work through a series of processes and find themselves to a greater or lesser extent 'advising', 'steering', 'mediating', 'supporting' and 'holding the school to account'. While each governing body will decide for itself how it should be involved in the running of a school, like other partners it should demonstrate a commitment to continuous improvement, both in terms of improving the quality of education for the pupils and also in developing its own learning capacity and that of most of the whole-school community. This will mean establishing positive relationships between governors and school leaders based on trust and transparency, where there is open discussion among governors, the head, staff, and parents to ensure that there is a shared understanding about roles and responsibilities.

Absolute clarity about the different roles and responsibilities of the headteacher and governors underpins the most effective governance. As so often in school

A
B
C
D
E
F
G
H
I
J
K
L
M
N
O
P
Q
R
S
T
U
V
W
X
Y
Z

improvement, the process runs most smoothly when school leaders and governors behave with integrity and are mutually supportive. Governors have a vital role to play in policy-making, development (planning, and monitoring and evaluation), and will wish to be informed and inform themselves about the school's strengths and weaknesses so that they can work effectively to secure continuous improvement. Certainly, the time and expertise of governors needs to be deployed to focus more strongly on strategic direction, to set high expectations and ask challenging questions based on high-quality training and information.

Many of the more successful schools have smaller governing bodies with the right skills to champion high standards and act decisively. For governing bodies as a whole, the creation of the right committee structures and accountabilities, a rolling programme of progress reports critically analyzed, is vitally important. The role of individual governors in key school groups such as the Raising Attainment Group is also critical to the school's capacity to drive itself forward as well as being a vital backbone and backstop. Good partnerships with governors are essential if school improvement is to be sustained. Governing bodies have a vital role in establishing a collaborative culture that encompasses staff, pupils, parents and the wider community. Governors can make schools better by shaping and guarding the values and vision of the school through its key roles of strategic planning and monitoring and evaluation. The new Inspection Framework (2012) gives governors a chance to re-formulate its structures and processes around the four key areas of leadership and management, standards, teaching and learning and behaviour, and to make a telling contribution to the school's self evaluation statement. Outstanding governance supports honest, insightful self-evaluation by the school, recognizing problems and supporting the steps needed to address them.

Further reading
See OfSTED report on School Governance.

G is for Grammar of school improvement

 Change is the sum of a thousand acts of reperception and behaviour at every level of the organization.
John J. Kao

Over many years working on school improvement we have worked out a particular grammar to provide a common language of analysis, discussion and debate. This grammar is made up of the following parts:

- *Punctuation:* 'Butterflies' (see throughout the book), very small initiatives taken by schools which have a disproportionate effect as catalysts for improvement and taken together affect climate.

- *Nouns:* The key factors of school effectiveness such as:
  - vision, values, culture and ethos
  - leadership
  - teaching and learning
  - CPD
  - the curriculum
  - the learning environment
  - school partnerships.
- *Verbs:* The processes of school improvement described by us as:
  - Leading at every level – while recognizing the need for different styles in different circumstances and at different times.
  - Managing and planning – again at different levels, ensuring that everyone plays their part in getting the detail right.
  - Learning, teaching and assessing – the bread, butter and jam of schooling. It occupies everyone's time.
  - Creating a fit environment – visually, aurally, behaviourally and in a way that encourages learning.
  - Developing staff – not just teachers but all staff, by making good appointments, providing thorough inductions and extensive further professional development, which combines individual and collective need.
  - Involving and connecting – with parents and the community – sometimes overlooked, but it is key that the school is accessible to all who might benefit and contribute.
  - Self-evaluating and critically reviewing – an activity that prompts gradual or great change and is crucial to the progress of the school.
- *Adjectives:* The descriptors of successful practice which are illustrated throughout this book.
- *Adverbial clauses:* Critical interventions which are directly focused changes of policy and practice such as:
  - Seeking improved standards of attainment through new assessment and data systems.
  - Whole-school participation in action research.
  - Increasing the range of personalized learning opportunities.
- *Tenses:* Planned changes over time which make up the melodies and rhythms of school improvement.

A
B
C
D
E
F
G
H
I
J
K
L
M
N
O
P
Q
R
S
T
U
V
W
X
Y
Z

A
B
C
D
E
F
G
H
I
J
K
L
M
N
O
P
Q
R
S
T
U
V
W
X
Y
Z

H is for Headteachers spending their evenings and weekends balancing work and home life

If reading and writing are best done alone, it follows that they will happen outside school days and terms. The arrival of email is a sore test of any head's determination to use that time for reflective reading. Given the continued though diminishing flood of paper, any head needs some system to keep on top of the task of 'seeing wider and further,' while dealing with the sheer volume of day-to-day business. That's why one head, who has claimed never to use her computer during school hours, explains how she makes it happen. She has an agreement with her PA and office manager to spend 15 minutes each morning after they are first in, with an equivalent session each evening, picking up her folder of items and post. The post that they have sifted is dealt with either at home or before everyone arrives the next morning; 'my selected emails are marked as unread with the urgent ones in red and I deal with them on my laptop out of school hours'. But that does mean that successful heads get up and arrive early and leave and go to bed late. They know that those are the times when they wrestle with the strategic and with downright boring or painful chores. Intricate personal, legal and budgetary matters can be incredibly time consuming. Judicious and skilled delegation will take you far and needs to be mastered. Indeed, in many matters of appeal, they are essential and, in the end, there's no avoiding a lot of apparently unproductive time. Governors' meetings are outside school time, as are the many school sporting fixtures, musical events and celebratory occasions. 'Showing interest in something I was not originally or naturally much interested in is one of the first unexpected things which I discovered in headship' was how one head who had overcome a lifetime's lack of interest in sport, put it.

It's in the evenings – well those that are free of school engagements – while the family are watching television, that heads read articles, or alternatively, in the early mornings before the rest of the household is awake. Eating either at working breakfasts or in restaurants in the evening can often also be part of the rhythm of the heads of larger schools. Taking on the tradition of the 19th century legends like Arnold, their families will sometimes be ensnared in school related activity. Some parts of the holiday are not sacrosanct either. One successful head spent at least half her three weeks in France last summer putting together a very impressive 'So you want to be a head one day?' course which she then ran for 17 volunteers from the staff on Friday afternoons. Time outside school on these sorts of task will vary widely. Sometimes it's very heavy: at others it's blissfully peaceful.

H is for Headteachers teaching, learning and assessing

Many studies of school leadership envisage a time when headteachers of schools or groups of schools will not have had teaching experience. That seems to us an improbable recipe for success: after all, even Education Officers in local authorities were expected to have done some teaching. Certainly, it's the perception of those heads who have been very successful – and of their staff – that part of their credibility comes from their expert interest in teaching and, of course, learning and assessment. 'If I'm not seen as a reasonable practitioner, I'm simply not credible in the staffroom,' is how one head put it, as we reflected on the desirability of being seen to do playground duty or take over the teaching of a Year 9 class on a Friday afternoon. There are many ways for heads to demonstrate their interest in teaching.

Regular teaching?

How they demonstrate their teaching is a different matter. Probably it's not sensible for the head to have a regular teaching slot. (Mind you: ask any head of a two or three teacher primary school and while they might agree, they will comment that 'chance would be a fine thing!') In a large school however, apart

A
B
C
D
E
F
G
H
I
J
K
L
M
N
O
P
Q
R
S
T
U
V
W
X
Y
Z

from anything else, the head will get dragged away too often to be fair to the pupils. Of course, school assemblies need to be stunningly brilliant occasions in the very successful schools and the head must be seen as a good performer. They should also circulate every tutor group; where there is a difficult issue to talk out with pupils, the intimacy of the tutor group is the right vehicle for doing it.

Teaching pupils is one thing; teaching adults another. Yet like the good teacher, the successful headteacher, by the use of 'appreciative enquiry', is an excellent coach. Conversations with staff seek to identify what's good in their practice and how it might be extended, by supporting the member of staff's assumed ambition for excellence. So they facilitate visits and show interest in the outcomes. They encourage teachers to have videos of their own practice. They celebrate the faculty, which has created a bank of videoed key lessons, so that pupils who miss lessons – or who don't understand the point at the time – can refer to them later. In their teaching, they know that they have to model excellent explanation and story telling and high quality questioning. Indeed, it's worth adding as an aside, that they are better at asking the right questions, than in hurrying to provide answers, tempting though it is to do so. But 'questioning' raises the issue of the heads themselves providing an example of being a learner. Respecting the expert knowledge of the subject specialist is the obvious everyday way of doing so. It's the head's job to bring all this expert knowledge together so, coupled with their own greater understanding of what is happening beyond the school, they can make for a greater sense of the whole. In that sense they are what Michael Fullan has called 'knowledge creators'. They may even have a research project of their own and they certainly encourage further study among their staff. They find articles to share with individual staff. They rotate the role of 'chair' in meetings of the senior team and encourage faculty leaders to do the same. Informally, they ask speculative and genuinely enquiring questions and formally they may even have a shared 'learning plan' for the year. Their interest in assessment shows not merely in their regular 360 degree feedback exercises, but in their often demonstrated commitment to improving on their own previous best. They are interested in the changes in external assessments and, of course, keep abreast of OfSTED changes in inspection practices. These activities can take up anything from two to ten hours in a week.

H is for Homework

Homework is the most vexed and least researched aspect of school life that may affect school improvement. Parents have a love-hate relationship with it but are quick to see when a school says one thing but does, or rather doesn't do, another. So although parents and staff all too frequently have a thankless task of nagging unwilling youngsters – teenagers especially – parents are the first to complain when the good intentions at the start of a school year fall by the wayside after Christmas. Staff are similarly ambivalent. Governments are clear that it matters: indeed in the late 1990s Michael Barber, then leading the

Standards Unit in the Department for Education, produced a paper that showed the impact of homework on pupil outcomes.

In fairness, how can a school not be interested in and seek to affect what goes on in the 80-85% of a pupil's waking time that occurs outside school? However, much of a chore it is to set and mark – if of course it is of a sort that needs marking – most schools realize that it is something on which they need a clear and consistent rationale. Moreover, it is one where 'singing from the same song sheet' is key to the perceptions of parents and pupils of the school's efficiency and effectiveness, indeed whether they care.

So what do really good schools do? Is there anything within a homework policy and practice that has a significant impact on pupil outcomes? We think there is and that any primary or secondary school will be better able to form a view as to what those issues are by visiting the Gov.uk website (reference below). From that they will get a feel for the right sort of tasks and times to give to different age groups. They will learn there the obvious points about the need for homework clubs, the chances which now exist for e-referencing via the school e-learning platform or intranet and the way teachers at the leading edge are using texts and specially created social network sites to promote beyond school learning. What they won't find are two observations which we think worth repeating here.

First that homework provides a grand opportunity for family learning, especially in the years of transition in Year 7 and secondly that as one head so wisely commented, 'If you want it taken seriously it has to be part of the rituals – rewards at assemblies and 'prize givings' for the best homework of the week / year, faculty prizes and reviews and of course performance management arrangements. Otherwise nobody thinks you take it seriously. In my view you have to model it and it can form part of an individual's 'learning plan' for the year'.

In the section on lesson planning (see L is for Lessons) we refer to 'flipped lessons' which we think transform homework for the better.

2 Homework tips

1. Create a numbered, indexed 'Homework book' – clearly on the e-learning platform if you have one – so homework tasks can be drawn from it and referred to by students and parents.
2. As part of 'the way we do things' school policy, all teachers set the homework at the beginning, not the end of the lesson.

A
B
C
D
E
F
G
H
I
J
K
L
M
N
O
P
Q
R
S
T
U
V
W
X
Y
Z

A
B
C
D
E
F
G
H
I
J
K
L
M
N
O
P
Q
R
S
T
U
V
W
X
Y
Z

H is for Hope

We rest our case in this entry on four quotations.

> Hope is definitely not the same thing as optimism. It is not the conviction that something will turn out well, but the certainty that something makes sense, regardless of how it turns out. It is hope, above all, that gives us strength to live and to continuously try new things, even in challenging conditions.
>
> Vaclav Havel

> Teaching is an act of hope for a better future...the reward of teaching is knowing that your life has made a difference.
>
> William Ayers

> More than anything else, more than expectations, passionate engagement or standards, teaching is about hope. Every child is the teacher's hope for the future. Education happens when hope exceeds expectation. Teaching is what makes the difference.
>
> Andy Hargreaves and Michael Fullan

> History says, Don't hope
> On this side of the grave,
> But then, once in a lifetime
> The longed – for tidal wave
> Of justice can rise up,
> And hope and history rhyme.
>
> Seamus Heaney

H is for Hyacinths

Hyacinths are important to teachers and their leaders. Let us justify our assertion. It is most vividly explained by a story. Sir Alec Clegg was arguably the best Chief Education Officer ever. Certainly he would rank among the top two or three. He plied his trade in the old West Riding and achieved remarkable innovations in education – for example, initiating a burgeoning of the arts and music as part of the curriculum which in time was to transform every aspect of our national life. He also inspired loyalty and outstanding practice in the schools of the West Riding so that any self-respecting teacher wanted to work there.

In retirement he would tell a story of visiting his aunt when he was a teenager. She was a foreign languages teacher in Grantham and took in private pupils one of whom was the young Margaret Thatcher (née Roberts). Clegg was to cross swords with her later when she was Secretary of State for Education and he always argued that she had never noticed the sampler on his aunt's wall which read:

'If, of fortune thou be bereft,
And of thine earthly store have left,
Two loaves. Sell one and with the dole,
Buy hyacinths to feed the soul.'

He used the verse to argue for balance in the curriculum as he recognized what for some pupils was a loaf, for others would be a hyacinth: indeed it underpinned his drive for the expressive and performing arts and his valuing of craft as well as the academic subjects and a rich balance of skills, knowledge, values and ideas in the curriculum.

It is our contention that today Clegg would have put another interpretation on the need for hyacinths. In Clegg's day stress wasn't acknowledged as a real issue in working life but now as the speed of life has accelerated, it is. So getting a balance for each individual between loaves – the things we have to do – and hyacinths – the things we enjoy doing – is vital. One consumes energy, the other creates it.

So, wise headteachers are always looking to find the hyacinths in their staff's background and present pastimes so that they can encourage them to give them a full rein in school life and beyond, so that staff don't burn out. And they are mindful of their own hyacinths too.

I is for Inclusion

We have a separate entry for Special Educational Needs and Disabilities because of course ideas of inclusion have raged across the educational landscape at a professional and political level ever since the vigorous promotion of secondary comprehensive schooling in the mid-1960s. We should not forgot that it wasn't until 1971 that children who attended what were called Junior Training Centres were legally declassified from being deemed by medical colleagues as 'ineducable' and handed over to the care of local education authorities and renamed Educational Sub Normal schools Severe or ESN(S) where they were counterpoised with ESN(M) – i.e. Moderate.

When newly reorganized comprehensive schools' headteachers and staff were asked to consider under the banner of 'inclusion', the inclusion of such children, and others with physical or sensory impairments, within their mainstream schools, two things happened. First, many of them – as indeed did their primary headteacher colleagues – gulped and protested that they weren't equipped to teach 'children with such great special needs' – although they were more confident when it came to children who were academically accomplished but suffered from physical or sensory handicap. Secondly, their colleague heads in special schools unsurprisingly agreed. Nevertheless, the debate about abolishing special schools continued for at least 25 years across different parts of the country as people talked about the continuum of 'locational', 'social' and 'functional' inclusion or integration. Indeed, in many parts of the country there are examples of that debate being brought to practical impressive and uncontentious conclusions.

So that is one set of inclusive arguments. There is, however, another which affects each and every school and in almost all aspects of school life. Obviously something like the admissions policy and practice is either inclusively or exclusively inclined. But so too is the language it uses, how the curriculum is organized, what priorities are adopted in setting the timetable and what is celebrated at assemblies and awards evenings. Marking and the displays are either inclusively or exclusively inclined. Almost all a school's organizational practices (its behaviour policies and practices in particular) and the teachers' daily practice in the classroom and the corridor have messages about inclusion. For primary schools it causes arguments about the impact of within class groupings – or setting – according to ability and the need to avoid children losing confidence as a result of their slow development in the basics. Teachers in both primary and secondary schools are careful to find imagery in their storytelling which appeals to all youngsters and to make sure that they have 'buddying' systems which ensure that newcomers are welcome and any difference of background is celebrated.

I is for Induction of...

Staff

The essential details for the staff induction programme – the underlying policy and the details of the practices – will be included in the staff handbook. But induction deserves special mention as it becomes a vital support to maintaining consistency especially where there is high staff turnover. Staff induction must encompass all staff: teaching and support alike. It should contain a common element for all with faculty-based (including administrative team function) elements. The timetable will usually be on an annual cycle which will offer opportunities, for those who arrive either at the beginning of the school year or during it, to have a brief, repeated, general introduction. This should be followed by a sequence of modules, carefully focused on what the school knows are the vital elements in 'singing from the same song sheet'. In addition, there should also be a guide for part-time and supply staff, so they too know what it is they are expected to do to support the school. New heads of department and senior leadership team members will have an assigned mentor either from within or sometimes outside the school.

The best schools we know ask all new members of staff, after they have been in post for a year, to look at their experience and make recommendations for improvements. This helps to keep their induction programme fresh.

A
B
C
D
E
F
G
H

J
K
L
M
N
O
P
Q
R
S
T
U
V
W
X
Y
Z

Pupils

All schools will have induction arrangements for new intakes whether in Year 1 or Year 7 or some other point of transfer from other schools. But pupils arriving randomly at other points in the school year are a common phenomena for schools with very high 'churn' of pupils, often called mobility. Large estates of social housing in urban areas will know how family issues can easily lead to youngsters moving school. Whatever the reason, schools know that it means that extra effort has to be made with 'settling' the new pupil in. So more than one 'buddy' fellow pupil is key for such a newcomer and making enquiries on a daily basis about possible bullying won't come amiss. Alerting staff who will come into contact with the new pupil at staff briefings and making sure a member of the senior leadership team talks with the newcomers in the corridor are both common practice. We were impressed with one school we know which has photos and pen descriptions of 'New pupils this week' on the staff noticeboard.

I is for Inspection

Quite simply, I believe we need radical improvements to the education system in this country. And I believe that inspection...can help to make this happen.
Sir Michael Wilshaw, HMCI

The publication of inspection reports is an important part of making schools accountable to parents. At its best, inspection can confirm school self-evaluation, boost staff morale, and stimulate further improvement, but at its worst it can have the opposite effect. There is a considerable debate as to whether inspection is a major tool of school improvement or whether it is simply an accountability measure confirming good practice and identifying those schools where children and young people are being let down.

The OfSTED framework has been updated and changed several times but the new inspection framework (2012) concentrates on four main areas: pupil achievement; the quality of teaching; leadership and management; the behaviour and safety of pupils. There is also a focus on the needs of all pupils and in particular pupils who have special educational needs or who are disabled, as well as the promotion of all pupils' spiritual, moral, social and cultural development.

There is general agreement that the *Framework for Inspection*, setting out appropriate criteria and providing grade descriptors, provides good guidance in terms of school self-evaluation and school improvement. However, there is less agreement on the usefulness of inspection reports themselves to drive forward improvement. The reports do identify the key priorities for improvement which is clearly helpful but there is often little in them which helps the school identify the 'how' of improvement. To put it another way, inspections clearly provide appropriate accountability and challenge but not support. Of course, inspectors argue that having identified the key issues, it is then up to the school to navigate its way forward seeking support elsewhere. At its best, schools will receive from inspection enough guidance to propel themselves forward and make incremental improvements through monitoring visits. At its worst, the key priorities are identified again and again and just as the pig being constantly weighed doesn't gain weight, so the school being constantly monitored doesn't improve. Other forms of inspection such as survey visits or subject inspections are carried out in all schools. These are very useful to schools as they result in published, good practice reports which are of benefit to the system as a whole as is the *Annual Report of HMCI.*

Inspection is likely to remain a permanent feature of the education landscape and schools therefore need to get the best out of this process. Certainly an inspection framework helps schools to be clear and robust about their self-evaluation processes which then drive their improvement. Schools should have quality standards with quality assurance systems in which case inspection can be used to affirm and confirm good practice. However, arguably the system could deal with 'underperformance' and 'failure' in a better way triggering a set of support mechanisms to guarantee eventual success. It may be that, when there is a maximum number of Teaching Schools and National Support Schools led by National Leaders of Education, together with structural solutions where appropriate, there will be an automatic support system to get behind rather than on top of schools.

We have hesitated to offer schools advice about how to prepare for and manage OfSTED inspections, but we have observed that the quality and consistency of OfSTED can vary and that any sensible and successful school will not be going into 'unannounced' inspections unprepared. Among the obvious things they will consider are:

- Ensuring from time to time that they are checking out how an active OfSTED inspector rates the school's own self-evaluation. (This is relatively easy to ascertain since the major inspection firms use self-employed consultants as team leaders).
- Knowing how the data will / can be interpreted particularly in respect of levels of progress.
- Having a good tracking system so that individual teachers (and departments in secondary schools) can talk about where youngsters are in terms of progress.
- Being really secure on senior leadership team rating of teacher lessons and steps taken to improve teaching.
- Ensuring that key members of the governing body can demonstrate they are critical friends rather than uncritical supporters.
- Having a 'live' self-evaluation system in use and well known by those OfSTED will encounter including a dynamic website.
- Making sure that the school avoids defensiveness in its reactions to the inspection process even when, as sometimes happens, they are unreasonably provoked!

A
B
C
D
E
F
G
H
I
J
K
L
M
N
O
P
Q
R
S
T
U
V
W
X
Y
Z

I is for In-School Variation (ISV)

For years researchers have argued with each other about whether it is the variation between one school and another or within schools between one teacher and another that is the more important. Is it teacher effect or is it school effect? We think it is both although we acknowledge that an Organization for Economic Cooperation and Development survey of 2002 suggested that 'in-school' variation was four times greater than 'between-school' variation.

Certainly, there are three main aspects to ISV: first, as it affects different groups of pupils, for example, boys and girls, children from different ethnic backgrounds, children from 'at risk' backgrounds (see F is for Failure); secondly, as it manifests itself in differing pupil performance among the various faculties in a secondary school or between literacy and numeracy in a primary school; and thirdly, as it shows in the different performance of individual teachers. All three aspects can be improved. An excellent guide to an approach to any one of these issues was developed recently by a joint study involving the National College and the Training and Development Agency for schools. Put simply it will involve a step-by-step approach involving investigating reliable data, evaluating that and other more qualitative evidence and arriving at a plan.

We have been impressed by one head who told us, 'I see in-school variation as a springboard for discussion and debate. So it isn't simply that we discuss 'residuals' in exam performance each year and how it compares with the national position – though we do that and make it part of our self-evaluation framework and review of each department and a part of our learning walks – we also established a working group of six 'Young Turks', all in their second or third year of teaching and in different departments and led by a middle manager. They were each given a £500 honorarium – to be paid at the end of the task – to examine the phenomenon and produce an agreed short report covering its impact here when compared with another school where the data suggested it was better and 1000 words each for how things could be improved both in their own faculty and across the school as a whole'.

I is for INSET (or occasional days)

Ever since Secretary of State, Kenneth Baker, introduced what were named eponymously Baker days, schools have used or misused them in a variety of ways.

Clearly when they occur is a matter of some concern to parents, so they need to be calendared and discussed with governors from time to time – indeed we consider a governors' feedback on their use wouldn't come amiss. Those who have made the most of occasional days, have focused on using them for professional development of one sort or another. Among those uses have been the following:

- Using one of the days for whole-staff review of a practice recently introduced – such as vertical tutoring, or curriculum change – preceded by a small group of staff collecting evidence and presenting position papers. The day, which also sometimes has a student group feeding back on their perceptions, leads to 'adjustments' for improvement.
- A residential every three years where staff re-examine the vision and aims of the school, or its teaching and learning practices. This will increase the likelihood of more 'singing from the same song sheet' and is best scheduled as a day tagged on to a holiday.
- Visiting another school which is in session, in groups of two or three or in faculties in order to 'observe' teachers. The 'learning walks' need a very clear focus with a view to extending the school's management organizationally and / or teaching and learning practice. This always requires a follow-up scheduled set of meetings.
- Turning over a whole day to pupil feedback led by student leaders.
- Bringing in a national expert for the day or a half day to run a workshop on a topic related to the school improvement plan.
- Sharing a day with another school / schools to take advantage of more numbers when arranging a national speaker / workshop leader.
- Sharing a day with partner primaries to discuss transition in detail.

I is for Interim Executive Board (IEB)

 It's skills with strength that governs a ship.

Thomas Fuller

An Interim Executive Board (IEB) consists of a small group of experienced and expert people (typically three to five) who are appointed to replace the governing body of a school for a temporary period, in order to secure a sound basis for further improvement and promote high standards of educational achievement. This usually happens when a school goes into special measures or is experiencing significant turbulence. When in office, IEBs act as the governing body of the school and take on their responsibilities, including the management of the budget, the curriculum, staffing, pay and performance management. IEBs can be an effective solution in schools where a step change in the leadership and management is required for a temporary period. They are best used when the governing body is providing insufficient challenge to the headteacher and senior management team; or where there has been a breakdown in working relationships which is having an impact on standards. IEBs would normally be in place for a year until new governance arrangements can be put in place. In our experience their great advantage is that they can act very quickly to stabilise and improve a school although care has to be taken to maintain effective communication with all the stakeholders, particularly staff and parents.

With the increasing tendency of schools being 'forced academies' as they fall below the 'floor targets', IEBs are being used by LAs – themselves under pressure from DFE – to ensure local compliance with the national agenda.

I is for Interventions to raise school standards

> ❝ **Success comes in cans;**
> **Failure comes in can'ts.**
>
> Anon ❞

These interventions can be defined as focused programmes of educational activities which are designed to make a distinct difference to present practice. They will usually have a significant impact on teacher's behaviour as reflective professionals, on pupil development and learning, and on whole-school culture. As intervention is such a generic term it is necessary to make a distinction between large-scale interventions as major case studies of educational change, small scale interventions which are designed to make an immediate difference and classroom interventions which we have covered elsewhere. For example, changes in the curriculum and assessment practices involve a major re-appraisal of the school's provision and procedures with significant elements of training and professional development.

Examples of small-scale interventions are many but in school improvement terms these most often refer to the extra things a school does to raise standards, particularly with very critical year groups such as Year 6 and Year 11 who face external assessment. Key to this is the rigorous analysis of pupil progress data through pupil tracking systems. This will often reveal groups of pupils or individual pupils who are being left behind. As a school can only be considered effective if it promotes progress beyond what should be expected, given prior attainment and development factors, for all its pupils, schools devise a programme of interventions to secure this. The interventions with pupils to raise standards are many and varied but they will rely on forensic analysis of data, continual assessment of pupil progress, review of targets and consistency of practice across all teachers and support staff.

One of the most common interventions is a programme of one-to-one tutoring, coaching, mentoring or other support at critical moments on a pupil's learning journey. This demands the harnessing of all the schools' human resources – teaching assistants, teaching associates, adult volunteers, other pupils, and the better use and organization of teacher time. While there is a tradition of one-to-one tuition in schools such as peripatetic music teaching, sports coaching, reading recovery tuition, specialist teaching assistants, personalizing support for a wide range of pupils to make sure they progress academically is a greater challenge.

However, in many schools it is becoming a sophisticated operation so that apart from the timetabled lessons pupils now expect some additional provision to secure progress at the required rate and to succeed in external tests and examinations.

Some examples of secondary interventions at Key Stage 4:

- published programme of 'intervention' opportunities before and after school
- one-to-one provision in English and mathematics
- saturday morning school – occasional intensive sessions
- easter school
- residential study time
- senior leadership team mentoring of 'critical' students
- parent / pupil attainment evenings
- re-grouping and re-setting
- rewards and incentives
- homework clubs
- subject surgeries
- master classes.

Some examples of primary interventions at Key Stage 2:

- one-to-one provision in English and mathematics
- guided groups for provision teaching in English and mathematics
- breakfast learning e.g. 'Bright Start Clubs'
- booster revision classes before and after school and targeted at weekends and holidays
- parent / child and teacher reviews of progress
- gifted and talented workshops
- ICT groups using the Virtual Learning Platform
- mentoring 'critical students'
- links to outside support e.g. The Children's University.

In both primary and secondary schools in university cities there is a growing movement of engaging voluntary help on a one-to-one basis from undergraduates.

Further reading
See U is for University links, see C is for Classroom interventions.

A
B
C
D
E
F
G
H
I
J
K
L
M
N
O
P
Q
R
S
T
U
V
W
X
Y
Z

J is for Job descriptions

Not everyone would consider job descriptions vital to the smooth running of a school but they couldn't be more wrong. Sloppily put-together job descriptions can sap energy; written imaginatively they release energy.

Crucially, they will relate to the staff handbook in the sense that the description of 'lead' and 'support' responsibilities for different aspects of school life will be reflected in the language of the job descriptions. So too will they relate to the tasks necessary to carry out the policies. The best schools now avoid a long list of duties ending with the catch-all 'and such other duties as may from time to time be determined' preferring instead to list 'primary' or 'lead' responsibilities along with 'secondary' and 'support' responsibilities – the latter usually in teams. Job descriptions are closely linked to 'performance management' or 'staff appraisal' or 'professional development'. Different schools use different language according to the climate they are seeking to encourage for those closely related activities and the emphasis they think appropriate for individual staff discussion.

In the best schools, job descriptions are provisional and subject to review and change after a specified period. In this way, leadership can be reviewed and rotated to the benefit of the individual and the school as a whole. What is absolutely crucial is to look at the policies and practices which are held dear to the school and put the job descriptions alongside, to make sure that job descriptions are so framed as to cover the eventuality of someone falling ill or leaving and a treasured small initiative being then allowed quietly to disappear.

Put in all new teaching job descriptions the expectation that if candidates are to teach examinable classes they will do a stint as an external examiner and give them an honorarium in addition to the examiner's fee for doing so.

J is for Judgement

 The seal of knowledge is in the head; of wisdom, in the heart. We are sure to judge wrong if we do not feel right.

William Hazlitt

Judgement is one of the most elusive issues in school improvement. We mean by this the skill to choose sensitively and accurately when or whether to do something. There will be a host of occasions in all aspects of school life where members of staff at all levels of seniority are exercising judgement. Before picking out a few we believe the most important of all is trying to assess sound judgement when employing new members of staff. This is why, in the section on that topic, we explain that the more you can push the questioning to what the candidate *has* done which turned out well or badly, the more you can assess their judgement. Providing them with a case study which asks them what they would do if confronted with such a situation can also reveal much about judgement. Of course this affects governors too especially when making headship appointments.

There are all sorts of aspects of school life where judgement is key such as:

- what priorities govern the making of the timetable
- whether or to what extent, when and how to 'set'
- how to involve parents / guardians at an early stage so issues don't escalate
- when to exclude and how to keep staff on-side in difficult behaviour issues where perhaps their judgement was at fault
- how to judge what each member of staff needs to bring out their best
- when to move to 'capability' procedures with a member of staff
- how to avoid being a 'bull at a gate' when introducing change and ensuring in process that that all stakeholders are consulted in the right order and to the right extent and occasionally deciding that the change has to wait
- what to insist on as part of 'singing from the same song sheet'.

And for the classroom teacher there are myriad lesson by lesson – even second by second – judgements including:

- when and how to change seating plans
- when to diverge from lesson plans

- how to ensure fair distribution of questions
- when to 'tactically ignore' behaviour
- how to divide time for individuals between 'appreciative enquiry' and 'problem solving'
- when to use comparative and summative assessment with individual and groups of pupils.

For the primary home class teacher and secondary form tutor there are yet more judgements as there are for all the support staff.

Broadly speaking, the experienced leader will know that the guiding principles in making these judgements are to stick to the stated values of the school and to ask how far the answer to any of them will help the least advantaged members of the community and be sure it won't make their lot worse. That is to say try to live by the values of equity and equality.

When someone is new to a job, inevitably their judgement will be hampered by unfamiliarity with the context, though of course there is a natural predisposition which you will have discovered at interview. So it's as well to bear in mind how job descriptions are best constructed with emphasis on responsibility, and why mentors and coaching are crucial, not to mention how delegation is exercised and how, through induction and CPD, judgement is developed.

K is for Kes factor

It was a discerning secondary head who brought this factor to our attention. She was remarking on the film and the book of the 1950s (*A Kestrel for a Knave* by Barry Hines) which tells the story of a northern boy and his preoccupying interest in kestrels and his own 'Kes' in particular. The boy was seen as a failure at his secondary school who were unaware of this consuming pastime.

We agreed that the story was indicative of three important factors for schools to consider. First, that everybody is the richer as an adult for having an interest which is going to be a lifelong interest which is fulfilling for them and which perhaps involves the development of some skill in which they can take pride. Second, this skill or interest may not be part of school life – as with Kes. Third is the importance of the teacher / student relationship.

A colleague of ours who is a headteacher has resolved that her school is going to set itself the challenging target of asking each of their school leavers what their particular 'Kes' interest is. It seems to us a very timely and appropriate thing to do at a time when the measures of school effectiveness are so circumscribed.

Our butterfly on the next page is a true one but we have no idea as we write what the outcome will be as it is in the summer of 2012 that the schools decided to do it.

A
B
C
D
E
F
G
H
I
J

The Kes factor

Description

Secondary heads in West Sussex and in Suffolk held separate conferences in July 2012 and some of those attending resolved to return to their schools and enquire of their partner primary schools the names of the youngsters who were coming to secondary who were most at risk of 'learning to fail' – that is to say, they had risk factors in terms of low attainment levels and other challenges. Of each of these youngsters the heads were going to ask what the youngsters were good at or interested in – if you like, the 'Kes' factor. Their intention and resolve was that each of their senior leadership team would talk informally with one of these youngsters remarking that the primary school has said how good they are at whatever it is they have been told. Their intention is to continually follow up with conversations in the first term and make sure the tutor does too and do whatever it takes to convince the youngster that they are noticed and valued.

Comment on impact

The hope is of course that the outcome of this comparatively simple strategy will be that at least a few of the youngsters will increase their confidence and self-belief to the point that they will take advantage of some of the one-to-one programmes and make progress in their learning. Checking with some of the heads in the autumn term we can report enthusiasm and a determination on the part of one to extend the practice to a chosen few with blockages to their learning in Years 8 and 9. (See also H is for Hyacinth.)

L
M
N
O
P
Q
R
S
T
U
V
W
X
Y
Z

I have come to the frightening conclusion: I am the decisive element in the classroom. It is my personal approach that creates the climate. It is my daily mood that makes the weather. As a teacher I possess tremendous power to make a child's life miserable or joyous. I can be a tool of torture or an instrument of inspiration. I can humiliate or humour, hurt or heal. In all situations it is my response that decides whether a crisis is escalated or de-escalated; a child humanised or dehumanised.

H. G. Ginott
Teacher and Child

A
B
C
D
E
F
G
H
I
J
K
L
M
N
O
P
Q
R
S
T
U
V
W
X
Y
Z

K is for Key expenditures of time by school leaders

Time is vital for everyone, but for none more so than busy headteachers. In the primary sector moreover, heads often arrive in the post after the unreal experience of a 'timetabled' day as a teacher who is governed as no other professional is, by a contrived set of predetermined activities.

Two cautions and a health warning

The first is pretty obvious: namely that headteachers, whether they are successful or not, are deeply conscious of the fragmented nature of their days: they flit from one activity to another, sometimes spending very short time spans on any one activity before moving on to another. The successful heads know this to be a tendency of the job, but guard against life becoming ad hoc: they know that over a day, they may not achieve the allocation of time to plan that they want, but that over a week or a term, they can and will. Distraction is inevitable – but in the long run, it can be defeated. Secondly, you will find that when you add up the time spent on all of the different tasks, they add up to more than a week's worth of working hours. That's because the key starting point is that successful leaders use time twice or three times over. They have mastered the skill of doing things simultaneously rather than sequentially – not in everything, of course, but in many tasks. While they are doing their regular 'daily round' of the classrooms, they may also be doing business with a visitor, or reinforcing a 'singing from the same song sheet' message with staff. Quantitative surveys of the use of time, of which there are many, may serve solicitors, architects and accountants for cost allocation to charge clients but they are a dangerously misleading way of measuring headteachers' time. And that brings us to a health warning. We used the words 'dangerously misleading', because the great problem with successful headteachers is that they are so committed.

They worry that if only they had devoted more time to this or that person or activity, then the outcome (in their private and unvoiced opinion) would have been better. They, too, will quickly feel guilt regarding the contested issue of how they use their time. Indeed, as an antidote to guilt, it is probably as well to say that whatever the pattern of their time, successful headteachers need time off – not particularly to think, but to draw breath and recharge. That won't be on a daily or weekly basis, but it will be taken in dollops every now and then.

We have referred here to headteachers but we think it applies to deputies and heads of department too. What we have set out in the references at the end of this section are essential reading for school leaders wishing to make the best use of their time. It is recognizable territory for the stand-alone head of a primary,

secondary or special school. But it will not be for the system leader or the
executive head of more than one school whose role is analogous to that of an
education officer in a small local authority in the sense that they are necessarily
more detached from the everyday running of the school. They too, however,
have their 'optimum use of time' rules and many of them derive from the other
entries to which we now refer.

Further reading

See also A is for Acts of unexpected kindness; S is for Sitting on the wall not the fence; S is for
Skalds not Scolds; H is for Headteachers teaching, learning and assessing for most of their time; H is
for Headteachers spending their evenings and weekends balancing work and home life.

K is for Knowledge creation and innovation

 The capacity of a school to mobilise its intellectual capital
is critical, for this is what fosters new ideas and creates new
knowledge, which leads to successful innovation in making the
school more effective.

David Hargreaves

As well as their core purpose schools are in the business of developing new
knowledge and practices to drive their improvement. This may relate to better
classroom organization, improved pedagogy, advanced use of ICT or a range of
innovations improving provision.

David Hargreaves has written extensively about the three elements of school
capital as being organizational, social and intellectual. (See *Working Laterally:
How Innovation Networks Make an Education Epidemic*, 2003.) He defines
intellectual capital as an 'endless supply of focused intellectual curiosity with
effective knowledge sharing which build capacity'. Some individual schools and
groups of schools, through collaborative learning environments, are creating
knowledge through innovative practice in school improvement. In both student
learning and staff learning they are using the techniques of modelling, peer
learning, team teaching, coaching, mentoring, peer review and action research
to build up their knowledge of what works. By keeping these under review and
anticipating changes they make these work even better while innovating and
trying new strategies. They sustain intellectual curiosity and the capacity to
innovate through seeking and modelling best and next practice both in their
own school and with other schools. Some schools deliberately challenge their
staff and students to create new knowledge and practice by organizing learning
in different ways e.g. specific 'super' learning days and weeks. Others encourage
different parts of the school to build knowledge creation and innovation into
all their work programmes. Some capture their new knowledge capital in their

A
B
C
D
E
F
G
H
I
J
K
L
M
N
O
P
Q
R
S
T
U
V
W
X
Y
Z

virtual learning environment platforms, or in the form of learning narratives, case study publications and annual teaching and learning conferences with appropriate research papers. Of course, it is one thing to systematically create knowledge, it is another thing to effectively transfer this knowledge. Inside schools there is a lot of established practice on the operation of professional learning communities (see P is for Professional learning communities) and the growth of collaboratives, chains and partnerships of schools should assist this in particular Teaching Schools and their Alliances (see T is for Teaching schools). George Berwick's book *Engaging in Excellence – The Approach, Vol 1,* 2010, sets out the key components of effective knowledge management, the virtual spiral of knowledge development and how knowledge can be best transferred and volume 3 in this series will concern itself exclusively with knowledge capital.

With regard to innovation generally it is best to remember that this is a process not an event, it is about creating a market for ideas through smart experimentation, it is often re-combination rather than invention, and above all it is about moving from good practice to best practice, replication and then scaling up.

 Innovation is a change that creates a new dimension of performance.

Peter Drucker

L is for Lavatories

For generations, secondary school lavatories have either been locked or are places where pupils visit only 'in extremis'. As a result children's bladders over the years have suffered in ways best left to the imagination! It doesn't have to be like this, as our primary schools have always shown. Secondary colleagues will counter that by saying that teenagers are different and of course they are right. Some secondary schools now see the lavatories as a touchstone of whether the improvements they've made are simply skin deep.

Involving what's called 'student voice' (see S is for Student voice) they suggest to the school's council issues that are concerning them and seek students' comments on the issues and ask about omissions. The school's council are then provided with a budget either for the school or a part of the resources required to solve the particular project. They are guaranteed to raise issues which affect the students' environment and so the lavatories are very likely to be on their list. There are many solutions to this perennial problem now claimed by schools. The best ingredients, apart from pupil involvement in identifying solutions, include refurbishment, installation of smoke detectors that only go off in the main office (so miscreants can be caught with a 'smoking gun' as it were), and then regular inspection of the toilets either with paid attendants or regular patrols of school council members and staff of the school.

L is for Leadership

> **Level 5 leaders blend extreme personal humility with intense professional will.**
>
> Jim Collins

The topic of leadership has attracted more attention than any other aspect of school improvement. Indeed, it has prompted the establishment of not just the National College of School Leadership but a whole set of leadership centres regionally based on groups of local authorities and universities. It is one of the processes we have highlighted in our grammar of school improvement and in the introductory section. We believe that it is best shared or distributed – among staff whether of phase, faculty or school and with pupils, governors and parents. There are many parts of the rest of the book which deal with leadership and we cross-refer to them here.

First, there is the question of appointing leaders among staff (see S is for Staff appointments). When appointing school headteachers however, there are extra considerations: it is often the case that governors have never had the experience of choosing a head. To expect them to do this unaided is to ask for trouble, for, like any other activity, practice if not making perfect, certainly makes less imperfect. The school chains have an advantage in this respect and our knowledge of the best of them suggests that they seem to have learnt from what was required by law after the Education Act of 1986 when the final selection of a head was shared by a panel consisting of equal numbers on the one hand of governors and on the other of what was then called the local educational authority (LEA) – now the local authority (LA). This device ensured that neither could railroad the other into a favoured internal or external appointment and that among the LEA representatives there developed an expertise over a period that was invaluable to discerning governors. Of course all that has gone though the 'chains' have the potential to re-establish such practices with equal numbers of experienced personnel from the chains and governors making the appointment. For other governors wishing to avoid mistakes, clearly reading and following some of the simple advice under S is for Staff appointments will help, but we would strongly advocate using proven expertise either from a reliable, experienced consultancy possibly one recommended by the LA, or better still the Association of School and College Leaders or the National Association of Head Teacher nationally, or of course the National College itself. Certainly, the process needs to be rigorous and should contain more than one stage and a series of challenging tasks.

Michael Fullan has set out a good visual way of considering the qualities and characteristics of what we might be looking for in school leadership as follows:

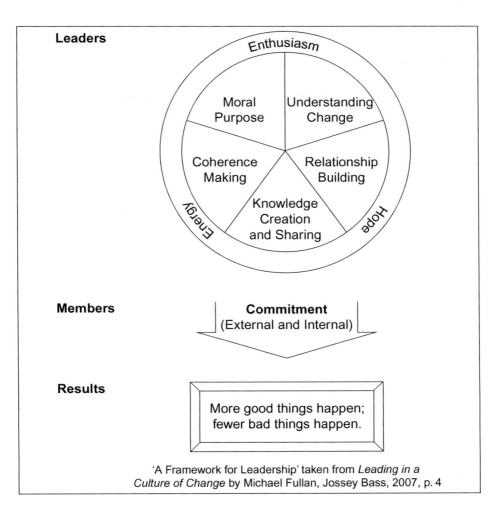

'A Framework for Leadership' taken from *Leading in a Culture of Change* by Michael Fullan, Jossey Bass, 2007, p. 4

School leaders, on taking up an appointment, prepare themselves for the first stage of headship – initiation (see F is for Four stages of headship). They are clear about their Values (see V is for Values), help everyone to become involved and contribute to the vision for what the school might be like after a few years (see V is for Vision and vision statements).

Then they are embarking on the second stage of headship – the developmental. Meanwhile, they are carrying out the essential tasks (see E is for Essential tasks of school leadership), learning to manage their time (see H is for Headteachers spend their time and K is for Key expenditures of time by school leaders) and becoming masters of the art of delegation (see D is for Delegation). They understand the nature of complex change and any changes they introduce benefit from that understanding (see C is for Change).

They will have read about leadership and understand the need to be a role model for learning. Most successful leaders relate to the following four habits as characteristics of successful school leaders. They need:

- *Unwarranted optimism:* this echoes the framework Fullan advocates and it appeals to the experienced hard-pressed leaders as they reflect on the number of occasions they have had to appear determinedly up-beat when, at the time, it was hard to see their way through the apparently insurmountable difficulties confronting them.
- *To regard crisis as the norm and complexity as fun:* as anyone familiar with school life will know, there will be no shortage of opportunity for this to show itself.
- *An endless supply of intellectual curiosity:* if the leader isn't speculating about ideas and possibilities – especially those offered by others – a school starts to stall and teachers lose their creativity.
- *A complete absence of paranoia or self-pity:* leadership can be lonely and difficult decisions sometimes are made when there is a real danger that you can start to feel sorry for yourself.

Sharing a room to share and grow leadership

Description

The description of this butterfly demands the story that brought it to our notice. The head in question was one of those headteachers who made us feel we were 'no better than we ought to be'. This was usually a good sign in our experience! She taught us a lesson we have never forgotten. We were both separately lobbied by her for extra accommodation. Her school was on a challenging estate in east Birmingham and was bursting at the seams. We visited separately and both of us were taken on a conducted tour which ended in her office which she shared with her two deputies.

Anyway, she got her extra accommodation and we visited again, and after our tour of the new accommodation we visited her same office which she still shared with two deputies, though they were different ones as the others had moved on to headship. This time we couldn't resist the obvious question, 'Why do you still share a room with your two deputies?' We received the following rejoinder: 'Oh, you aren't one of those traditional status seekers are you who only want the job so you can have an office of your own? Surely everybody nowadays shares an office with deputies. It's such a good way of talking issues over as they crop up and very good staff development.'

The incident brought home the changed nature of headship. It really was the case a generation ago that, if they wanted to – and of course many did not – heads could treat their job as an end in itself. Headship represented status in a deferential society. All they had to do was repeat last year's timetable, make sure the 'No Parents Beyond This Point' sign was in place and join the local Rotary club – yes it was mainly a male preserve. No exam results were published. SATs didn't exist. HMI would visit on average once in 20 years and if they did, they would leave a private short supportive note of their visit rather than send a judgemental letter to parents.

That world with its low expectations of what's possible has given way to a more ambitious one albeit also more participative, disputatious and accountable. Nowadays there's no hiding place for inadequate heads.

Comment on impact

We noticed that the school was outstanding at producing future heads and when we researched further by talking with those who had benefited, they all commented on the fast learning involved. We could also see that it aided delegation and shared leadership as well as more efficient and timely management.

L is for Learning

 Learning is the whole business of the school: it deserves to be at the forefront of the minds and conversations of everyone.
Tim Brighouse

At the heart of any really successful school is 'teaching which leads to learning'. Ultimately, after pupils' work has been successfully assessed by the teacher, the process should begin to enable the pupils themselves to assess their own work, as they become increasingly autonomous learners.

The model of progress here is summarized in the sequence:

- dependent = shallow learning
- independent = deep learning
- interdependent = profound learning

Some of the suggestions within S is for Student voice illustrate ways in which pupils can be more involved in their own learning and make progress on this continuum.

Of course, it can be argued that the reference to Judith Little's research into successful schools (See T is for Teachers and teaching) are schools where:

- teachers talk about teaching
- teachers observe each other teaching
- teachers plan, organize, monitor and evaluate their teaching together
- teachers teach each other;

A
B
C
D
E
F
G
H
I
J
K
L
M
N
O
P
Q
R
S
T
U
V
W
X
Y
Z

is all very well, but somewhat limited. What if we changed it to the following:

- staff talk about learning
- staff observe each other's learning
- staff plan, observe, monitor and evaluate their work together
- staff learn from each other;

that way we should be forced to think of all the staff and what they all contribute to learning. It would have implications for staff meetings and those who belonged to the School Improvement Group. The third point of reviewing together would ensure that, at the time of self-evaluation, everyone's contribution was valued. There would be implications for staffrooms too. Finally, it forces us to ask ourselves: is teaching leading to learning or does everybody else have plans for improvement in their own performance and we have forgotten to do one for ourselves?

Some organizations have gone further and introduced 'Learning plans for the year', ensuring all staff are clear and reminded of the difference between 'predictions', 'expectations' and 'targets' and that the watchword for every lesson is not 'What am I going to teach?' but 'What are the youngsters going to learn?'

Improving staff knowledge of new children's literature: an agenda item at staff meetings

Description

One of the phenomena of today's age is the burgeoning area of children's books. It is immensely difficult for teachers to keep up with what is available. One school helps crack that issue by having as a standing item on staff meeting agendas 'new books'. At each meeting teachers take it in turns to describe a new book they have used with their class and give it a rating. The deal is that another teacher either in the year above or the year below then commits to use it at some point in the year and report back.

Comment on impact

The school claims that over the course of the year staff more easily keep up with what has been published and that the impact on discussion being about 'teaching and learning' rather than transactional business is significant.

L is for Learning narratives

 Give enquiry and reflection pride of place.

Louise Stoll

We have talked elsewhere about case studies of excellent practice and 'butterfly' collections but learning narratives are short, sharp (about 1000 words) pieces related particularly to pedagogy and the practice of teaching and learning. Teachers are natural researchers and in almost every lesson they are constantly analyzing and refining their practice. Groups of primary and special teachers sometimes reflect together over practice with particular years or groups of children and resolve to try a new approach or plan something differently. Similarly, secondary teachers, often in curriculum areas, will reflect about teaching a specific subject to different groups. This collaborative reflection can often be captured best through learning narratives that establish the focus of the enquiry, describe what has been done differently and evaluate impact. If time for collective reflection is built into the 'meeting' cycle either in years, phases, or curriculum areas then these could be written up collectively as a series of enquiry narratives. Some schools as part of their internal review and quality assurance processes ask that a set number of these are produced. These then can be published annually by the school for themselves and other schools, demonstrating the quality of reflective practice and reflective practitioners which is real self-evaluation and a driver to constantly improve teaching and learning.

Further reading
See A is for Action research.

L is for Learning styles

 The fact that teachers are thinking from the learner's end has to be a good thing.

Guy Claxton

The concept and practice of identifying learning styles of children in order to teach better can be controversial. The most commonly used system in schools is the VAK model of classification, which divides children into visual, auditory or kinaesthetic learners: those who like to look, those who like to listen and those who learn best through physical activity, sometimes called 'active learners'. Most learning styles analysis relies on self-assessment questionnaires completed by children. This has obvious defects; many school activities are not purely visual, auditory or kinaesthetic, but a mixture of all three. Even if we accept that

A
B
C
D
E
F
G
H
I
J
K

M
N
O
P
Q
R
S
T
U
V
W
X
Y
Z

children learn in different ways, most teachers agree that a preferred learning style is simply an acquired habit and that children need to experience other styles. Most schools that embrace the concept of learning styles try to encourage teachers to make lessons accessible to all students by including visual, auditory and kinaesthetic elements. They believe that it is equally important for teachers to analyze their own style of learning and teaching. Most teachers, they argue, allow their own style to become their habitual teaching style – to the detriment of those students who learn in different ways.

The danger with other rigid classifications of children's learning preferences is that children will be labelled and forced into a narrow view of their own abilities. However, some mechanisms for assessing learning styles take a more holistic view and look at a wide range of issues under the heading of 'Learning styles'. For example, there are learning styles analysis profiles based on a wide series of questions grouped under categories that are brain based, sensory, physical, environmental, social and attitudinal. The outcomes or profiles avoid labelling children by describing preferences and flexibilities in the spectrum of issues involved. Nevertheless, it seems that learning style models are still an oversimplification of the complex way in which children process information. However, the debate over learning styles has at least encouraged teachers to examine their own practice and explore a wider repertoire of teaching strategies. Perhaps instead of talking about learning styles, we should talk about learning skills and provision of an environment most suitable of learning, whether that is individual, group or class work, the availability of learning technologies or aural stimulation.

L is for Learning walks

It is one of life's great ironies: schools are in the business of teaching and learning, yet they are terrible at learning from each other. If they ever discover how to do this, their future is assured.

Michael Fullan

The aim of learning walks is to see how enquiries in the form of structured, focused visits to schools and classrooms can contribute to school improvement and self-evaluation. Sometimes this is practised within a school but it usually applies to formal visits to the learning areas of other schools. A learning walk is certainly not an inspection nor a sight-seeing trip. It is a rigorous and robust enquiry process which requires a focus on chosen, shared issues to explore learning.

A learning walk works best when schools decide on a clear focus linked to a commitment to use the evidence gathered to improve practice e.g. closing attainment gaps, English as an additional language (EAL) provision and specific aspects of teaching and learning. The principle behind this activity is that schools can learn from each other about best practice in different contexts. To be most effective this exercise needs to be approached by everybody with professional commitment, appreciative enquiry, trust and generosity of spirit. In process terms normally schools in particular networks identify areas of best practice validated by internal quality evidence and / or OfSTED inspection evidence, or other review evidence. Each school then commits to hosting visits to any of their designated areas of best practice together with the provision of appropriate documentation and resources. Learning walks seem to work best as a half day activity allowing for a short tour focusing on the learning environment but particularly on 'deep dives' into two specific areas with time for a final discussion to discuss common issues and share insights. The 'visiting' school then reflects and evaluates what changes in its practice it is going to make and the host school also reflects, as a result of observations, how it can improve its already good practice. Within a network, all schools commit to host and visit a set number of times in a year and use this as a way of further school self-evaluation and improvement.

Further reading
See www.learningwalks.wetpaint.com

L is for Lesson plans

When we started teaching it was rare, especially for experienced teachers to have detailed lesson plans! Now the frequent observation of teachers by senior staff and peers – not to mention inspectors – will mean that the teacher will hand over lesson plans outlining activities, lesson objectives and a variety of activities to ensure there is pace and involvement of each and every pupil. Teaching and learning is clearly the most important part of school improvement: improve the lessons to the level of the best and huge improvements for students will occur. We have begun to move on from basic models of the three-, four- or five-part lessons with learning objectives and plenaries.

A recent development has been the 'flipped lesson'. This involves the teacher videoing their 'explanation' sessions and setting the homework which involves the pupils looking at it either on the virtual learning environment or the intranet and then spending the lesson with the pupils doing the follow-up work and the teacher offering coaching advice to individuals or groups of pupils. Another example of this 'flipped approach' is to ask the pupils to research the issue on the internet as homework and then to be prepared to present to the class.

A
B
C
D
E
F
G
H
I
J
K
L
M
N
O
P
Q
R
S
T
U
V
W
X
Y
Z

Nevertheless, there are some time-honoured aspects to teaching which any school's policy and practice will cover as they seek to move from 'good' to 'outstanding'. Among them will be the use of questions and storytelling in teaching.

Further reading

See is Q for Questions and S is for Storytelling.

There are numerous websites on lesson planning and flipped lessons, the most encouraging and revealing of which is http://transformededucator.blogspot.co.uk/

L is for Library

School and public libraries

Some newly-built schools have foregone a library space. We think that this is a mistake even though we know that there is a sea of change brought on by the revolution in communication technologies, and a different approach to public library policy and practice as a result of this and, of course, public expenditure cuts. For example, we know that in France it is now fashionable to call what were once 'bibliotheques', 'mediatheques' and one local authority has called their public libraries 'ideas stores' while others have seriously discussed closing many of their libraries. The future of the book is in question and some American states have decreed that all text books should be online.

So change is rapid and inexorable.

For primary schools at least there is still the task of ensuring that all children can read and while we know that the book corner is a vital part of each primary classroom we believe that burgeoning children's literature and change in family habits mean a primary school library is vital to a school. The school library services have disappeared and it requires groups of primary schools to work together in order to make sure that through their book and library policies and practice they should be able to optimise the chances of all children acquiring the reading habit. 'Book floods' – a rich collection of the best books imported for a period – are ideal but difficult to organize. Easier to arrange are visits from storytellers who may have the skills to train up teachers to be storytelling fellows among the staff and so promote better writing among children as well as a love of books.

For secondary schools this has always been a problem, but most schools recognize just what a difference a really well run library can make both to the environment for youngsters and for staff. To be well run there needs to be a close liaison between the school librarian and the ICT facilities manager. One head we know ensures they share rooms so that it is more likely they bounce ideas and possibilities off each other: 'You can promote some joint visits through performance management so that they share some professional development opportunities'. The library itself can be used to promote subliminal messages through display and can be open from dawn to dusk so students from backgrounds that are not conducive to study can use the space when they wish. Heads of department too can order books for specialist areas of the library: indeed it should ideally be part of the teaching and learning policy so that separate book collections don't start appearing in faculty areas but are maintained centrally in the library.

Staff libraries

One of the features of great schools is that they have a staff library, not least because staff are encouraged to read widely about education. This means there is an expectation to add to the staff library and to use chapters / extracts from some of the books to promote discussion about teaching and learning in staff and school meetings. Many schools locate staff libraries in staff workrooms but that perhaps misses a trick, after all there is no reason why a section of the school library shouldn't be devoted to it and a few schools do just that.

With the increasing tendency for schools to cluster together in partnerships, there are greater possibilities for sharing an approach to libraries to take full advantage of the fact that over 80% of secondary schools have a trained librarian.

Further reading
For expert advice, consult the School Library Association which gives much helpful advice: www.sla.org.uk

L is for Literacy

 Finding ways to engage pupils in reading may be one of the most effective ways to leverage social change.
OECD Report.

Every school knows the importance of doing well in literacy (speaking and listening, reading and writing): after all its results in English – and mathematics (see N is for Numeracy) – key stage tests and GCSE exams will heavily influence how the school is judged by the public and OfSTED.

So it deserves an entry of its own in this book. We examine first the theoretical case for the current emphasis and then illustrate ways in which schools seem to be successful in improving outcomes for children.

A
B
C
D
E
F
G
H
I
J
K
L
M
N
O
P
Q
R
S
T
U
V
W
X
Y
Z

The case for literacy

The most recent annual reports of HMCI, other reports by OfSTED and independent research have drawn attention to the crucial importance of literacy in improving children's life chances but also to the fact that the attainment of particular groups of children and young people in literacy falls far below that of the rest of the population. The underperformance of those from low-income families is very marked, particularly at secondary level. The Communication Trust, which is funded by the DfE to raise awareness of speech and language issues, highlighted the following:

- vocabulary at the age of five is a powerful predictor of GCSE achievement
- two thirds of seven to 14 year olds with serious behaviour problems have language impairment
- 65% of young people in young offender's institutions have communication difficulties.

In the White Paper, *The Importance of Teaching* (2010), the government outlined its intention for OfSTED to concentrate in the new school inspection framework of 2012 on the teaching of reading and on pupils' literacy skills by the time they leave primary and secondary education. The guidance and training materials for inspectors available to all schools makes this explicit, relating to reviewing literacy across the curriculum, monitoring attainment in English, tracking groups of pupils and reviewing pupils' work and teachers' marking. The recently published Standards of Teachers taking effect from September 2012, make it clear that all teachers should 'demonstrate an understanding of and take responsibility for promoting high standards of literacy, articulacy and the correct use of standard English' and that, if teaching early reading, 'demonstrate a clear understanding of systematic synthetic phonics'. There is much debate about synthetic phonics and particularly about a test being introduced in 2012 for all six year olds. To many, it seems an unwarranted intrusion into teachers' professional judgement and the best and most successful teachers maintain that synthetic phonics is just one in an armoury of techniques they will deploy to overcome different children's barriers to reading success. Of course, too, there is a strong professional argument for saying that in the UK we focus on reading too early and rightly argue that speaking and vocabulary understanding are vital precursors to the process of learning to read. Nevertheless, for the moment schools and teachers must work in a context where synthetic phonics is part of a tight accountability system for literacy.

What schools are doing about it

As part of their ongoing school improvement strategies, and in the context of current accountabilities, many schools are reviewing and re-focusing their literacy policies and practices. Of course, context and current performance varies considerably but there is no substitute for a continuing, sharp analysis of progress data, especially around the performance of different groups indicating the need for effective intervention.

Through reports, research, peer reviews and partnership working, schools are sharing best practice in promoting literacy, focusing on a consistency of approach across the curriculum. Some of this includes:

- A strong focus on literacy in the school improvement plan with a specific literacy action plan.
- Senior members of staff with excellent knowledge of literacy and its pedagogy coordinating the plan and a literacy development group.
- Quality professional development for all staff with high expectations for pupils' achievement in literacy.
- Inter-school partnerships for English departments and literacy coordinators to learn from each other's practice.
- Carefully planned provision – including one-to-one support – to meet individual needs.
- Monitoring outcomes in literacy and evaluating the effectiveness of action and provision.
- Making the best use of libraries. (See L is for Libraries.)

In our visits to schools we have glimpsed imaginative ways of promoting literacy in both primary and secondary sectors. We have set out two butterflies at the end of this entry which may appeal but there are others. In the Ark Academy in Brent, for example, all teachers are teachers of reading and all staff are trained how to teach reading as part of staff induction. The school day starts with a 20 minute reading lesson for every student where teachers explicitly teach students skills: they develop vocabulary; teach them to read aloud with expression; how to skim, scan and summarize; how to question a text and much more. The reading programme is a major priority for the school in which they invest considerable resources. For them reading is never an extra initiative or an intervention programme: teaching reading is one of their core purposes. By prioritizing reading in this way they hope to deliver the very best results for the vast majority of students, despite large numbers joining them with poor reading skills. Of course, it is a new school with all the advantages which that brings in ensuring every member of staff is singing from the same song sheet.

In another existing school, in Key Stage 3 the English, history, geography, RE and science departments take it in turns to lead a whole-school termly emphasis on various aspects of syntax and grammar. Another has created a 'Language for learning and thinking' thesaurus intended to sort out the language which individual departments know is vital to have a chance of accessing the curriculum in Key Stage 4 and thereby increase their pupils' chances of exam success.

Further reading
See also OfSTED Reports on *Excellence in English* and *Moving English Forward; Action to raise standards in English* and *The Literacy Leader's Toolkit* by Graham Tyrer and Patrick Taylor.

A
B
C
D
E
F
G
H
I
J
K
L
M
N
O
P
Q
R
S
T
U
V
W
X
Y
Z

Extending pupils' vocabulary

Description

Led by the head of Year 8, after consultations with all heads of department, a secondary school decided to introduce a weekly vocabulary competition.

Each department took it in turns to announce at the Friday and Monday briefings, the three words which all teachers of Year 8 classes during the week had to incorporate within their lessons with appropriate definitions. So science, for example, one week chose 'analysis', 'hypothesis' and 'investigation'. Then each teacher, in addition to posting the words and definitions on the interactive whiteboard, added two more words of their own choosing.·

The subsequent competition involved all Year 8 students at the end of Thursday putting their selection of the three common words in the 'Vocabulary box' – with the first correct solution drawn at Friday's year assembly winning a prize. (They had eight forms of entry and eight winners, one per tutor group.)

Comment on impact

'Singing from the same song sheet' – or achieving consistency – without inhibiting teacher individualism is a perennial issue for urban secondary schools in particular. This is an example of achieving that which affects the curriculum.

What the 'butterfly' achieved was simple but impressive cooperation between the head of year and the heads of subject departments over a whole-school issue – extending language competence and understanding, without which youngsters have less hope for exams and life generally.

Heads of year and heads of department were considering similar but different awareness raising, cooperative efforts and competitions for other year groups based on other common issues e.g. mathematical challenges.

Have you met the Book Wizard?

Description

The head explained that the vital thing for children in later childhood – and certainly before going on to secondary – is to find an 'enthusiasm' which might turn out to be a lifelong interest. So she enlists staff and members of the community who she knows will be infectious communicators of their enthusiasm to read and talk to students. She notes down those children who are particularly inspired and makes sure they are supported in their interest. Then she brings in the Book Wizard. It is perhaps worth explaining that her theory is that children of that age are fascinated by Merlin, Harry Potter and all things magical. So she and her school have established that there is such a thing as a Book Wizard who seems to have a role in the arrival of books for the library and all things literary and magical about the school. The head says that her children understand that one of the things the Book Wizard does is send books to children from time to time. So the school has a supply of really good books and when the time is right they write an appropriate inscription and message from the Book Wizard, wrap up the brown paper and take it 20 miles away and send it through the post to the child's home address.

Comment on impact

It is easy to imagine what happens next. There is excitement both at home and later in the school when the child sees the wonderful arrival of the Book Wizard's present. The school believes it reinforces the motivational combination of an enthusiasm and its potential for causing a spurt in reading.

L is for Local Leader of Education (LLE)

Local Leaders of Education (LLE) provide leadership support and expertise to headteachers in a local area where schools are not making the progress expected of them. The concept of LLEs is built on a coaching model. Recruitment is carried out by the National College through a participating local authority only and to a bespoke local authority timetable. It includes a four day training programme held jointly with the local authority. An LLE spends approximately a day or half a week in the school being supported and will draw on a wide menu of activities in their coaching and mentoring role.

A
B
C
D
E
F
G
H
I
J
K
L
M
N
O
P
Q
R
S
T
U
V
W
X
Y
Z

The level of support is not at the depth or intensity provided by LLEs and their schools but does constitute an important additional resource in terms of school to school support. The precise focus of LLE work varies but it is usually where the headteacher would benefit from peer challenge and support to ensure a greater pace of improvement or where the headteacher is looking to develop fresh perspectives on issues presenting considerable challenge. Deployments usually last a year but could be longer depending on regular reviews of progress. Most local authorities now have a cadre of LLEs and similar to NLEs the White Paper anticipated an expansion of this programme to some 2,000 by 2014/2015. Evaluations from schools reveal good support for this approach to school improvement, stressing the importance of confidential collaboration and coaching. In many areas National Leaders of Education are working in tandem with LLEs to maximise the support available to local schools.

L is for Lunch hour

Chances are that when the school consults its school council on plans and priorities, it will also receive comment on the lunch hour and the queues. Lunch hours too can be transformed: solutions range from condensing the lunch hour to abolishing it altogether.

The former can involve:

- ensuring that all support staff have duties in their contract to help with supervision
- providing a rich range of activities, run either by the permanent staff, senior trained pupils with staff supervision or 'bought-in' entertainment
- having a clearly thought-through and implemented practice of music, played by a DJ – a rota of 'wannabe' pupils – during the lunch hour or as background calming music to modify behaviour. (Certain music affects mood – and of course disposition to learn – in different ways)
- changing the nature of the playground. Here, the pioneering work of 'Learning through Landscapes' has meant that the conventional tarmacadam can be transformed into a varied sequence of spaces defined by plants, structures and sculpture
- welcoming pupil access to the carefully designed and well-supervised range of ICT facilities, including those permeating the library, where pupils can pursue their 'independent study' or 'homework' assignments.

The abolition of the lunch hour has been implemented by a few schools. Anybody embarking on that option needs to visit a school that's done it and reflected on the outcome. Schools we know that have done it are The Compton in Barnet and Ninestiles in Birmingham. Each refurbished their dining area and catering facilities, a solution incidentally frequently pursued by those wishing to minimise queues. Then the two schools tackled the timetable, so pupils from different age groups (linked to faculty or subject) are off-timetable at different times. For instance, between 11.45 am and 1.30 pm, groups have their lunch together in a sitting of no more than 250. During their 'spare' time, after eating and while others are learning, the pupils are encouraged to pursue studies or take part in supervised playground activity. Both schools report 'transformation': by choosing different age groups to eat together, they have minimised large peer group behaviour problems.

A
B
C
D
E
F
G
H
I
J
K
L
M
N
O
P
Q
R
S
T
U
V
W
X
Y
Z

A
B
C
D
E
F
G
H
I
J
K
L
M
N
O
P
Q
R
S
T
U
V
W
X
Y
Z

M is for Marking

Not many teachers will say they enjoy marking, although they know it's such an important part of teaching and assessment. Long gone are the days of '$\frac{3}{10}$ try again' at the foot of a piece of homework. Those who are mastering the practices of AfL or formative assessment will relate to the following story. A visitor to a London comprehensive school was let loose with members of the school's council for half an hour. To break the ice he asked which teacher marked their work best and why? The body language of the teacher at the back of the room left him in no doubt that she thought this question 'off limits'. (When her name was mentioned a couple of minutes later however, she was all smiles and told the visitor afterwards what a good exchange it prompted!)

A youngster from Year 7 volunteered that Mr Hodge the geography teacher was very good at marking her work because 'he tells you what you do wrong and explains how you can get it right'. Another pupil agreed but added that Mrs Blair was better because 'in English when you've handed in your work, Mrs Blair does the same but if you only do what she has suggested you won't get top marks. You have to think for yourself about how to improve it to get that.' It soon emerged that all the English teachers did the same. This example however was trumped by a girl who was in Year 9 and advanced the claims of Mr Bailey the music teacher. 'You see' she explained 'I play the cello and I sing and when I do Mr Bailey tells me how I can improve. But it's got to the point where when I play or sing I can tell how I can improve. Mr. Bailey calls it meta-cognition.'

The story serves to illustrate a school which had a very highly developed teaching and learning policy and practice and that probably marking policy was a departmental responsibility within some broad school guidelines.

In the primary sector marking practice has developed a lot in the last few years to a level where leaders of successful schools will be confident that:

- individual teachers know exactly where each of their pupils has reached in their framework of progress in English and mathematics and will be raising with the school leaders their concerns if they have any about any individual pupil. In short it is less about the senior leadership team monitoring and more about the teachers knowing the tracking framework so well that he / she is alerting the leadership team to any issues.
- the marking practice in classrooms will mean that there is reflection time at the beginning of lessons where the dialogue shows how the pupil has understood their peers' or their teacher's comments.

Some primary schools have learned from the best early years' practice where teachers look at camera recorded examples of pupil talk and activity, and then decide what this evidence and examples of pupils' work are actually telling them about progress.

In one secondary school we know, two departmental meetings a term are used to look at pupils' work and debate the marking of it. Another agrees to let newly qualified teachers mark some of the head of department's class's work and vice versa. Of course they learn in the process. In the primary years now, Year 5 and Year 6 teachers deliberately extend the examples of pupils' marking their own and other pupils' work, as this really explores and develops in-depth AfL. They say it can't be real formative assessment unless the pupils themselves own it.

But our prize memory is one school where each term, as a matter of course, each member of the leadership team including the head takes on the marking of a class set of work of one of the teachers. The impact in terms of debate and the knock-on to real departmental review and performance management is considerable.

Ask each faculty to have their own explicit 'marking' policy and practice that is reviewed every two years. Encourage 'same subject, different set' teachers to swap sets for marking once a term.

A
B
C
D
E
F
G
H
I
J
K
L
M
N
O
P
Q
R
S
T
U
V
W
X
Y
Z

M is for Meetings

Successful schools ring the changes of their meeting schedules from time to time to avoid, as one head put it, 'them becoming a complete waste of time'.

It is all too easy in any organization for meetings to become predictable and worse still, an occasion for people to deliberately get on each other's nerves.

So the best schools have written ground rules such as:

- timed item agendas
- avoiding 'cheap shots'
- starting a meeting with a round-robin of things that have gone well
- sharing the duty of the chairing of meetings both to avoid one dominating but also to train future leaders
- avoiding admin/business items and making sure the discussion is focused on teaching and learning, assessment and the curriculum
- scheduling meetings in the school calendar.

As we have shown elsewhere we think there all sorts of ways in which meetings can be made more worthwhile by planning agendas in such a way that discussion of the worthwhile issues takes precedence.

Consider the following butterfly.

Rotating staff, faculty and phase meetings

Description

Knowing that what teachers talk about influences whether a school succeeds or not, a primary head decided that meetings needed to be entirely about teaching, learning and assessment. Business, she decided, can easily be covered by staff briefings, the staff notice board and the e-learning platform.

So she decided to rotate staff meetings from one classroom to the next with the first item on any agenda being the host describing why they organize the room in the way they do, how they involve the pupils in classroom management and what they intend to do next in display. Staff are asked to comment on one aspect they particularly like in the display and why. The head said that once everyone had had a go, the next meeting was devoted to a discussion of display in the school's corridors with an analysis after school visits elsewhere of what they might do to provoke more thinking.

A
B
C
D
E
F
G
H
I
J
K
L
M
N
O
P
Q
R
S
T
U
V
W
X
Y
Z

Comment

The intervention cost nothing, set the tone for changed discourse in staff meetings and led to some discussion of the best use of teaching assistants in the school. Soon she had added other standing items to the agenda with the similar intention of reinforcing discussion of teaching and learning.

Clearly, although this is a primary example it is easy to see how the same approach, slightly modified could apply in secondary schools with faculties taking it in turn to host and explain. It is also easy to see how faculty or phase meetings could be so organized.

M is for Mindset

 If parents want to give their children a gift, the best thing they can do is to teach their children to love challenges, be intrigued by mistakes, enjoy effort, and keep on learning.
Carol Dweck

The same could be said for schools too. Carol Dweck's research over 20 years and her book *Mindset* (2006), robustly tackles the issue of whether intelligence is fixed or expandable and convincingly demonstrates that individuals can become more intelligent. The key to expandable intelligence lies far more in self-belief than it does in any hypothetical notion of 'ability'. Carol Dweck calls this belief a 'growth mindset' or 'mastery orientation' where for example, children and young people can be convinced that putting in the effort of learning is likely to bear fruit both in terms of making progress and in terms of strengthening intelligence itself. Her research reveals that in USA schools there is often a 'fixed mindset' or 'helpless prone orientation' in which effort often feels pointless. Different mindsets come from the way parents, teachers and older children respond to a young person's successes, struggles and failures. As both Bill Lucas and Guy Claxton have pointed out in various publications, such as *New Kinds of Smart*, (2010), schools should be a place where you can 'get smarter', not simply a confirmation that some are both intelligent and others without the appropriate brain power cannot achieve. A teacher's job is fundamentally to develop more intelligent learners: cultivating dispositions to create active learners, developing and sustaining growth mindsets, helping pupils with the right tools and strategies, and helping them to reflect on their learning in order to improve.

When devising their curriculum and grouping strategies, schools do have to consider current levels of achievement or performance, but these should not be a fatalistic ability level which predicts all that can be expected of students. We have all been in the presence of teachers who can inspire children to considerable achievements not only in a single lesson but over a long period of time. Such teachers care nothing for the notion of 'fixed intelligence' but concentrate on the unlimited potential of young minds. However, there are other teachers who consciously or unconsciously have fixed the ability levels of their pupils in their minds partly as the result of a very rigid setting and organization of learning opportunities. School improvement ultimately depends on what teachers do and think in the classroom and if there is a culture and mindset that limits potential and achievement only to those who are perceived to be 'able', then the school will not succeed.

Further reading
See also Matthew Syed, *Bounce – The Myth of Talent and the Power of Practice.*

M is for Moral purpose

 Moral purpose of the highest order is having a school system where all students learn, the gap between high and low performing becomes greatly reduced, and what people learn enables them to be successful citizens and work in a morally based knowledge society.

Michael Fullan

One of the great drivers of school improvement is a strong sense of moral purpose articulated particularly by school leaders. All other capacities should be in this service. Most school leaders are absolutely committed to making a positive difference in the lives of individual children and young people and those of the teachers and staff as a whole. That is the major reason why they came into the profession in the first place. They demonstrate this through personal attention and concern for individuals. However, to make a real difference, they have to transform the culture of the school as a whole so that all pupils and staff benefit in terms of achieving desirable goals and that continuous improvement is built into the system sustained by organizational change.

Such a culture of improvement will include:

- a relentless focus on student achievement
- tackling barriers to learning
- setting high expectations
- forensic analysis of data and stretching benchmarks
- high leverage interventions
- building collaboration and capacity
- unwavering resolve and active engagement
- powerful partnerships with parents and the community
- securing sustainability.

In such a culture collective attitudes, beliefs and values, together with shared knowledge and skills, facilitate success. Passion and purpose is mobilized effectively across the entire school community and is exhibited daily through the actions of individuals. There are high levels of trust and integrity. Relational trust with a strong press for moral purpose produces tough cultures of disciplined enquiry and action. The brutal facts have to be confronted if all pupils are to achieve their potential.

Moral purpose dictates that schools should be engines of social mobility, helping children to overcome the accidents of birth and background to achieve much more than they may ever have imagined, but to really encourage change it is necessary to make a difference beyond the school. The overall environment of the school system must improve for all schools to continually improve. The moral imperative has to be a collective endeavour whether through local authorities, dioceses, chains, federations, partnerships or collaboratives.

To some extent the White Paper of December 2010, signalled the way through with emphasis upon building greater capacity in the school system as a whole, where the best schools and leaders take greater responsibility and extend their reach and the most effective practice spreads more quickly. Thus there are now enhanced number of Local and National Leaders of Education, National Support Schools and Teaching schools (see N is for National Leaders of Education and National Support Schools and T is for Teaching schools) actively demonstrating that they care about other schools and their children through sharing their expertise which then drives instrumental change. If we accept that all our futures depend upon the quality of education for all children than everybody has a vested interest in raising standards across the board. The most effective school leaders see and appreciate the larger context in which they operate and the values of the moral imperative. They will demonstrate this daily, both in their own schools and through their work in the school system as a whole.

Further reading
See C is for Culture of schools, V is for Values, Michael Fullan – *The Moral Imperative of School Leadership.*

 Scratch a good teacher and you find a moral purpose.
Michael Fullan

A B C D E F G H I J K L M N O P Q R S T U V W X Y Z

N is for National Leader of Education (NLE) and National Support School (NSS)

> You cannot help someone get up a hill without getting closer to the top yourself.
>
> General Norman Schwartzkopf

National Leaders of Education (NLE) and National Support Schools (NSS) were first established in 2006 with the primary purpose of raising standards by harnessing the skills and experience of the best school leaders, as well as their schools, to support those that needed to improve. These are not confined to one phase of education but are active in primary schools, special schools and secondary schools including Academies. The criteria for being designated an NLE are demanding requiring the following:

- Headteachers of schools that have been judged by OfSTED as outstanding in leadership and management.
- The leadership capacity to support and achieve improvement in other schools without compromising standards of the 'home' school.

- A track record, experience and capability to lead schools out of the most challenging circumstances, providing intensive support at all levels.
- The ability to lead one or more schools in addition to their own, at any one time.
- The ability to provide expert advice to Ministers on future development strategies.

NLEs and NSSs were originally a lynchpin for raising standards in the three city challenge areas of London, Greater Manchester and the Black Country but now they are a force in every region of the country. The White Paper of December 2010 pledged to increase their numbers from 500 to 1000 by 2014/2015 so that schools wanting this kind of support could find it easily. This decision was based upon a number of evaluations describing the impact of NLEs on their schools which demonstrated that nationally, schools being supported were improving at a significantly faster rate than other schools. Further, the 'home' school improved too – a 'win-win' combination. The evidence showed that struggling schools benefited hugely from working alongside a strong school and where appropriate taking on their systems, skills and expert practitioners to get them moving in the right direction. Sometimes the struggling school was also able to provide examples of best practice to benefit the stronger school.

In school improvement terms the NLE/NSS concept is different from other support models that rely on consultants or advisers who have left the frontline of school leadership. Such models, by their nature, cannot draw upon the current practice or skills of other colleagues, that is, the senior and middle leaders and expert practitioners whose contribution to achieving improvement is fundamental. However, the entire NLE/NSS programme is dependent upon brokerage and effectively matching schools together. This responsibility lies with the National College and their regional staff who work with local authorities, school leaders, governors, sponsors and other agencies to help match the needs of underperforming schools with the particular skills of appropriate NLE / NSS. The College operates a target figure of 80% deployment at any particular time.

Since 2006 there have been different types of support. Some have been unplanned in response to an emergency in another school such as breakdown of leadership or a critical inspection report. Others have been planned and prepared for in advance in response to ongoing anxieties and concerns about a school's performance. These circumstances allow more time for the analysis of the need and the nature of the support required and also gives the opportunity to scope the task and direction of the mission. However, the basic tasks have always been the same:

- providing expert diagnosis and helping to construct an improvement plan
- supporting and challenging through firm, focused conversations: coaching, mentoring, modelling and monitoring
- devising bespoke solutions
- building capacity and securing sustainability.

Although the major task of an NLE/NSS has always been to support underperforming schools, since 2010 there has been a changing school

A
B
C
D
E
F
G
H
I
J
K
L
M
N
O
P
Q
R
S
T
U
V
W
X
Y
Z

improvement strategy leading to a new education landscape. NLEs sometimes now find themselves developing national teaching schools, leading the growth of chains of schools, establishing new school groupings across the boundaries of phase and type of education and helping to support the creation of Academies. NLEs are operating on a wider canvas bringing their strategic expertise, commitment and credibility to education policy. They are the education system's entrepreneurs, leading improvement and innovation with their staff. They are now at the forefront of developing new models of education and taking on some of the toughest performance challenges. However, with the trend towards greater diversification of school supply, NLEs and NSS are faced with an increasing range of options. As the new OfSTED framework changes and formerly 'satisfactory' schools are placed in a new category of 'requires improvement' there will be a greater demand for their services alongside Local Leaders of Education. They may choose to move their school to Academy status and 'formally' support another school as part of this accreditation, take over a 'failing school' via a Trust or Federation or concentrate on leading a teaching school and supporting other schools through this mechanism.

Some have chosen to develop their own 'chain' of schools and team up with another education provider to open new schools. It will be crucial to the school improvement system that the best school leaders and schools are used to optimum effect, which will mean that the National College will need to align criteria for different schemes and provide guidance to outstanding leaders around the various wider leadership roles open to them.

Whatever route the NLE / NSS take to support school improvement there should always be a fundamental moral purpose of supporting the education system to do the best for all children and young people. This demands generosity of spirit, determination, resilience, persistence, hope and optimism.

Further reading
See Robert Hill and Peter Matthews – *Schools Leading Schools II – The Growing Impact of National Leaders of Education.*

N is for National teaching schools

 The network of Teaching Schools will include the very best schools, with outstanding and innovative practice in teaching and learning and significant experience in developing. These schools are best placed to lead system-wide improvement in an area.
The Importance of Teaching, The Schools White Paper, 2010

In the autumn of 2009, following consultation with schools, the National College and Training and Development Agency for Schools (TDA) drew up proposals for a new single designation for schools to be named national teaching schools. The new teaching schools model drew on existing TDA training schools, the National College City Challenge project and designated leadership partner schools. The vision for national teaching schools was underpinned by a number of fundamental principles:

- the focus on the quality of teaching and leadership
- a progressive continuum of professional development provision from initial teacher training (ITT) to leadership
- a collaborative, school-led approach
- a system that provides high quality training and development
- a simple, non-bureaucratic and flexible approach.

Subsequently the White Paper in 2010 outlined plans to raise standards and improve the quality of teachers and school leadership through school-to-school support and peer-to-peer learning. A new national network of teaching schools was proposed modelled on teaching hospitals. Outstanding schools, providing they were also outstanding for teaching and learning and met other criteria such as a track record of effective school-to-school support, were to be given the role of leading the training and professional development of teachers, support staff and headteachers as well as contributing to the raising of standards through school-to-school support. The National College was charged with developing and quality assuring the designation of teaching schools and establishing a network of around 500 teaching school alliances by 2014/2015. Teaching schools are expected to build strong alliances with other schools, some of whom will become strategic partners, especially where this is a particular expertise. They are also expected to build relationships with other organizations and institutions such as universities and, where appropriate, local authorities.

The elements that make up the teaching school role are as follows:

- *Initial Teacher Training (ITT).* The White Paper vision is that teaching schools will take a key role in managing and quality assuring ITT across their partnership, to ensure that all ITT reaches the highest standards and contributes to raising standards. This might involve working towards becoming a fully accredited ITT provider or taking responsibility for the strategic leadership of ITT across the alliance, strengthening work with university partners.
- *Continuing Professional Development (CPD).* As part of the eligibility criteria teaching schools will already have been undertaking a significant amount of CPD activity. However, this has been expanded to include a range of professional development opportunities for teachers and support staff that work in schools across the alliance. Teaching schools will identify other schools and individuals that have the capacity and willingness to work outside their own school, to deliver bespoke or generic programmes as well as coaching and peer-to-peer support. They also have the job of designating Specialist Leaders of Education on behalf of schools in the alliance and brokering their support.

A
B
C
D
E
F
G
H
I
J
K
L
M
N
O
P
Q
R
S
T
U
V
W
X
Y
Z

- *Leadership Development and Talent Management.* Teaching schools will increasingly have a role in identifying and developing the leaders of the future. This may be through one of the National College's existing leadership programmes or by offering placements, mentoring and coaching to trainee heads as part of the National Professional Qualification for Headship (NPQH). It may also include shared delivery of leadership development programmes with other partners such as universities.
- *Support for Schools.* Increasingly, teaching schools and their alliances will have a range of National and Local Leaders of Education, and Specialist Leaders of Education to call upon to help them with their school-to-school support function. Working strategically with a range of partners including local authorities, teaching schools work to help schools out of low OfSTED categories, to help them secure performance above floor targets, provide executive leadership of a federation or collaborative, or provide extra leadership in a struggling school.

At the time of writing (2012) there are currently just over 200 teaching schools and alliances in operation and they are responsible for assuring the quality of the work they undertake and the impact it makes. There has as yet been no national evaluation but there are many examples of very effective school-to-school support and practitioner-to-practitioner support including coaching, mentoring, and modelling best practice. Increasingly, schools should seek to be part of teaching school alliances so that they can take advantage of particular school improvement programmes.

N is for Numeracy and the development of mathematical language

 Improving student motivation to learn mathematics is important for raising school attainment and for encouraging young people to pursue careers in fields requiring high levels of mathematical knowledge.

Report on Mathematics Education in Europe: Common Challenges and National Policies

We have referred elsewhere to literacy (speaking, reading, writing and communication) across the curriculum but the development of mathematical skills is also vital. Both the White Paper on the *Importance of Teaching* and the subsequent Wolf Report on vocational education, stress the importance of teaching English and mathematics as the bedrock of education. In the new inspection framework OfSTED in judging achievement, will assess standards attained by pupils in reading, writing, communication and mathematics across the curriculum. As with literacy, there needs to be a planned whole-school approach to whole-school numeracy. We have listed these elsewhere in the entry L is for Literacy, so you can see that we think this should include deliberate professional development for staff, the monitoring and evaluation of outcomes and a carefully planned provision to meet individual needs. In the case of mathematics and numeracy there are many websites which are familiar to schools and OfSTED surveys on best provision in the teaching of mathematics. In particular the National Centre for Excellence in the Teaching of Mathematics has published a range of research reports and projects e.g. *Mathematics Matters*.

Some schools have stressed the importance of the development of mathematical language throughout the curriculum and this can be linked to the language of school improvement. For example:

- share vision and value
- make things count
- add value
- multiply good practice
- make a difference to standards
- estimate impact
- calculate the leverage of interventions
- future proof systems.

Further reading
See Jo Boaler *The Elephant in the Classroom: Helping Children Learn to Love Maths* and The National Centre for Excellence in the Teaching of Mathematics: www.ncetm.org.uk

A
B
C
D
E
F
G
H
I
J
K
L
M
N
O
P
Q
R
S
T
U
V
W
X
Y
Z

A
B
C
D
E
F
G
H
I
J
K
L
M
N
O
P
Q
R
S
T
U
V
W
X
Y
Z

O is for Optimism

Perpetual optimism is a force multiplier. The ripple effect of a leader's enthusiasm is awesome.

Colin Powell

We have talked elsewhere about 'energy creators' as a vital factor of school improvement and that of course is closely aligned to 'optimism'. Most people expect their leaders to see more of the total scene than they individually can do, so a lack of optimism insidiously undermines their morale. In a sense, leaders need vision and those who accompany them need to feel that they have seen the other side of the mountain. If leaders are pessimistic and show it to others, there is clearly a problem in the longer vision leaders are tacitly credited with possessing. One commentator once said that 'unwarranted optimism' was the real key to leadership and a momentary reflection on the apparently irresolvable crises of school life confirms it. Some schools have built the term 'relentless optimism' into their common language reinforced by everyday behaviour. Good teachers are invariably optimistic, positive and enthusiastic. When we read memories and reminiscences on the theme of 'my best teacher' we read about enthusiastic, committed and inspirational teachers who made learning exciting and who believed in the capacity of children and young people to do well. Good teachers build confidence, competence and self-esteem among all pupils and their goal is always the highest quality of learning experiences so that aspirations and ambitions can be met. The great reward of teaching is that 'teachers affect eternity; they can never tell where their influence stops'.

Martin Seligman in his book *Learned Optimism: How to Change Your Mind and Life* shows the value of being positive, how it improves health and how it can transform our ability to persist rather than give up in the face of difficult events. Cultivating positive mindsets helps people to work better and achieve more.

Schools would do well to consider their strategies for creating an optimistic learning atmosphere from cheerful 'good mornings' from all staff and students to the regular use of positive language, detailed attention to the conduct of meetings and assemblies, and the promotion of a positive learning environment. Schools should be places where everyone in its community tastes the confidence and optimism that comes with success in some form or other.

There is one point of caution, namely the danger of not facing or analyzing the real situation: this is always a necessary precursor to optimism.

Further reading
See M is for Mindset and H is for Hope.

Schools are institutions in which the work is directed to the future; they should have no place for someone who is pessimistic about it.

Bodil Jonsson

A
B
C
D
E
F
G
H
I
J
K
L
M
N
O
P
Q
R
S
T
U
V
W
X
Y
Z

I was supposed to be a welfare statistic…It is because of a teacher that I sit at this table. I remember her telling us one cold, miserable day that she could not make our clothing better; she could not provide us with food; she could not change the terrible segregated conditions under which we lived. She could introduce us to the world of reading, the world of books and that is what she did.

What a world! I visited Africa and Asia. I saw magnificent sunsets; I tasted exotic foods; I fell in love and danced in wonderful halls. I ran away with escaped slaves and stood besides a teenage martyr. I visited lakes and streams and composed lines of verse. I knew then that I wanted to help children do the same things, I wanted to weave magic…

Evidence submitted to 'The National Commission on Teaching and America's Future'

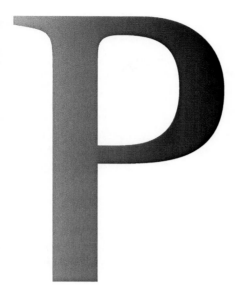

P is for Parents and carers

 You get nowhere if parents aren't behind the school wanting the best from it for their children and the best for it as a school.
John Macbeath

There is compelling evidence that parental aspirations, expectations and involvement have a major impact on their children's achievement. Parents also have an impact where they have contact with schools to share information, and where they participate in school events, the work of the school and in school governance. One of the most comprehensive studies by the Department for Children, Schools and Families in 2008 *The Impact on Parental Involvement on Children's Education,* found parental involvement in schooling for a child between the ages of seven and 16 was a more powerful force than family background, size of family and level of parental education.

Good schools think strategically about the ways in which they can involve parents more and more deeply in supporting their children's learning. Good practice in early years has led the way in working with parents as partners in their children's learning and growth. Workshops and discussion groups, at which parents can see and understand how children are learning in different areas of the curriculum, can help them to gain access.

Of course, involving parents can be socially complex, especially in areas of high deprivation or where children are vulnerable. In these situations schools will draw upon good partnerships with other agencies such as social services, youth offending teams or voluntary organizations. There should be a common core of building trust with parents, establishing a dialogue about their children's learning and providing information on what they can expect from their school and the progress their child is making.

Beyond this universal provision, good schools have thought through where more focused energy may be necessary, particularly for families with specific additional needs and where parents may be hostile to involvement with the school and hard to reach. Particular attention is required to deal with the needs of children in care, which ought to be the school's top priority.

Key features of effective work with parents include:

- Accessible literature covering what all parents want to know about the school, which also includes a website and regular newsletter. The school's website has a large parents' section with a wide range of activities e.g. helping children gain literacy and numeracy skills. There are also links to other educational sites.
- Information being made available to parents on what they can expect from the school regarding individual pupil progress. This ideally and increasingly includes access to schemes of work and learning materials.
- Frequent communication, telling parents clearly how their children are doing but also about the variety of learning events that they can attend.
- Mechanisms for parents to give feedback on the quality of education, for example through regular surveys of parental satisfaction, which of course should feed into school evaluation.
- Home-school contracts to support learning at home in cooperation with the school, which may involve particular partnership schemes such as home-school planners, home-school reading diaries, sending books or work home, lending libraries for toys and books for younger pupils or homework diaries for older pupils. In this sense parents are not only involved with the school but demands are made of them to contribute to their children's learning.
- Regular consultation and review sessions with the parents and also with students – particularly in secondary schools. Students can review their work with the form tutor and their parents and agree targets for further progress. Many schools, through 'achievement days', are now encouraging the student rather than the form tutor to lead the review, thereby taking full ownership of the issue.
- A termly class meeting in primary schools to explain to parents the nature of the coming term's curriculum and how parents can reinforce this at home (backed up by resource materials). We know one school where emails go out to parents every week about what the children will be doing in class the following week giving the opportunity to reinforce the curriculum at home.
- Thematic parents' evenings or open weeks around such topics as the teaching of reading and numeracy or the use of ICT, at which parents can understand and participate in the learning process and support their children

appropriately. Some schools invite parents to work alongside their children in a particular subject area.

- Opportunities provided by the school for parents to enhance their own learning, sometimes gaining 'access' qualifications, for example communication skills, parenting skills, health and safety education and IT. In primary schools in particular there may be a parents' room or base that can be used for a variety of activities and courses.
- Celebrating success through exhibitions, class assemblies, display of pupils' achievements and performances in music, dance, drama and sport.
- Parents and community members becoming involved in the teaching and learning process as learning assistants (volunteers or formally employed), working alongside teachers or taking up other functions within the school.

The effort to draw in parents by establishing meaningful partnerships can be considerable, but the prize is great. Good schools think through the style and tone of contacts that are set in the first place by the head and senior leaders. However, essential to success is the consistency with which they are maintained by all staff. Consistency of approach to pupils' work and behaviour also makes a strong contribution to the home-school partnership. Parents need to feel that the school is a community of which they are a part, with welcoming signs and easy access. Above all, parents should feel welcome in the school and be actively encouraged to participate in the life of the school through informal contacts, social events, as volunteers in the classroom and through lots of inclusion in the work their children take back and forth between home and school. Parental views are now often sought both informally and formally through survey and questionnaires, and OfSTED invites parents to rate their children's school online using a parent view questionnaire. Good schools will make sure that they take parents' views seriously and act upon them.

Further reading

See DCSF, *The Impact of Parental Involvement on Children's Education* and OfSTED, *Parents, Carers and Schools*.

 If schools start by assuming that parents are co-educators, then they will work to find ways of including parents in having a say in shaping the school's priorities.

Kathryn Riley

P is for Partnerships

Schools ought to belong to at least three partnerships if they have aspirations to serve their pupils better.

1. First, there is the partnership which is locally based and focused, usually with local authority support, on services and discussions and actions arising

from the needs of children and families who need interdisciplinary support sometimes from a variety of agencies such as social services, health, housing, as well as 'beyond the individual school' expertise from, for example, psychologists. These partnerships have different names and require lots of patience as the various agencies dance to slightly different tunes. So deciding in advance what days of the week case conferences will be called so that year planning becomes easier can reduce wasting time. Induction for each profession, which involves time spent with another discipline, will also make the work of the partnership easier and more productive. See below for some rules of partnership.

2. The second partnership which we believe every school should have – and it's not locally based – is with other schools. This will involve inter-school visits for 'learning walks', sometimes exchanges of staff and a clear agenda of planned action, all focused on a school's priorities. Often some CPD events arise from the partnership, which is usually for a fixed term with an intention to review and change membership in order to keep ideas fresh. Typically there will be a mix of differently OfSTED-rated schools although certainly at least one that seems exceptional. There may or may not be Local or National Leaders of Education in the group.

3. The third partnership essential to any school is its international partnership arrangement. For an island people within a shrinking global world, and where in poorer areas children do not often visit their city centre and where the other side of a city might be a million miles away, widening horizons is crucial. Schools should have a range of international partnerships for a variety of purposes such as curriculum projects, school building, learning languages, learning about different cultures, plus of course school visits. Staff visits to other partner schools in different countries have also been pioneered by some schools. As one head told us, 'The international dimension is so important in a country that is now so multicultural. Exploring what an international partnership can mean seems therefore an essential part of enabling students to have a better understanding of the wider world in which they live, besides being culturally enriching for our whole community.'

Of course there are other partnerships – for example for post-16 courses, or some overt sharing of services as schools become more independent but see the benefit of sharing. Partnerships, however can be confusing and are often time-wasting because participants haven't agreed on certain essential ground rules before embarking on the arrangement.

Some questions for partnerships to consider:

1. *What are the shared and agreed values and principles?* Of course this won't be an issue in the first type of local partnership outlined above, but it may influence your choice of partner in any school improvement partnership or indeed others designed for different purposes.

2. *Is there a statement of the overarching purpose of the partnership?* One of the schools on which one of us sits as a governor, belongs to a City Wide

Learning Partnership involving six schools and a college. It soon decided it needed to answer this and the next question clearly.

3. *What are the agreed detailed purposes?* For example, a partnership could have any or all of the following – CPD or ICT development, curriculum development, research, bidding for a worthwhile joint project, after school and school holiday provision or shared residential facilities.

4. *Who leads on the various detailed purposes and for how long?* Unnecessary irritations and misunderstandings occur – not to mention resentments – if the partners are not clear on this from the beginning. So if a group decides to look at literacy for example they might have a lead practitioner for a two to three year period (and a head chairing the group headed up by that person) but at the end of this period the lead and chair come up for review with the expectation that somebody else takes on the responsibility.

5. *What are the agreed success criteria for each detailed purpose?* It focuses the mind to have clear criteria by which to assess the effectiveness of the partnership.

6. *When is progress to be reviewed and how?* Any school acting by itself would always ensure a review of the effectiveness of any of its activities. So this is all the more important for shared activity with other schools.

7. *How is finance to be arranged for the partnership? Who agrees the budget?* This may require participant schools to pay a small percentage of their budget to cover the costs of the partnership (see 11 below). On the other hand some of the costs may depend on participation in a particular activity. Being clear what the costs are and how they will be shared is something that needs agreement near the beginning. Moreover, employing somebody often means forming a limited company, community interest company or a trust. These considerations probably won't apply to belonging to the first or second form of partnership outlined at the beginning of this entry.

8. *When and how far ahead are meetings scheduled?* There is nothing more irritating than finding clashes of important meetings in your diary. So if a partnership is going to flourish at least annual dates need to be in diaries so that school calendars can bear them in mind.

9. *How within each participating institution is the work of the partnership reported and are job descriptions clear on the role of partnership working?* It isn't simply job descriptions. Are there reports of the work of the partnership to staff? Is it an item on the governors' meeting? Can people see the benefits of the partnership work? All these are needed to get support. Partnerships which have a CPD purpose and enable staff to visit other practitioners are usually more popular than others.

10. *Who is the chair of the partnership as a whole? For how long?* See the answer to question 4 above. The heads who enter into the partnership often defer to one of their number as the initiator but for the partnership to flourish rotation of leadership in a planned way is key.

11. *Are we using the partnership to lever in extra funds?* One of the attractive features of partnerships is that they appeal to funders so this should be an early discussion point. Clearly, understanding priorities of potential grant making bodies such as Esmee Fairbairn, Paul Hamlyn, Rowntree, Nuffield

A

B

C

D

E

F

G

H

I

J

K

L

M

N

O

P

Q

R

S

T

U

V

W

X

Y

Z

and Leverhulme is also necessary to avoid abortive and time consuming failed bids.

12. *Who is the progress chaser / expediter?* Of all the points made here this is the most important. We have all arrived at meetings embarrassed to discover the mention of our name in the last set of minutes as having promised to do something which we have forgotten to do. So having someone whose job it is to make us efficient is key to the success of a partnership just as it is within any school.

P is for Pastoral

Primary and secondary schools have always had their differences in terms of pastoral care: it was always assumed that the structure and typically smaller size of primary schools meant that everybody shares in the vital pastoral aspect of school life.

From the moment of secondary school reorganization along comprehensive lines, two factors emerged. Secondary schools became larger and typically two sets of staff from former grammar and secondary modern schools had to be accommodated. So nothing was more natural than that there should be heads of department (HoDs) and heads of year (HoYs) for grammar and secondary modern former teachers respectively. This curriculum / pastoral split was replicated at deputy head level and persisted for years. Its disadvantage was that it tended towards unhelpful demarcation that hindered seeing the whole student and assessing their possible progress. Everybody did their job conscientiously but the structure got in the way of some pupils' optimum progress. More recently this structure has given way to one that focuses on progress, especially so far as levels are concerned. Nevertheless, most senior leadership teams see the need for ensuring that the strategic overview of pastoral needs is in someone's portfolio. The detailed practice, however, will lie either in vertical tutoring within 'houses' or by HoYs with key roles for the Special Educational Needs and Disabilities Coordinator.'

Further reading
See K is for the 'Kes' factor, P is for Personalized learning, T is for Tutor and tutor period and Y is for Year heads. The National Association for Pastoral Care in Education (NAPCE) runs a journal and keeps enthusiasts abreast of latest developments see www.napce.org.uk

P is for Peer learning

 A pupil is a great resource.

Hudson Stuck

There are three main types of peer learning. Firstly, peer tutoring which involves one pupil teaching another where peers are usually at different academic levels and often at different ages. For example, a common approach is getting sixth formers to help Year 7 and Year 8 particularly in literacy and numeracy. Some schools have gone further through systemizing employing 'gap year' students as subject specific coaches to current sixth form students. Some primary schools, using a programme originating in Fife, hold paired reading schemes with pupils aged seven and eight working with ten and 11 year olds. Evaluations show that this is beneficial to both sets of readers: the younger pupils have quick feedback and encouragement and the older pupils develop their own reading skills in carrying out the task. Similarly in mathematics with a system of 'duology' the older pupils can encourage their tutees to discuss the progress used to solve mathematical problems.

Secondly, cooperative learning commonly occurs in groups of four to six members working towards a common goal which is likely to require discussion of differing points of view. This process helps to develop listening and speaking skills and better pupil engagement. Thirdly, collaborative learning also occurs in similar group sizes but here each member of the group has a specific task to undertake and the group can't succeed as a whole unless each member is successful in their individual role.

Generally speaking, peer learning of all varieties works better in primary than in secondary schools because of the organization of classrooms. However, increasingly peer learning is becoming part of the Key Stage 3 curriculum – particularly in Year 7 where there is often a 'Competence' or 'Learning to learn' curriculum. Some schools have gone further and have challenged pupils to design, plan, deliver and access units of work for others – in other words co-constructing learning. We are familiar with one example where a small number of sixth form philosophy and ethics students planned and delivered a GCSE unit for Year 10 religious studies on 'Life after death'. When evaluated it was found that pupil outcomes when taught by other pupils were at least equal to those when the lessons had been planned and delivered by staff. Furthermore, the sixth form students gained a great deal, developing a range of skills including presentation, communication, teamwork and creativity.

As with other aspects of teaching and learning, teachers working individually and collectively have to strike the right balance between the focus on themselves as presenters and informers of knowledge and peer tutoring, cooperative learning and collaborative learning. One thing is for sure, pupils are a great resource.

A
B
C

P is for Peer review

D
E

While peer review is important within a school, it is vital outside the school.

F

Many local authorities, chains, trusts and collaboratives of schools are encouraging the process of peer review whereby schools review each other's performance often using OfSTED criteria. These are reviews not inspections but they have the great merit of being conducted by current practitioners with the objectives of being solution focused rather than simply judging current performance.

G
H
I

J

In the interests of rigour it is important that senior leaders are trained as reviewers, which offers professional development opportunities, and that there is an agreed formal process and programme, but the emphasis is on sharing the best practice to enable the school to improve further. We have talked elsewhere about 'critical friends' and being part of a peer review programme offers that opportunity both in conducting and receiving a review. Peer review can be thematic e.g. literacy, numeracy, inclusion, behaviour, or can provide a more in depth look at the quality of education provided. For example, Challenge Partners, a group of over 200 schools, have come together to fund a peer quality assurance programme including two-day reviews and reports looking at performance relative to the most recent OfSTED inspection and the sharing of outstanding practice.

K
L
M
N
O
P

The important point is that being prepared to engage in scrutiny by peers and for peers will help the school improve. The peer review process can be a vital element in transferring and managing knowledge as an ongoing process rather than a one-off event.

Q
R
S

Further reading
See C is for Critical friendship.

T
U
V

P is for Performance management

W

X
Y

The skill for the successful school leader is to get the right balance between personal accountability and the accountability of others.

Andy Buck

Z

It is not the intention of this section to examine in detail the regulations which exist and those changes that have come into force (September, 2012) but rather to consider performance management as part of school improvement. We can all agree that teaching and the leadership of teaching should be at the heart of any strategy for improvement. Elsewhere in this book there are several sections stressing the importance of leaders, showing their passion and commitment to teaching in everything they say and do, backed up by a commitment to high quality professional development. The debate is how effectively the quality of teaching is monitored and whether performance management systems are robust enough in rewarding those who teach and perform well, and doing something about those who consistently underperform. OfSTED has raised the stakes in this debate by indicating that it will inspect the correlation between the quality of teaching and salary progression and will examine performance management records. Most of the regulations relating to appraisal are not new. Schools must have an appraisal policy for teachers and an annual cycle for setting and reviewing objectives and issuing an appraisal report. All objectives should contribute to improving the education of pupils. What is new is that teacher's performance will be assessed against the relevant standards as well as their objectives and their role in the school. There are now new teachers' standards and these will be used as a formal part of the process rather than merely as a backdrop to performance management discussions. As well as this, most of the prescriptions of the 2006 regulations have disappeared including the limit on classroom observation.

The key to successful performance management as a driver for school improvement is a culture of honest self-appraisal throughout the school. The more that all staff become reflective practitioners who value feedback, and act upon it in a way that makes them more effective, the better the school becomes. Similarly the more that all staff, especially those in leadership positions, hold themselves accountable for achieving success the better the school becomes. In such a climate you only need two questions for performance management: 'what went well?' (www), and 'even better if' (ebi). Where these expectations are well established and there is real clarity and a shared understanding about the performance management process then decisive action can be taken if necessary to deal with underperformance, but in the main the process sustains better performance. There are of course some schools who have to deal firmly and decisively with underperformance as a pre-requisite of improvement and as part of their re-culturing strategies in developing a collective culture and a reflective, accountable, professional community. In these cases particularly, the clarity, communication and regulation of the performance management process is absolutely essential.

A
B
C
D
E
F
G
H
I
J
K
L
M
N
O
P
Q
R
S
T
U
V
W
X
Y
Z

A
B
C
D
E
F
G
H
I
J
K
L
M
N
O
P
Q
R
S
T
U
V
W
X
Y
Z

P is for Personalized learning

 Instead of a National Curriculum for education, what is really needed is an individual curriculum for every child.

Charles Handy

Personalized learning is about helping every child and young person to do better, which means tailoring education to their individual needs, interests and aptitudes so as to fulfil their potential, and give them the motivation to be independent, lifelong learners. For schools it means a professional ethos that accepts and assumes that every child comes into the classroom with a different knowledge base and set of skills, as well as varying aptitudes and aspirations.

Successful schools have thought through what constitutes effective learning in their particular context in order to raise the achievement of all pupils and put into place appropriate processes and practices. They will be aware of the dangers of young people's learning being dominated by judgements of ability that can profoundly affect their self-esteem and sense of identity. Students learn very quickly about their standing in comparison with their peers, and which category they belong to in terms of 'more able', 'average' and 'less able'. This kind of learning is often reinforced daily through a range of experiences, and it takes a conscious effort to practise 'learning without limits', so that young people's school experiences are not all organized and structured on the basis of judgements of ability.

The components of personalized learning can be summarized as:

- assessment for learning (AfL)
- effective teaching and learning
- curriculum entitlement and choice
- organizing the school for personalized learning
- beyond the classroom.

These five key components are integrated and mutually supportive. The use of ICT permeates all components as a way of enhancing creativity and extending learning opportunities. The Specialist Schools Academies Trust, in a series of pamphlets on *Personalised Learning* (2005–6) edited by David Hargreaves, suggested that schools approach the task of personalized learning through nine interconnected gateways and as a sequence of core themes or strands that capture what characterizes the pupils for whom learning is being successfully personalized.

These core themes are:

- engagement of the pupil in learning and schooling
- the responsibility assumed by the pupils for learning and behaviour

- independence in learning
- confidence in learning
- maturity in relationships and pupils taking ownership of their learning.

Schools will recognize this agenda as trying to do their best for every child and young person by adapting schooling to meet the needs of the individual, rather than forcing the individual to fit the system.

Most schools would claim that they give students individual attention, but those that are working hard on personalized education have realized that there is a lot more that they can do, particularly in allowing students opportunities to work at their own pace. Choice is also an important part of personalized learning, particularly in secondary schools, with the building of individual learning pathways. However, the constraints of syllabus, space, curriculum and assessment can make it difficult to offer a truly personalized form of learning, although there have been some innovative approaches through the benefits of workforce remodelling and more effective use of ICT. In the last analysis the curriculum must appeal to the individual or the group so the successful learner is engaged in the curriculum that the teacher has tailored to the world. For example, teachers have rightly criticized the 'one size fits all' National Curriculum and previously the National Strategies because they were often over prescriptive and could de-skill teachers by discouraging them from bringing their own views to the curriculum.

It also needs to be recognized that the school day and the school year provide only a small percentage of available learning time. That's why the suspended timetable involving a day or a week of learning is so important to successful learning.

To succeed in their hope of enhancing learning and achievement, schools must find new allies and build new sorts of connections to the community of which they are a part. One of the first key steps is to build mainly on learning partnerships with parents and carers, remembering that they are co-educators of children in tandem with teachers.

The most important attribute that schools can give students is the ability to learn on their own and to take responsibility for their own learning. While this can be encouraged through the formal curriculum in terms of flexible learning and independent learning, the provision of curriculum enrichment and extension opportunities creates a real opportunity to prepare for lifelong learning, whether through traditional extra-curricular activities – such as sport, drama, chess and other clubs and societies – or through study opportunities provided before and after school by breakfast clubs or at weekends and holidays – such as courses and residential learning experiences, Easter revision courses, summer schools or study extension with organizations such as the Children's University or Gifted and Talented Centres. Curriculum enrichment and extension allows for a greater flexibility of teaching and learning, particularly around techniques such as accelerated learning and concepts such as multiple intelligences. There are also

A
B
C
D
E
F
G
H
I
J
K
L
M
N
O
P
Q
R
S
T
U
V
W
X
Y
Z

extra opportunities for developing ICT skills. Above all, an improving school will provide these opportunities to improve motivation, build self-esteem, develop effective learning and raise achievement.

Further reading

See also A is for Assessment for Learning, P is for Peer Learning, C is for Classroom interventions and *Personalized Learning: Transforming Education for Every Child*, John West-Burnham and Max Coates.

P is for Planning for school improvement

 Leaders set the course for the organization; managers make sure the course is followed. Leaders make strategic plans; managers design operational systems for carrying out the plans.
K. S. Louis and M. B. Miles

The school improvement plan provides a clear and high-level statement to the whole school identifying what priorities have been established and what actions the school will take to address these priorities as well as the support and resources it is intending to use. It also sets out key accountabilities and success criteria as a means of whole-school self-evaluation. Beyond this, most schools and their governing bodies have a longer term (often three to five years) strategic plan focusing on developing the school's capacity for sustaining improvement and a set of goals demonstrating an ambition to be the best they can be.

It is salutary to remember that school improvement and development planning has only been a major feature of schools for just over 20 years. Following the Education (Schools) Act of 1992, which introduced a national programme of regular inspections, the first framework required a judgement on the quality of the school development plan, its usefulness as an instrument of change and development, and the achievement of any priorities set. This developed into an expectation (although it was never statutory) that there would be a school improvement plan along with a school evaluation form. For those schools who were judged to be inadequate (special measures or notice to improve) a post inspection plan was required which HMI monitored roughly every six months. In 2008, the National Challenge introduced the concept of Raising Attainment Plans (RAPs) for those secondary schools on or below floor targets (see R is for Raising Attainment Plans including RAP Management Groups). This was a tactical, short-term plan with a particular focus on increasing the number of pupils who achieved five A*–C grades with English and mathematics although there was also a focus on sustainable improvement which meant that the plan's priorities would affect other year groups. The methodology of RAP has been taken up by a wide range of schools, including primary schools, clearly focusing on attainment and progress and creating a sense of urgency and pace for improvement. Meanwhile schools also retain an annual improvement plan which determines all the priorities for improvement, agreed by governing bodies, and monitored and evaluated accordingly. As a sub-set to this secondary schools often have set departmental or faculty improvement plans and primary schools sometimes have separate phase plans e.g. Foundation Learning, Key Stage 1 and Key Stage 2.

School improvement planning incorporates at the extreme the micro (teacher's planning) and the macro (strategic planning) but the principles are the same: objectives, actions, resources, outcomes, monitoring and evaluation. Schools will find their own way to plan for improvement – the only test is whether the planning is smart and flexible enough to deliver real educational gains.

Further reading
See www.teachersmedia.co.uk

P is for Progress

 Our priority now is to ensure that no child gets left behind; we must create a reality where ever school and every pupil is making progress.

DfE Policy Statement

Schools have long been used to accountability and performance measures related to attainment with published data, allowing for league tables and local / national comparisons of performance. However, for many years the headline figures at Key Stage 2 and Key Stage 4 related to absolute scores rather than a measure of progress over time. The Department of Education now, alongside the anchor marks, measures progress across key stages in English and mathematics – three levels being expected from Key Stage 2 to Key Stage 4, and two levels being expected from Key Stage 1 to Key Stage 2. Both at Key Stage 2 and Key Stage 4 there are established average national medians for schools to benchmark themselves against. Measuring, assessing, reporting and stimulating progress – so that every child develops at the best pace, and no child gets left behind – is a vital measure as to the overall effectiveness of the school.

As we have said elsewhere, within every group of children there is a wide range of variation in terms of progress and attainment. Could we reduce disparities of ultimate achievement by focusing more on progress? Good schools track the progress of their pupils with rigour and vigour and adjust their teaching and provision to ensure that all make the best possible progress. They have tracking systems in place that are thorough, regular, individualized and well-maintained. Good schools use the data to focus on progress and better outcomes for every child regardless of circumstances. Periodically, they scrutinize additional evidence: folders of work, books, one-to-one sessions looking for evidence and

A
B
C
D
E
F
G
H
I
J
K
L
M
N
O
P
Q
R
S
T
U
V
W
X
Y
Z

gaps in achievement. Through often relatively small adjustments in the style and timing of ongoing classroom assessment, in the way pupils are engaged in their learning, in the way parents are helped to understand and support their child, every pupil can reach their full potential. Alongside this there should be the provision of individual tuition to lift the performance of those who entered the key stage already well behind trajectory or who fall behind during the key stage (progression tutoring). There should also be progression targets for particular groups most at risk of falling behind. Clearly, personalized teaching and learning to support progression is the key to success backed up by strong whole-school systems of assessment and monitoring. Some schools now write up individual pupil progress profiles, particularly those from underachieving groups, in order to demonstrate successful practice and interventions.

P is for Professional learning community

 An aspirational learning community is an inclusive group of people, motivated by a shared learning vision, who support and work with each other, finding ways inside and outside their immediate community to inquire about their practice and learn new and better approaches that will enhance all stakeholders learning.

(NCSL Document)

There are different interpretations about what this is, but in terms of school improvement, a professional learning community refers to the staff of a school who are mutually supportive with a collaborative and reflective approach towards investigating and learning more about their practice in order to improve pupils' learning. Key to this is learning together in a community of practice, and of course a school culture of collaboration, support and trust, is vital in this respect. There is nothing casual or loose about this – it is a serious enterprise underpinned by a specialist knowledge base, a commitment to sharing knowledge and developing new knowledge. It is a recognition of professional expertise and standards and the importance of collective learning beyond professional development which emphasizes only the development of individual knowledge and skills.

In a school that claims to be a professional learning community you would expect to see the following characteristics:

- A shared understanding which is written and articulated about pupils' learning and pedagogy.
- Collective responsibility for pupils' learning which helps to sustain commitment.

- A culture of reflective, professional enquiry often using the e-learning platform to disseminate information and ideas.
- Group, as well as individual, learning is promoted where all teachers are learners with their colleagues (usually working in small Teacher Learner Communities).
- An environment that supports innovation and experimentation to foster changes in practice.
- A capacity to engage more effectively in terms of knowledge transfer with other schools and education providers.
- Staff regularly and openly model their own learning.

The key features of a professional learning community are as follows, most of them illustrated elsewhere in the book:

- everybody is learning – all stakeholders
- peer observation and feedback
- learning walks
- student engagement in planning and evaluating the learning process
- collaborative reflection and knowledge transfer
- innovation and creativity
- coaching
- mentoring
- action research and action learning sets
- enquiry narratives and case studies
- teaching and learning alliances with other schools and universities.

Inevitably, a distinguishing feature of a professional community will be the quality of reflection, review and self-evaluation. The school is seen as a knowledge-creating institution auditing professional knowledge and managing, validating and disseminating new knowledge. Innovation and improvement promote critical thinking, build capacity and sustain vision – learning while innovating through good feedback systems. The school is visibly enquiry minded, geared to innovation and research, with a commitment to publishing learning narratives, case studies and organizing seminars and conferences. Most critically of all, as a learning community it is able to fully mobilize its intellectual, social and organizational capital to produce and sustain excellent educational outcomes.

Further reading
See A is for Action research, C is for Coaching and Case studies, L is for Learning narratives and *Professional Learning Communities* by Louise Stoll and Karen Seashore Louis.

A
B
C
D
E
F
G
H
I
J
K
L
M
N
O
P
Q
R
S
T
U
V
W
X
Y
Z

A
B
C
D
E
F
G
H
I
J
K
L
M
N
O
P

Q is for Quality assurance and quality control

R
S
T
U
V
W
X
Y
Z

Quality assurance differs from quality control: it is about ensuring that systems are designed so well that a high standard is assured when the system operates as it should. *Assurance* relies on performance feedback on what's working and what needs to be changed. *Control* relies on a range of checks to ensure compliance, so that when problems arise it's often the human who has not met the standard. It is best to focus on quality assurance but those systems do need to have underpinning controls.

Good schools have developed quality assurance 'maps' so that all staff leaders are aware of systems, procedures and accountabilities mapped out across the academic year. The performance management review cycle is part of this together with reviews of pupil standards, curriculum areas and the quality of teaching and key dates are set out a year in advance. The school self-review cycle is clear and well designed and feeds into the ever developing self-evaluation statement.

Many schools have developed a quality assurance intranet so that detailed guidance on specific aspects of quality assurance can be easily referred to e.g.

observing lessons, book looks, performance management, case studies, walk throughs, Raising Attainment Plans (RAPs) and RAP Management Groups, standards data and pupil progress interviews.

Q is for Questions

 The important thing is not to stop questioning.

Albert Einstein

Much has been written about sequencing, distribution and the rules of pause. Some schools, however, only allow pupils to put their hands up in certain prescribed and thought-through circumstances, preferring the teacher to direct questions of an appropriate nature to different pupils according to where they've reached in their learning. Other schools wishing to ring the changes have a 'question monitor,' with the teacher posing the question, again with careful consideration given to the level of difficulty, and the 'question monitor' picking one of the 30 sticks, each with a pupil's name from a beaker. But there is more to questions than the rules of pause, predetermined order, appropriate response and distribution.

Teachers are expert in four orders of question, each using the seven questioning words: 'when', 'where', 'what', 'why', 'who', 'which' and 'how'. First order questions are questions of fact; second order questions are those of inference; third order questions are 'surprising' questions; and fourth order questions are ones of 'conditional hypothesis,' preceded by the devilish 'if'! We sometimes think 'surprising' questions are the same as 'Fermi' questions. Fermi was an Italian nuclear physicist, who loved complex questions so, an example of a 'Fermi' question would be: 'How many piano tuners are there in New York?' Questions like this call for lateral thinking, estimation and justification of a hypotheses that leads to a conclusion.

Equipping pupils with knowledge of the seven question words and the four orders of question paves the way for good group work, because pupils are skilled in using questions. In addition to 'questions', teachers may look at each other's storytelling techniques, for as we have remarked, stories are at the very heart of successful teaching, since the mind-opening habits of the philosopher Plato.

One teacher we know uses the four orders of question as a foundation for training her class in better group work and as the basis for visits to places of interest where the pupils are expected to formulate questions rather than answers.

 I keep six serving honest men, (they taught me all I know). Their names are what and why and when and how and where and who.

Rudyard Kipling

A
B
C
D
E
F
G
H
I
J
K
L
M
N
O
P
Q
R
S
T
U
V
W
X
Y
Z

Q is for Quick wins

The journey of school improvement can be long and arduous and it is very important for everybody to feel that they are experiencing some early success or quick wins to sustain morale and momentum. These are often bound up within a particular context or culture and what one school might consider implementing with successful outcomes, another might feel it was a step too far. Certainly schools in OfSTED categories or schools struggling to improve need to find some quick wins to kick start their improvement. With reference to 'butterflies' (examples are provided throughout this book) we have seen many schools start by engaging the staff by simply asking everybody for one contribution of a small idea with high leverage. This provides some energy and engagement to sustain further improvements and leads to better sharing and dissemination of ideas related to school improvement. We know of other schools who have recorded quick wins through improving the learning environment with whole-school displays, achievement boards, improvements to resources and facilities and also attention to the staffroom itself. These can all provide a much improved work and social environment. Other schools have changed their break and lunchtime arrangements, in consultation with staff and students, to reduce overcrowding, improve behaviour and make the school day much more pleasant and purposeful. In terms of the student body, quick wins come from an enhancement of the student voice and translating that into a series of actions which demonstrate that students are being taken seriously. Of course, whatever the quick wins, they have to be part of a longer term, sustainable strategy of school improvement. Many of the butterflies in this book present the opportunity for quick wins.

Q is for Quotations

 It is a good thing to read books of quotations...the quotation when engraved upon the memory gives you good thoughts. They also make you anxious to read the authors and look for more.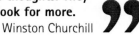
Winston Churchill

Readers of this book and our other publications, particularly *Inspirations – A Collection of Commentaries to Promote School Improvement* (2006), will appreciate that not only do we like quotations but we believe that regularly used and displayed in schools they can have powerful effects on everybody in the learning community. We know very few teachers – and fewer schools – who haven't found a quotation useful from time to time to either improve or reinforce a message, whether that be in assembly or in regular lessons or in the public areas. Along with anecdote they are the stock-in-the-trade of teachers keen to inspire children and young people. Some of the best quotations are butterflies, in that properly used they can have a disproportionate effect. As visitors to many schools in the country we collect quotations commonly displayed in the entrance foyer, the hall or on the walls. We have even come across one school whose idiosyncratic headteacher and staff decided at the beginning of one school year to introduce a 'quid for a quote' scheme which led to the schools' environment being transformed by over a thousand, framed quotations each 'donated' by a student and put into place by a member of the support staff whose duties included leading the visual environment of the school (a key post of responsibility). The following 'butterfly' explains the scheme:

Quid for a quote – a cost effective way of improving the learning environment.

Description

The headteacher believed that pieces of prose and poetry as well as snappy epigrams and other quotations are often an opportunity to stir the mind of the passer-by into profitable thought. He discussed his idea of 'quid for a quote' at a staff meeting. It was adopted enthusiastically.

So, at the start of the school year in each assembly, the head of year and one of the school leadership team talked about one of their favourite quotations. This was followed up in the tutor group. The first homework of term was for each student in the school to go home and discuss with their family or carer five favourite quotes, and we promised that if one were thought worthy of framing and hanging we would send £1 home to give to their favourite charity! So with a little bit of help from the design and technology department and support staff, 1,300 framed quotations were duly hung round the school.

Comment on impact

The visual, aural and behavioural environment of the school plays an important part in the likelihood of a school's success. Ensuring the visual environment is stimulating is always a problem. This scheme provided a simple way to raise awareness of the issue right across the school. However, we are sure that there are many others and would encourage all schools to give this some thought in their attempts to provide a stimulating learning environment.

It is fairly commonplace now for schools to use 'quotation for the week' as another butterfly to affect the atmosphere and ethos of the school. We know of more than one primary school which uses a readily acquired app which has an apparently never ending supply of excellent quotes!

 By necessity, by proactivity – and by delight, we all quote.
Ralph Waldo Emerson

A
B
C
D
E
F
G
H
I
J
K
L
M
N
O
P
Q
R
S
T
U
V
W
X
Y
Z

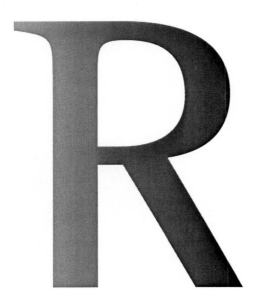

R is for RAISEonline

In the section D is for data we referred to RAISEonline which all schools tend to scrutinise in the autumn and after Christmas to see how they compare to other schools in similar circumstances. Those involved will be the senior leaders of the school and the governors but schools will also hope to ensure that heads of department and members of those departments become familiar with the implications.

Further reading
See D is for Data.

R is for Raising Attainment Plan (RAP)

Although most schools have always had some kind of RAP it has usually been subsumed under a school development plan or school improvement plan. Schools have learnt from the National Strategies and the National Challenge of the importance of a highly specific RAP which not only records the diagnosis, actions and support required to bring about improvement in attainment but also forms the central touchstone for monitoring progress.

The essential features for an effective RAP are:

- *Objectives*: a very clear focus on specific improvements in attainment
- *Actions*: clearly defined small steps
- *Responsibility*: clear lines of accountability
- *Personnel:* named appropriately
- *Outcomes:* specific success criteria
- *Timescale:* a series of milestones to be monitored
- *Resources:* e.g. staffing, funding, CPD time, external support
- *Monitoring:* a clear process for checking that planned actions have taken place on time
- *Evaluation:* assessing the impact of the planned actions on standards in the school
- *Reporting and accountability:* RAP management group, headteacher, governors, and other agencies.

Some of these may be said to be features of good planning generally but a high quality RAP creates a sense of urgency for achieving progress, translates priorities into action quickly, maintains a sharp focus on these, and is accessible to and understood by all staff. To act as a driver for monitoring and evaluation the original National Challenge suggested setting up RAP management groups (RMGs) comprising the headteacher, core subject leaders, other key staff as approved and a governor, meeting to monitor progress at least every two weeks. Some of that practice is also current today reporting to performance sub-committees of governing bodies. If a school is below or around floor targets for attainment then they will need something equivalent to a RAP and an RMG, but it is noticeable that schools that are performing well often adopt this methodology to make sure that they sustain success overall and also that they deal with very specific attainment issues, such as closing gaps between groups of children and young people.

Further reading
See P is for Planing for school improvement.

R is for Research

Research is important in successful schools for three reasons. It can:

- inform the curriculum
- be a defining theme of a school
- enable closer links with universities and the latest in research into specific subjects, how children learn and develop, what make successful techniques in teaching and school improvement.

A
B
C
D
E
F
G
H
I
J
K
L
M
N
O
P
Q
R
S
T
U
V
W
X
Y
Z

Informing the curriculum

At the primary level one of the traditional challenges for schools, especially as the accountability processes focus unrelentingly on SAT scores and levels of progress in English and mathematics, is how to keep creativity within the curriculum and find an antidote to 'drilling in the basics'. Traditionally schools have tackled this in part by having 'projects' which involve lengthy study by the class with ranges of wider skills for the pupil to master and exhibit and clearly defined first steps in being a member of a team and bringing a complicated task to a successful conclusion. Rather than call this approach a 'topic' some schools are calling the work involved 'research', recognizing of course the limits compared with adult research. Nevertheless, those that take this approach use the word to compare and contrast the work the pupils do with high level research and, in the process, introduce children to the notion of having a hypothesis, testing its validity and understanding the discipline of investigative field work and the collection of data and evidence. In doing so they introduce young children to scientific methodology, the world of provisional answers and the fun of discovery over a longer period.

Those secondary schools which have introduced early completion of GCSEs have often accompanied this with the undertaking of what has been called by some 'the extended study', which in effect is a mini-research project with all the advantages but at a more mature level than that outlined above. Schools which take this seriously report a huge improvement in students' essay writing in the humanities and in their approach to experiments in science.

Defining theme of a school

Clearly, a school which has adopted a research approach to the curriculum and student learning is likely to look more widely at school life. They encourage staff as part of CPD to try narrative enquiry and action research (see L is for Learning Narratives and A is for Action research) and some even have a 'visiting researcher' in the form of a researcher from a local university who has an annual slot on a staff meeting to report on the strength and research successes of her university. One school has a young researcher award for each year group which is presented at the annual awards evening.

Enable closer links with universities

Any school which has made research a defining theme of a school is likely to respect evidence rather than hunch. In their approach to self-evaluation and review they will want to be informed in their decision making by what the best evidence is in research.

The first thing they will want to do is pursue links with local and national universities (see U is for University links). In 2011, the Sutton Trust commissioned a really useful study by Durham University into what worked in terms of school level interventions. We have reproduced the summary of the research at the end of this entry. Our health warning would be to get the full report and then use it in an evidence-based review of all your school's practices to see where there might be a shift of emphasis. We think that it may persuade schools to take seriously some of the practices outlined under S is for Student voice.

Toolkit to improve learning: summary overview

Approach	Potential gain[1]	Cost	Applicability	Evidence estimate	Overall cost benefit
Effective feedback	+9 months	££	Pri, Sec Maths Eng Sci	☆☆☆	Very high impact for low cost
Meta-cognition and self-regulation strategies	+8 months	££	Pri, Sec, Eng Maths Sci	☆☆☆☆	High impact for low cost
Peer tutoring / peer-assisted learning	+6 months	££	Pri, Sec, Maths Eng	☆☆☆☆	High impact for low cost
Early intervention	+6 months	£££££	Pri, Maths Eng	☆☆☆☆	High impact for very high cost
One-to-one tutoring	+5 months	£££££	Pri, Sec, Maths Eng	☆☆☆☆	Moderate impact for very high cost
Homework	+5 months	£	Pri, Sec, Maths Eng Sci	☆☆☆	Moderate impact for very low cost
ICT	+4 months	££££	Pri, Sec All subjects	☆☆☆☆	Moderate impact for high cost
Assessment for learning	+3 months	££	Pri, Sec, Maths Eng	☆	Moderate impact for moderate cost
Parental involvement	+3 months	£££	Pri, Sec, Maths Eng Sci	☆☆☆	Moderate impact for moderate cost
Sports participation	+3 months	£££	Pri, Sec, Maths Eng Sci	☆☆	Moderate impact for moderate cost

Approach	Potential gain[1]	Cost	Applicability	Evidence estimate	Overall cost benefit
Summer schools	+3 months	£££	Pri, Sec, Maths Eng	☆☆	Moderate impact for moderate cost
Reducing class sizes	+3 months	£££££	Pri, Sec Maths Eng	☆☆☆	Low impact for very high cost
After school programmes	+2 months	££££	Pri, Sec, Maths Eng Sci	☆☆	Low impact for moderate cost
Individualized instruction	+2 months	££	Pri, Sec, Maths Eng Sci	☆☆☆	Low impact for low cost
Learning styles	+2 months	£	Pri, Sec All subjects	☆☆	Low impact, low or no cost
Arts participation	+1 month	££	Pri, Sec, Maths Eng Sci	☆☆☆	Very low impact for moderate cost
Performance pay	+0 month	£££	Pri, Sec, Maths Eng Sci	☆	Very low/no impact for moderate cost
Teaching assistants	+0 month	££££	Pri, Sec, Maths Eng Sci	☆☆	Very low/no impact for high cost
Ability grouping	±1 month	£	Pri, Sec, Maths Eng Sci	☆☆☆	Very low or negative impact for very low or no cost
Block scheduling and timetabling	±1 month	£	Pri, Sec, Maths Eng Sci	☆☆	Very low or negative impact for very low or no cost
School uniforms	±1 month	£	Pri, Sec, Maths Eng Sci	☆	Very low or negative impact for very low or no cost

[1] Maximum approxmate advantage over the course of a school year that an 'average' student might expect if this strategy was adopted.

Further reading

The other shortcut to an understanding of what research evidence is at least on teaching and learning, is to acquire a copy of John Hattie's latest book *Visible Learning for Teachers: maximising impact on learning* (2011). See A for Action research.

R is for Residentials

Schools which do not own their own centre for residential visits sometimes have longstanding arrangements with existing residential centres for pupil visits. This provides an embedded assumption in the school culture which underpins the value of it among the school community.

Best primary school practice includes curriculum-related residential visits, typically related to geography and environmental studies so that there is a well understood whole-school approach to residential trips. This is more difficult to achieve in secondary schools which are in general larger and organized within stronger subject bases. Good forward planning can minimise inter-departmental tensions.

Some schools have their own residential centre and for them there is never the need to make the case for the value of residential experiences for youngsters. The expectation for staff joining such schools is that they will take their part in residential activity and the programmes embrace all pupils visiting somewhere either at the end of Year 7 or at the beginning of Year 8. The purpose of these visits is both to bind teacher-pupil relationships and to extend their learning. They may provide a chance for intensive immersed learning, or for pupils to experience something new such as an outward bound activity centres. In addition there are field trips, music or sport camps or a trip may be part of training pupil leadership.

Of course, one of the attractions is that instead of having youngsters for such a short time each day (pupils between the age of five and 16 spend only 20% of their waking time in school) residential trips provide contact for virtually all of the waking time and therefore offer a better chance for staff to get to know youngsters and vice-versa.

The key to any successful residential experience is the most meticulous planning and attention to detail not just on health and safety grounds but to take full advantage of the extra time spent with pupils.

As we write this, we are aware of two key contemporary issues. First, the Paul Hamlyn Foundation has been backing a programme called Learning Away involving more than 30 schools engaging in a wide range of different residential programmes with a view to a reflective evaluative publication on their value. Secondly we know that the existing network of school residential centres which

A

B

C

D

E

F

G

H

I

J

K

L

M

N

O

P

Q

R

S

T

U

V

W

X

Y

Z

have been run (and the cause promoted) by local authorities are being threatened by cutbacks in local government finance.

We think that the first of these developments will add evidence to the claims for the value of residential experiences just at the point when existing capacity shrinks.

We would go so far as saying that we think that partnerships of schools and chains will have to pick up the baton of this cause because we are in no doubt that residentials will find a place in the list of 'experiences' we have noted elsewhere and that well thought through residentials are a feature of all successful schools. Somebody once said that 'A week's residential is worth half a term in school': we don't disagree.

Further reading

The most helpful website on school residentials is likely to be the Paul Hamlyn fund which is completing an evaluation shortly of funded programmes of different sorts of residential opportunities. See www.phf.org.uk

S is for Seating plans

Ever since the invention of the blackboard it became more and more common to organize desks and later tables so that every pupil could see the front of the room. This reinforced the traditional style of education, with pupils sitting to receive the teacher's attention. It could be argued that even with the invention of the interactive whiteboard, designed to make use of the latest technology, the tendency is still to have desks and tables facing the front, and commentators sometimes remark that classroom organization has not fundamentally changed despite many new buildings.

Many pupils do now sit in groups rather than rows, and the idea that they should work together, rather than simply passively listen to a teacher, is well established. There is quite a lively debate about seating plans and table arrangements including the effectiveness of columns, rows, the u shape, the horseshoe, a semi-circle or groups. There is a further debate about which pupils should sit where and how often this should change. Teachers, if left to themselves, favour the style of classroom arrangements which they feel best suits them but of course it may not suit the pupils. The answer clearly is flexible arrangements when organizing a classroom, and this is relatively easy for primary or special school teachers who tend to stay in the same space, rather than secondary teachers who may have to travel around several classrooms.

A
B
C
D
E
F
G
H
I
J
K
L
M
N
O
P
Q
R
S
T
U
V
W
X
Y
Z

However, increasingly, secondary provision is subject suited which makes bespoke classroom arrangements possible. Most primary school classrooms are laid out in a group setting all of the time but this can make it difficult for individual pupils to work on their own to complete tasks.

There is no right or wrong way to organize a classroom but it is important for schools and teachers to have a debate together and agree on some general principles, such as the necessity to rearrange classes for particular learning activities just as teachers of physical education regularly do in their learning areas. If the teacher is providing information directly then clearly sightlines are important, if the intention is to share knowledge and work collectively then small tables and groups might be best. Whatever the classroom arrangement, thought should also be given to specific seating plans to encourage proximal learning.

Proximal learning

Description

The school agreed that it was more effective to have one whole-school focus for lesson observations undertaken by members of the middle and senior team. Structured talk in pairs of proximal learning was an early focus and training on what made the proximal work effective was provided for all staff at a whole school INSET. It was then agreed that every lesson, in every subject for the term, would have a slot for paired talk for students. All observations would only focus on proximal work so teachers could really get this right. For example, proximal work could form part of a starter or plenary e.g. talk together for two minutes on five effects of tropical storms you learned in the lesson, or a longer exercise, having a discussion first and then completing a written element often on a shared piece of paper. Giving a set amount of time for the proximal task is key. Students experienced this approach across the school and they all soon became skilled at taking part.

Comment on impact

All students could do this. It worked powerfully and it developed oral work across the whole school. Having one whole-school focus for observations ensured the initiative – small as it was – became quickly and very effectively embedded into the school. All staff now talk about 'putting some proximal into the lesson' and staff share proximal activities that work particularly well. New staff observe lessons to see proximal work in action as it is such a key feature of the way staff teach. As a development it cost almost nothing and had a major impact. For boys (and reluctant writers) it enabled action first and writing second and it gave weaker students things to say. Working in pairs and not small groups meant no student could 'hide' or opt out and they all had to be engaged in the task. The quality of speaking skills improved very significantly in a very short time across the age, gender and ability range. This butterfly provides high leverage in improving teaching and learning.

S is for Self-evaluation

The intelligent school is greater than the sum of its parts. Through the use of its corporate intelligence it is in a powerful position to improve its effectiveness.
Barbara MacGilchrist, Jane Reed and Kate Myers

With the abolition of the school evaluation form it is even more important that schools develop their own robust, self-evaluation process and their own evolving school evaluation statement. The new, tighter inspection arrangements demand more, not less, self-evaluation by schools with the emphasis on capturing the real essence of the school. It is of course important that the school concentrates on the key OfSTED judgements related to achievement, the quality of teaching, the behaviour and safety of pupils and the quality of leadership and management. But it needs also to self-assess and be able to explain the extent to which the education provided by the school meets the needs of the range of pupils and how well the school provides for all pupils' spiritual, moral, social and culture development. Moreover, the school's self-evaluation statement should also bring out the unique and distinctive features of the school and the richness of its provision based upon quality assurance systems ensuring that systems are designed so well that a high standard is assured when the system operates as it should.

Everything depends on the quality of evidence the school is able to present and how it seeks to collect evidence as a matter of everyday routine and a culture that develops and sustains critical reflection and enquiry to secure continuous improvement. The culture of self-evaluation should be based on a collective and reflective intelligence covering the processes of collecting, analyzing, interpreting and monitoring a wide range of evidence to judge the effectiveness of the school to plan and promote improvement. The voice of all those who exercise judgement on the school should be part of this process: the head, senior leaders, middle leaders, governors, teachers, the whole staff, pupils, parents and carers and the community as a whole.

A
B
C
D
E
F
G
H
I
J
K
L
M
N
O
P
Q
R
S
T
U
V
W
X
Y
Z

Developing a culture of self-evaluation

- Time is built in for collective enquiry and reviewing evidence.
- The school practises 'appreciative enquiry' – appreciating the best of what is, envisioning what might be the best, promoting a dialogue for new knowledge, thinking and practice.
- The school tests its performance against the most stretching of benchmarks.
- 'Action research' is practised and written up to improve practice on a planned basis.
- The school programmes and practises professional and collaborative reflection with clear outcomes.
- Self-evaluation is practised by all members of the school community.
- Regular observation and evaluation of teaching and learning takes place.
- There are regular internal reviews of the quality of educational provision.
- The student voice has an impact on the school.
- The views of all stakeholders are sought on a programmed basis, e.g. annual parents' survey and contributions to parents view.
- All governors' meetings have a section devoted to self-evaluation and review and governors write a report on all visits to the schools.
- The school publishes annual collections of 'enquiry narratives' and case studies.

One of the best ways for the school to demonstrate its unique and distinctive contribution in terms of provision, participation and impact is the self-evaluation of its spiritual, moral, social and cultural dimensions. This will be particularly apparent in the provision and participation of a range of artistic, sporting and cultural activities and the complete range of activities requiring social skills. The contribution of the school to its community, national and international links and partnerships, offers a rich dimension as does care, guidance, health and well-being provision.

The best characteristics of robust and rigorous self-evaluation

- The school has a self-evaluating culture where collective review is used as an opportunity to increase the common wealth of intellectual curiosity, leading to an extension and sharing of knowledge and ensuring consistently high standards.
- The school as an organization is a learning system and learns its way forward, building in time for collective enquiry, reviewing evidence and continually striving for betterment.
- The school practises appreciative enquiry by distinguishing the best of 'what is', fostering a dialogue for new knowledge around 'what should be' and creating the vision for 'what will be'.
- The school's capacity for improvement is reflected in its strong culture of professional reflection and in its case studies of success, some of which are

published externally, but all of which bear testimony to an active, reflective, collective intelligence geared to school improvement.

- There is a continuous process of reflection that becomes implicit in the way staff think and talk about their work and keeps the school aware of its inner life.
- Self-evaluation at all levels is grounded in sophisticated, accurate and open analysis and is used unflinchingly to compare performance against the most stretching of benchmarks.
- The school takes full account of the views of pupils, parents and the community in evaluating its progress. It learns from its mistakes and accepts the challenge of continual improvement.
- The school makes good use of external critical friends, including peer schools at key points of its journey, to provide an open, rigorous reality check.

S is for School-to-school support

 In schools treading water, failure is no longer an option. Schools must either propel themselves forward, be towed, or sink.
Roland Barth

In terms of school improvement there has been a long tradition of schools helping schools organized through local authorities, federations and chains of schools. Typically, a headteacher might be seconded for a period of time to lead a school experiencing difficulties or a network of experienced senior leaders and teachers may mentor and coach other professionals. A central aim of the school's White Paper in 2010 was to create a school system that was more effectively self-improving and for schools to learn from one another, rather than the use of highly centralized approaches to improving schools. In this 'horizon shift' there was to be a high level of autonomy for individual schools with a whole system aim for excellence – comparisons to the rest and the best – with an emphasis on sharing strengths and tackling challenges. The best schools and leaders were encouraged to take on greater responsibility, leading improvement work across the system. To accelerate this process the numbers of National and Local Leaders of Education have been increased substantially together with the creation of 'Specialist Leaders of Education'; excellent professionals in leadership positions below the headteacher who support others in similar positions in other schools. On top of this national teaching schools were to be established. The landscape of school-to-school support has now changed dramatically and by 2015 there will be 500 national teaching schools with many expert practitioners, 3,000 National and Local Leaders of Education and 1,000 Specialist Leaders of Education together with local authorities and ever increasing number of chains, federations, trusts and collaboratives.

Of course, there are over 20,000 schools in England so it would be wrong to assume that all schools are supporting, or receiving support, from each other. Many schools are geographically isolated and others cherish their independence,

A
B
C
D
E
F
G
H
I
J
K
L
M
N
O
P
Q
R
S
T
U
V
W
X
Y
Z

although there are dangers here of decline. Some, it must be said, are selfishly guarding their best practice and reputation believing this keeps them ahead of the 'competition'. However, most schools are driven by moral purpose and are prepared to support others where they can and also recognize that they might gain from this process in terms of staff development and new ideas.

Of course, for many schools, school-to-school support may be based on a partnership of equals with a determination to learn from each other. These schools will get themselves into the best partnerships and collaboratives and seek to practice peer review to improve their practice. In this sense the school system will become a much more joined up learning community for the benefit of everybody where best practice can be shared.

Further reading
See N is for National Leaders of Education and National Support Schools, S is for Specialist Leaders of Education, N is for National Teaching Schools, C is for Chains and F is for Federations. See Robert Hill's book *Achieving More Together – Adding Value Through Partnership* (2008).

S is for Singing from the same song sheet

This is the most intangible and elusive, yet vital, part of a school's success and it lies at the heart of what headteachers call 'consistency'. Clearly, the larger the school, the more important and tricky the issue becomes, after all, if you lay down too precisely what everyone must do, then individual flair and creativity will wither. Moreover, the most imaginative, free thinkers among the staff will soon seek new pastures. At the other extreme, where virtually anything goes, the school begins to fall apart. So the smaller the school or department, the easier it is. It's pushing the case, but the more dysfunctional a school or department is, the more tightly the 'singing from the same song sheet' rule needs to be drawn up, agreed on and – most vitally of all – followed by everyone. The more successful, the school or department, the more leeway there is – not least for experimentation.

So, are there approaches which are absolutely essential in 'singing from the same song sheet'? We list below three practices, which any school will feel are susceptible to examination and debate. We just want to ensure that each school hits the right note in their own particular version of the song they are trying to sing together.

Lessons

Clearly, some agreement about the planning and recording of lesson plans is necessary. Whether it should be a three-, four- or five-part lesson will vary

within and between departments, or indeed be laid down within descriptors
of other possible models. But, for example, there will probably be agreement
about 'greeting and seating'. That is to say the teacher is expected to be at the
classroom door to allow pupils to go into the classroom to settle at their desks.
Of course, there's a world of difference between carrying out this process well
and not so well. Do you stand between the open door and the opposite door
post, increasing the likelihood of pupils brushing against you, while ignoring
them as they enter, except to rebuke them? Or do you spread the door open with
a welcoming arm allowing maximum space and have a word with every pupil,
perhaps beckoning a prospective troublemaker to whisper jocular threatening
sweet nothings in his / her ear? Once inside, is there a convention that all staff,
from the most to the least experienced, from the strongest to the weakest, sets
the seating that suits them best? Is this ritual signalled across the whole school
at year assemblies in the first week of each half-term?

The corridors

In one school, the pupils confessed to us that groups or gangs of pupils controlled
the corridors. The school, of course, was dysfunctional except, as the pupils
observed, for the mathematics department, where a strong head of department
had created an oasis of order. In another school, however, the conversations
between staff and pupils in corridors, at break times and at the start and end of
the school day were pleasantly casual and frequent. So, conversation in corridors
is an essential part of 'singing from the same song sheet'. In some schools, as we
note elsewhere, this includes some focused conversations with particular named
pupils who, for one reason or another, are deemed most at risk. Some minimal
ground rules on display are another feature of corridor policy for departments /
houses / stages. So, too, is agreement on the rapid retrieval of litter.

Behaviour

Unless there is consistency on expectations of behaviour, everyone in the
school suffers. There is an American programme called 'Consistent Management
Consistent Discipline' that has been tried by some schools in challenging
circumstances and all schools involved claim it is successful. When one describes
the main features, they seem obvious; staff agree that when a teacher wants
silence they raise their hands and expect the pupils gradually, but rapidly, to do
the same. The same practice continues in staff meetings. Every half-term, every
member of staff – even the best – allocates their revised seating plan for their
lessons. Pupils are prepared for it at year assemblies by the head of year and the
headteacher. Pupils apply for classroom jobs and are given them: one is to be the
'question monitor', involving using a beaker with all pupils' names on sticks and
choosing one randomly, whenever a teacher requires a respondent.

Primary schools will recognize the 'applying for classroom jobs' strategy and
they will use 'circle time' and train pupil mediators, both to be found in Year 7

A
B
C
D
E
F
G
H
I
J
K
L
M
N
O
P
Q
R
S
T
U
V
W
X
Y
Z

in secondary schools too, where the full array of peer tutors, peer counsellors and peer mentors reflect a structure that allows pupil involvement and pupil voice. All schools mark out a preferred ratio of rewards to sanctions, all are carefully recorded, as are minor and major incidents, so they can be analyzed and practice can be adjusted accordingly.

S is for Sitting on the wall not the fence

How you start the day each morning is important in any organization. Nowhere more so than in schools, where the teacher's every move can affect a child's disposition to learn. It's no different with heads. The morning habit of many a primary headteacher is to sit on the wall or stand at the school gate, where they can be seen having a cheery word with all and sundry as they run into school. 'It's the chance for parents to nobble me too, and,' one primary head added reflectively, 'how the majority do, which helps to set the tone for the awkward few parents, who otherwise could storm into school to vent their own frustration with life on me. Either I or the deputy does the same at the end of the day too.'

A successful south London secondary head in a large school does something similar when he stands every day in the entrance foyer for half an hour from about a quarter past eight, so that entering staff can buttonhole him and ask for a word later in the day, 'and I'll always make sure that I get back to them the same day. It's my interpretation of an 'open door' practice, because I am never in my office except for meetings.' Another head, can be seen on the City Road in Birmingham each afternoon supervising bus queues and waving to parents in cars picking up their children. Such heads are deeply conscious of their need to be accessible to all the school community, if not all the time, then at least at some point during the day. The head knows only too well, that the less time spent in the office the better.

The school walk

In the same spirit of being accessible, the practice of the 'daily school walk' is key. It means visiting all (and not avoiding some) phase or faculty areas, talking with kitchen or catering staff and having a word with cleaners, as well as all the other school staff – learning mentors, teaching assistants, ground staff, and the back-up administrative staff – who comprise the management engine of the school. When we use the word daily, we are not implying that all of these people interactions happen every day, but that time is built-in, so that they do happen with planned regularity.

Another successful head has devised what we would call a variant on this, by engaging in 'pupil tracking', accompanying a couple of pupils throughout a school day – at least once a term, 'you can learn a lot in a day about what is worrying kids – and, of course, it reduces the need to do as much formal monitoring of lessons that way'.

'Sitting on the wall' also symbolises the need for the head to be at the edge of the organization as it were, the main conduit to the world beyond the school. So lunchtime patrols of the local community, the shops, the streets, enable the head and leadership colleagues to take the pulse of what is happening, as well as providing opportunities to visit fellow workers in the local health clinic, neighbourhood office or advice bureau.

'Not sitting on the fence' is a caution not to equivocate or procrastinate too often. Schools are places where people are quick to detect whether a delay to give due consideration to a difficult issue, or to secure consensus about something, is genuine or merely a device to conceal a head's lack of moral backbone and failure to be consistent. It's as well not to dwell too much on the negative, so it's probably not sensible to provide examples. All of us can bring them to mind. But the head who becomes 'invisible' to the community, by spending too much time in the office or outside the school, is in danger of not sitting on the wall often enough and thereby forfeiting the confidence of staff. Sitting on the wall in its many manifestations – school walks, lunchtime tours of the local area, pupil pursuits – can take up 25-30 hours a week.

S is for Skalds not scolds

The word 'skald' is reserved in Scandinavian folklore for the poets who told stories to warriors before battle. The stories were always positive and reminded people of past great deeds, as well as impending future triumphs. I suppose in our culture Shakespeare's construction of Henry V's speech before Agincourt is an equivalence.

It's the same with heads. There is a touch of the 'skaldic' about all the successful ones. They use awards days to reflect out loud that: 'Last summer's results at GCSE were the best ever however you look at them. But this year's Year 11, who are with us tonight, are the best year group we have ever had, so we know that next summer will be better still. And when I look at last summer's Key Stage 3 results and talk with the head of Year 10 we know this trend will continue'.

Assemblies are the same with tales of sporting and other success achieved and impending. Staff briefings are occasions to tell of the brilliant way a member of staff dealt with a pupil in the corridor and can be followed by a low-key apology for mentioning it 'because I know it's something that all of you do... but I was just reminded of the quality of our staff when I saw it.' The art of the headteacher, as skald or storyteller, encompasses imagery, metaphor, simile, analogy and an unerring sense of timing and occasion.

A

B

C

D

E

F

G

H

I

J

K

L

M

N

O

P

Q

R

S

T

U

V

W

X

Y

Z

Assemblies, staff meetings, parents' evenings, concerts, plays and major occasions are all key opportunities not to be easily passed up. Outside the school, too, the canny head repeats some of the best stories as, in an accumulating received wisdom, do other members of staff. They know that the perception of more good things than bad things happening is one of the vital factors in school success.

The dictionary definition of 'scold' is 'to use undignified vehemence or persistence in reproof or fault-finding'. It is a quick and certain way to lose goodwill to emphasize the negative on public occasions. That way failure is at your elbow in no time at all. Yet heads can so easily fall victim to the habit. They are stretched and pulled every which way and, of course, they are often dealing with crisis or instances when 'singing from the same song sheet' has become discordant or totally ignored. That's the time to remember that more good than bad things are happening, or if they are not, that a positive 'can do' spirit will ensure they do. If the head isn't an energy creator in their interactions, then nobody else can fully compensate. Being a 'skald' probably takes up three to four hours each week...and not being a 'scold' a lot longer! It should not be confused with talking which happens all the time – but it does embrace both speaking to large and small groups and telling stories.

S is for Spiritual, Moral, Social and Cultural education (SMSC)

 The climate and ethos of the school enabling pupils to grow, flourish, become confident individuals and appreciate their own worth and that of others.
OfSTED Guidance

The great regret expressed by thoughtful school leaders is that the understandable focus on attainment in measurable, and therefore relatively easily accountable processes sometimes cause schools to neglect what might be called the 'education of the spirit'.

As our opening quotation from OfSTED shows however, there is perhaps a pressing need to give the matter focused attention.

SMSC education is where a school can make a unique and distinctive contribution to the tutoring of children and young people in terms of provision, participation and impact. This gets to the heart of the climate and ethos of the school and its shared values and beliefs. In the Inspection Framework of 2012 OfSTED defined SMSC as:

- provision and participation in a range of artistic, sporting and cultural activities

- provision and participation in a range of activities requiring social skills
- contribution to the community and charities
- the impact of care and guidance provision
- the benefits of the contribution of citizenship education
- health and well-being provision
- international links and partnerships.

It would appear from guidance to inspectors, that other aspects such as community cohesion and the impact of the 'specialism' where relevant should also be incorporated. The evaluation schedule also takes account of SMSC through leadership and management, achievement, the quality of teaching and behaviour and safety. Indeed, the grade descriptor for 'good' states that 'deliberate and effective action is taken to create a cohesive learning community by promoting the pupils' spiritual, moral, social and cultural development'. However, SMSC education is less a question of precise definition but more a state of being and living every day in a complex community that makes up a school. We have referred elsewhere in the book to a school's 'X factor' which is often best described through the high-quality relationships that exist in a very positive climate for learning. Similarly, the entry on the culture of schools reinforces the motion of culture as the glue that should hold everyone together and be a positive force for well-being and development. The provision and impact of SMSC education is the best visible expression of this culture which results from the school's application of its vision and values, expressed through the way the school community relates to each other and works together for the benefit of all. Schools should always be in a position to describe and articulate the impact of this provision and demonstrate its impact upon the life and soul of the school.

The following quotation will appeal to the more romantic:

> Education is the lure of the transcendent – that which we seem is not what we are for we could always be other. Education is the openness to a future which is beyond all futures. Education is the protest against present forms that they maybe reformed and transformed. Education is the consciousness that we live in time, pulled by the inexorable otherness...To interpret the changingness of human life as 'learning' and to rein in destiny by 'objectives' is a paltry response to humankind's participation in the divine or eternal.
>
> D. Heubner

Further reading

See K is for 'Kes' factor, T is for Tutor and tutor period, T is for Timetable and E is for Experiences, enrichment and entitlements, and also E is for Ethos.

A
B
C
D
E
F
G
H
I
J
K
L
M
N
O
P
Q
R
S
T
U
V
W
X
Y
Z

S is for Special Educational Needs (SEN)

Primary and secondary schools wrestle with the complexities over Special Educational Needs (SEN), also referred to as Special Educational Needs and Disabilities (SEND).

Local authorities (LA) usually prioritise SEN pupils in their admission criteria and some schools have specialist units and therefore close links with specialist services in the LA even if they are Academies.

This entry examines two issues, namely:

- possible ways to organize posts and responsibilities for SEN
- the latest evidence of how best to deal with pupils with SEN.

The background is that LAs have always found it difficult to moderate schools' own assessment of individual pupils who may have different levels of SEND. They will probably find that no easier over the years ahead as pressure on LA spending and growing demand for the best resources to overcome a perceived barrier to an individual's learning combine to make the issue even more complex and fraught. This is set against a background in the UK both of proportionally more SEN (in some cases the figure is double) than any other developed country being identified and government legislation tackling these issues which raise considerable and understandable emotions. Whatever the outcome of that combination of pressures there is one more constant factor where SEN is concerned. By definition the more complex or uncertain the need, the more likely it is that a range of professionals and their agencies have to be involved and there is always the possibility of a referral to tribunals or courts.

With that background it is unsurprising that formal paperwork, increasingly electronically located, has formed a major part of the life of the person responsible for SEN to cope with.

Possible ways of organizing for SEN

At the primary level, especially for a small rural school, it is hard to escape the conclusion that belonging to a partnership, or federation, of small schools for this purpose and engaging someone in a shared post who is administratively good and efficient is the ideal way to discharge the paperwork burden of SEN.

Such an approach is possible in urban primary schools too. In the latter there will be likely be an interdisciplinary and agency partnership (see P is for

Partnership) which tries to coordinate the multiple needs of children from less advantaged backgrounds and complex needs. We are not suggesting that the teachers and head can divest themselves of responsibility for SEN. Quite the reverse. They must lead but need not get ensnared and bogged down by paperwork which others can do. At the secondary level similar approaches have been tried in federations.

The latest evidence of what works with pupils with SEN

The latest research in the field has focused on an intervention from *Achievement for All*, which reveals the intervention, involving pupils in Years 1, 5, 7 and 10 and reports improvements in English, mathematics and other attainments, attendance and behaviour when compared with similar pupils in schools which were not a part of the intervention.

Like all research into what appear to be successful outcomes, it seeks to identify the key factors in schools where the success was greatest. These were:

- leadership by the headteacher or member of the senior leadership team
- regular review of pupil progress by teachers, both in respect of data and in discussion with pupils themselves
- parents more involved in review
- multi-channelled communication with parents
- greater range of professionals having access to pupil data and sharing implications.

The research and the details of the study can be found at www.afa3as.org.uk.

What is clear is that the results are significant for pupils who are not on School Action Plus or with Statements and as such are helpful for schools trying to wrestle with the wider problems of SEN.

Further reading
See also I is for Inclusion and *Achievement for All* by Sonia Blandford and Catherine Knowles.

S is for Specialist Leader of Education (SLE)

We believe that SLEs will be beneficial for all parties involved – not only for schools receiving SLE support, but also for the individual SLE and his or her own school.
National College of School Leadership

A
B
C
D
E
F
G
H
I
J
K
L
M
N
O
P
Q
R
S
T
U
V
W
X
Y
Z

Specialist Leaders of Education (SLEs) are outstanding middle or senior leaders in positions below the headteacher, for example, assistant heads, subject leaders or school business managers, with at least two years experience in the leadership of a particular area of expertise. They have the capacity, skill and commitment to support other individuals or teams, in similar positions in other schools. They act as 'system leaders', supporting individual leaders and teams in other schools by using coaching or facilitation approaches that draw on their knowledge and expertise in the leadership of their specialist area. This may involve a variety of support models, including diagnostic visits, one-to-one or facilitated group support. Regardless of the type of support delivered, the aim is always to contribute significantly to improving outcomes for children and young people, through developing the capacity of peer leaders in other schools.

This recent initiative is a way of formally recognizing those outstanding leaders who have a track record of supporting others and have specialist expertise from which other schools can benefit. This can boost their morale and provide a renewed sense of purpose. We know already some of the benefits for schools in receipt of SLE support – peer-to-peer support is really valued as being credible, rooted in current practice and drawing on real experience. An SLE brings a fresh perspective to specific challenges or issues, as well as the benefit of their specialist knowledge and expertise and crucially schools find that accessing support in a particular area can have a marked impact on school improvement and performance overall.

The designation of SLEs was introduced in the 2010 school's White Paper and recognizes the important role that many senior and middle leaders play in school improvement. Teaching schools are responsible for the designation, brokering and quality assurance of SLEs. Around 1,000 SLEs have already been designated and this will build to 5,000 designations by 2014/15 in line with the expansion of the teaching schools model.

S is for Staff appointments

Successful heads agree on many things – indeed a collection of what they agree on would be a handy 'All you need to know about leadership' guide for newcomers to the role. Getting all staff appointments right would be in that list. They know that because most heads will admit they have got it wrong sometimes and, of all their mistakes, regretted that one the most. Being fussy about appointments is to avoid the pitfall of appointing in haste and regretting at leisure.

Of course, 'getting it right' – or perhaps reducing the odds of getting it wrong – is worth a lot of effort. As we point out elsewhere, putting right wrong appointments can be a painful, complicated and costly process. And the longer you leave facing up to it, the more difficult it becomes.

So what are the lessons from successful 'appointers'? One head once remarked, 'you can sort out some of the dangers before you even receive applications'. She went on, 'how you frame the advertisement and the further particulars can ensure you put off those who don't want to walk the extra mile or who have no sense of humour. If you are up front about the importance of extra-curricular activities in the life of the school, if you describe the place as one where staff are always trying something new and are encouraged to do so and even take risks, then the cynics or those who regard teaching simply as a means of earning a living will be put off from applying'. In a large secondary school, another head asks staff to let any contacts they have know that there is a job going and to tell him if the person applies, making it clear that it would be improper to raise false hopes. He explained that he was simply anxious not to miss the chance of getting good people in the frame and that it had never been a problem when an applicant recommended by a colleague hadn't been appointed and that on the other hand he had once picked up an excellent head of English through this device. Being involved in ITT either through the Graduate Teacher Programme (GTP) or PGCE is another way to grow your own candidates. Many schools over the years can point to a steady supply of 'proven' permanent members of staff, because of course, teaching practice can tell you more than any interview.

A primary head believed that the fact that she encouraged applicants to visit the school before making their application also helped, 'You can tell a lot when they are here, especially from the questions they ask. It often saves a lot of time'. When pressed, she agreed that the fact that someone didn't necessarily take up the offer prior to making the application wasn't necessarily the end of the matter since there might be good reason why it wasn't practical. Rather she said that often some of those who did visit revealed themselves as a person to shortlist.

Idiosyncratic systems for shortlisting abound. (There was once a head who confessed that unless candidates either played a sport or were interested in music, he didn't shortlist them! One could see what he was getting at.) Shortlisting is never a task for one person and is a good development opportunity for both senior and perhaps a more junior colleague. Once shortlisted, I admire the head who says she visits a candidate's school to see them 'in situ' if she can, if it's a post with responsibility.

At interview itself, a tour of the school accompanied by pupils – some schools at both primary and secondary level have systems for getting student views of candidates, which are invariably reliable and at secondary level can involve student feedback on the teaching itself – can be extended to be more specific. For example, in one primary school candidates are asked at interview to critique the display they have seen. In another, the candidates were forewarned that this would be a question at interview and the school put up an inappropriate display panel to see if anyone noticed. At another, they were forewarned to read online the school's pedagogic policy and practice and then asked about it at interview.

As Andy Buck points out, great schools have to be absolutely sure that the successful candidate understands and subscribes to the school's core values and beliefs. Questions are best rooted in ascertaining what candidates have *actually* done – giving illustrations from their practice – to back up their sometimes naturally idealistic claims of what *should* be done. The interviewing panel ideally should involve someone with whom the successful candidate is going to work closely as well as a reliable member of the governing body where appropriate.

In summary, don't offer a permanent appointment if you are in any doubt.

S is for Staff development

'It starts with the adverts and further particulars which highlight what we offer and our belief that it's the bedrock of our success' said one head. Unsurprisingly, all the job descriptions in the school had a common expectation that postholders have 'responsibilities' and 'rights' in their own further learning. In their first three years in the school any newcomer had a personally allocated budget to spend on CPD and joined a general school and bespoke faculty induction programme. Two unusual features stood out. First, each was asked to suggest a feature encountered in an earlier employment which in their opinion was exceptionally good in motivating staff or pupils. Secondly, each was forewarned that at their first annual 'development of performance', which was scheduled for six months after their arrival, they would be expected to offer one suggestion about what they thought the weakest feature of the school was. 'That's when we also ask them what really motivates them in their professional and private life so we can suggest ways in which they might bring it into school life' the headteacher said, as she explained that she saw her two main tasks as building the capacity and creating energy among the staff (see E is for Energy creators).

The head went on to describe a bewildering array of practices: bursaries for young staff to attend subject association and professional conferences; opportunities for young staff to have stints in senior leadership teams and other ad-hoc focus task groups; an expectation that everyone will do a stint as an external examiner, 'We give them an extra honorarium, beyond the examining board fee as an incentive. It's so important that all teachers know what the exams require'; a school-based 'action research' focused masters group run by the local university. The school also employed two ASTs who facilitated peer observation and led the debate about what made outstanding learning, teaching and assessment. All staff had an opportunity to observe others' practice and sometimes, through the use of privately videoed sessions, their own. The school offered two fellowships each year to staff who wanted to pursue some small action research project in curriculum development or pedagogy. If successful the 'fellows' received a personal honorarium of £1,000 plus £3,000 to be spent on visits, time off and resources to support their idea.

Every other year one of the five professional days at the school is used for staff in twos and threes to visit another school which is in session, to learn and report back on a feature of curriculum or school life they have agreed to observe closely. This is followed by a residential conference where the school seeks to learn from that process.

You have to admit it was impressive. It came as no surprise that there were regular timetabled sessions – every fourth week – when the staff ran regular in-service sessions for each other. Nor were we surprised that they regularly used the amazing website of TES and their series on professional resources. The budget? The head explained that the 5% they earmarked for all this, including the cost of part of the ASTs, was sacrosanct. 'But we all agree it's worth it'.

Sharing good practice

Description

A school firmly believed in the maxim that 'the biggest and most underused resource teachers have is each other'. But they also realized that they had to do something more than merely exhort colleagues to share good ideas. So they formally introduced, as a matter of policy, 'sharing good practice' as the first item on the agenda of every departmental, middle management and staff meeting.

One member of the senior leadership team was responsible for organizing which teacher was to present, on what topic, at which meeting, thereby ensuring that there was a broad range of contributions, from different subject disciplines. All the slots were short, a maximum of ten minutes and colleagues were encouraged to be as interactive with their peers as they would be with their students.

Many of the presentations were subsequently published in the staff bulletin and put on the CPD section of the e-learning platform.

Comment on impact

The impact was very powerful indeed. Staff came away from meetings with practical ideas they could use in their lessons the next day and it proved an excellent way of initiating cross-subject / discipline working arrangements. Another remarkable development was that although it began with senior staff, gradually the policy embraced everyone so that for example, second year teachers offered ideas to more experienced colleagues. In that school everyone was providing an example of learning. It was particularly high leverage in terms of staff development and the improvement of learning and teaching.

Further reading
See C is for Continuous Professional Development.

A
B
C
D
E
F
G
H
I
J
K
L
M
N
O
P
Q
R
S
T
U
V
W
X
Y
Z

S is for the Staff handbook

The staff handbook is the school bible and is at the heart of its smooth organization. Time and time again, schools which fall into difficulty realize too late that they've allowed their staff handbook to fall into neglect and it is therefore overlooked. First, even in the smallest schools, there needs to be a staff handbook, which includes in loose leafed form all the school's policies and practices – it can be a simple A4 sheet for each policy and practice. On this sheet will be a brief statement of both policy and the implications for practice, with the name of the member of staff responsible for leading the next review of policy and practice and the date on which it is to be reviewed. It would include the names of the teams of people responsible for implementing different aspects of the practice. When there is any change – and with changes in staff, this is inevitable – the revised version is formally included as an item of information at staff briefings and the replacement sheet inserted in all copies. Usually there is a copy in the staffroom, faculty areas and the school office.

The best schools now have their staff handbook in electronic form and readily available to all through their e-learning platform or intranet.

S is for Storytelling

Ted Wragg once remarked that teaching could be summarized as: explanations, questions, assessment and experiences. By that he meant that if you could master what was involved in those four, then learning would be happening and we would have a successful educational experience. At the heart of explanation is the art of storytelling. Teachers quickly learn that well told stories have the virtue of enthralling the pupil and enabling a point or an elusive concept to be understood. Nowadays, the use of visual and auditory technologies has transformed what is possible in this respect in a way that could only be dreamt of by earlier generations. We know many secondary schools where assemblies are choreographed brilliantly with film and archived materials to make points in a riveting way which is truly memorable. Few English or history teachers would now ignore the wealth of film material that reinforces great literature or periods of history and geography comes to life through TV programmes interspersed with subtle and skilled questions, tasks and reinforcements of learning.

Allied to the art of storytelling is the alter ego of teaching. Just as the nursery teacher sends 'teddy bears' home to have adventures with pupils, who come back and create pictures and stories of what's happened, so the same teacher uses the teddy bear as another character to stimulate pupils' talk. The primary teacher continues this practice for a time and is alert to the use of puppets. But it continues into secondary school, not in the form of puppets, but sometimes with lifelike figures in the history room (Henry VIII say) or in science (Darwin), and to these figures the teacher from time to time defers. They have imaginary conversations on the phone and, in the digital age, have orchestrated 'e-tutors' to whom the pupils can turn. One school has an enthusiastic teacher who has his very own 'Avatar', a constructed and moving figure on the screen with a programmed voice. We are of course in the foothills of our journey to exploit the learning technologies.

Finally, we must mention the Story Museum in Oxford (www.storymuseum. org.uk) a new charity with national ambitions. In their early work they have a skilled visiting storyteller – nothing unusual in that, as lots of primary schools have access to an informal network of storytellers – but this particular storyteller sees his role as enabling teachers (and pupils for that matter) to themselves become excellent storytellers and in the process extend their modelling of writing. The schools so far involved are convinced that the impact on Year 6 writing is significant.

S is for Student voice

 The key worker in a school is the student. The only important product is his or her learning.
Theodore Sizer

Student voice has rightly emerged as a vital ingredient in discussions about the next stage of school improvement and it features strongly in debates about the future of schooling. For example, people talk about 'co-construction' of school experiences, where the co-constructors are the pupils. That is to say, they are partners with staff in planning devising and delivering the outcomes. Like so many 'taken for granted' desirables, the detail of what's involved is often assumed rather than spelled out.

Charles Handy once put his finger on why student voice is most elusive in the 11–16 secondary school when he compared primary pupils to 'workers' who were always busy with tasks to complete and sixth formers to 'clients' who made choices about what they would and wouldn't do. By contrast, he suggested, students aged 11–16 were neither 'workers' nor 'clients': they were more like the cars on the assembly line with different people giving them a bit of physics, followed by mathematics then art and so on as the timetable and the years passed until they are released after GCSE.

Of course, his imagery was fanciful but it has sufficient truth in it to strike a chord and perhaps to explain how in the difficult adolescent years the school's concern for discipline and conformity gets in the way of developing pupil

A
B
C
D
E
F
G
H
I
J
K
L
M
N
O
P
Q
R
S
T
U
V
W
X
Y
Z

responsibility and leadership. School councils are often as far as it gets and even then the participants are predictable in their backgrounds: often the school's council's influence on school life is marginal. Some schools, however, have gone further and involved pupils not just in specific leadership initiatives but enabled them to influence departments and faculties as well as engage in leading learning and having a real say in every aspect of school life.

In some secondary schools, the school council is elevated to, and recognized as, a fundamental part of student voice: it is even called 'student voice' and instantly takes on a whole-school dimension. In the same schools opportunity is provided, during tutor time, for all students, along with their tutor who is part of the group, to voice their concerns and raise issues for the council to consider. These sessions are led by the council representatives who offer the issues raised for the next council meeting to consider. The meeting is timetabled and held within two weeks of the student voice tutor session. The representatives report back to the tutor group two weeks later on the outcome and further discussion takes place. All this takes place within each half term. This managed, student-centred approach to school council with student voice at its heart gives the whole process democratic credibility; student ownership and a direct input into school improvement. All students are encouraged to take part and everyone's opinion is judged to be valid and valued. This, in turn contributes to raising self-confidence and esteem; responsible and respectful communication and an awareness that their views matter and that taking part can make a difference.

Of course, it's easier at primary level and all self-respecting primary teachers involve the pupils in the daily management of the classroom allocating pupil monitors to apply for different tasks and then carry out their regular 'jobs'. It's surprising that on transfer to secondary school this habit simply stops, when in Year 7 there would be renewed willingness in most pupils to impress.

Recognizing that pupils need a voice, most primary and secondary schools have a school council. Without careful planning, however, this can soon become an irrelevance so it must have consequences for the whole-school community. Among the vital ingredients to its success are:

- A budget with strings attached i.e. it needs to affect the whole school environment.
- Task groups, to which other pupils need to be co-opted, charged with investigating various real issues in the school, for example attendance, homework, marking practices, extra-curricular activities, school rules and sanctions, reviewing student surveys, induction and 'buddying' arrangements for new arrivals, their school's communication policies and practices.
- Codes of operation – minutes, chairing, progress chasing prior to meetings.

Nowadays, schools councils often need to be related, in large secondary schools to year councils and / or houses / colleges or the emerging 'schools-within-schools' often with vertical tutor groups.

Whatever the state of a school's council – and it's obvious from what we have written that we see it as the central framework on which to hang pupil involvement – we believe students should be legitimately involved in most of the school's activities and certainly as follows:

- *within the classroom* – in managing roles and in self-assessment as part of AfL
- *as peer tutors* – an excellent way of learning and modifying behaviour for older pupils who are tasked to help younger ones. (It is interesting that the Sutton Trust review of what interventions have the most impact on school outcomes scores peer interventions among the top three)
- *as peer mentors* – within and beyond the classroom / tutor group
- *as peer counsellors and mediators* – to aid behaviour in and around school and act as a guard against bullying. (Some schools have pupil juries to deal with bullying and other disciplinary issues)
- *as 'community workers'* – helping locally as part of citizenship programmes.
- *as editors and contributors to a magazine produced by pupils*
- *in interpreting and reporting back on the annual review (through pupil surveys such as those offered by PASS, Keele University and NFER) of school ethos and students' commitment to the life of the school and their willingness to learn* – such reports are fed to the senior leadership team and governors.
- *as observer members of the governing body and its sub-committees*
- *as part of the appointment process for new staff* – including the head.

Pupils as Headteachers...for a day

Description

Among one of the most interesting practices we came across was a junior school which held a 'Headteacher for a day' scheme as part of children's day each year. It involved six pupil candidates from Year 6 putting themselves up for election two weeks before local council elections. Each had to publish manifestos and attend a kind of 'hustings' for questions and answers in front of staff and pupils. Voting took place on local election day and all staff and pupils are eligible to vote, other than those who are late. The winner was announced and become 'Headteacher for the day'. Aided by a cabinet of fellow pupils, he or she set out proposals for the day for consultation with staff and pupils. Other tasks included taking the 'praise assembly', giving out 'achievement of the week' awards, having tea (along with the cabinet) with their favourite members of staff and preparing a newsletter for parents about their experience as headteacher. The day usually ends with a talent session.

Comment on impact

From such a story, it's possible to imagine all sorts of new ways to involve pupils. It might even be a topic for the School Improvement Group to discuss for as we pointed out in our introduction real pupil involvement is probably the key to a school achieving real success in the balance of teaching and learning.

What follows are some brief suggestions from a secondary school in West Sussex. They are in addition to all the time-honoured and familiar ideas of school council, year council etc. referred to earlier (see also L is for Learning).

15 tips for making the students' voice heard

1. Make sure you use pupils to buddy any new pupil: we find two each is much better than one.
2. Try making an expectation that all sixth formers spend at least a specified time in lessons lower down the school and in primaries for their after school clubs. Incorporate it into their reports.
3. Make 'pupil presentations' a planned part of lessons and establish a rota whereby pupils take turns to lead parts of lessons.
4. Pupils introduce all new topics: they are told what it will be and given free rein to present it however they like. Teachers feed back on how they have done and have a term prize for the best.
5. Use pupils to lead revision lessons in Year 11.
6. Make sure class captains have jobs to do.
7. Let students with 'expert' knowledge teach the class.
8. Train a group of students – perhaps those thinking of going into teaching – review teaching and learning in the school.
9. Seek pupil feedback on 'what went well' and 'what could be improved' in lessons – 'even better ifs' (EBIs).
10. Each year, each faculty trains up a group of pupils in charge of display and allows the pupils to set up new displays for every faculty shared area and head of department's room.
11. In art and design have one-to-one peer assessment of photography portfolios.
12. Have pupils in rotation on reception and feed back their performance in reports.
13. Involve students in twos and threes as co-mentors and coaches so they try to solve issues about learning before going to the teacher.
14. In our faculty we all get pupils to put answers on the interactive whiteboard and have a rota of 'lead' questioners for them to ask the questions at a given point in the lesson.
15. Each faculty has a 'subject council' so pupils can feed back on quality of lessons and curriculum.

For student voice to be fully justified as a priority within any school, a commitment is required to develop the personal skills of young people so that they feel able to express themselves in safe learning environments, where people show respect for one another and are prepared to listen and be open-minded. These skills have to be learned, practised and developed. For some innovative schools this is done as a matter of course and students are encouraged to question, to be curious, be imaginative and seek challenges. But for most schools a framework is required to allow all staff and all students to experience and nurture student voice in this creative way. Experience indicates that tutor time is an excellent place for student voice to be developed. In such a setting, with no performance pressures applied, teaching and learning can experiment with group work, student lead presentations, performance and celebration. The added benefit, of course, is that since all tutors are usually classroom teachers, then methods successfully applied during tutor time can be transferred to subject lessons and student voice then genuinely takes on a whole-school dimension.

Perhaps one of the most successful ventures we have seen is in Somerset where two comprehensives, the Blue School in Wells and Chew Valley, have transformed our view of what is possible. They run a programme called 'Learning to lead' which involves upwards of a third of each school's 1,000 plus pupils. Students self-elect to one of a series of teams with intriguing titles, each of which has a clear purpose. So the 'book worm team' encourages students to read, the 'we love science' team works with staff to improve the educational experience, the 'chicken team' takes responsibility for the school coop, and the 'green team' predictably, consists of those with a strong environmental mission. Admittedly, there were one or two obscure and idiosyncratic examples such as the 'lizard team', which seemed anxious to set up a solarium in every classroom. But the most impressive thing was the way in which they came together collectively in the school forum. So well established is it in the Blue School, that they have just built an impressive sustainable round, wooden building as a student-run office centre where the teams can meet and develop their projects and meet 'in the round'. Apart from self election and being open to mixed-age membership, the other guiding principles include the important one that every activity has to be of value to the community, whether that is defined as the school, the town and surrounding villages or more widely and internationally. In that sense all the teams are different from the normal menu of extra-curricular activities such as sport, drama and debating. We saw an application of the same principle in a nearby primary school.

Further reading
For further detail visit www.learningtolead.org

S is for Success

What is a successful school? How would you recognize one? Does it necessarily have school uniform and is there an honours board? Do you need to see the key stage and examination results? Where do those excellent musical, arts exhibitions and performance productions fit in? If you think it is all these things how do you recognize success in primary schools or special school?

Is success only to be defined through the OfSTED inspection process? Is it

A
B
C
D
E
F
G
H
I
J
K
L
M
N
O
P
Q
R
S
T
U
V
W
X
Y
Z

to be affirmed or denied by the views of parents and governors or people in the school's locality, the shopkeepers, neighbours and local employers? Is it to be won or lost by the messages and views of the staff who happen not to be teachers at the school: the caretaker, the secretary, the technician, the teaching assistant, the learning mentor, the school meals staff? Is it to be seen in the behaviour of the children both inside the school or arriving and leaving? Is there a way of comparing the success of a school in a prosperous, leafy middle-class area with another school in a deprived inner city or a small rural school with a large urban school?

Unlike a company with a profit and loss account, a school's balance sheet is difficult to read and its successes may not show up in any case until years later. Some things are clear. If a significant number of pupils don't make progress in literacy and numeracy, if there is always a significant gap between the performance of groups of pupils, it pupil exclusions are common, if the staff turn-over is very high, if there are fights every day in the playground, if there is little pupils' work displayed in the classroom and what there is has been there all year, if the teacher cannot tell you about promising signs in the development of each and every pupil in their classroom, then you have got serious problems. If you add to that few extra-curricular activities, a library empty of students, no learning before and after school, musical instruments lost or broken, high absentee rates and a high incidence of staff sickness, then you have found a disaster.

We make the assumption that those involved in every school will want to make it a happy and successful place. If you scratch the surface hard enough, all staff, when they are appointed to this post in the school, will reveal a dream or a vision of how things could be in their classroom and in the school. Schools should be places where every one of its community tastes the confidence that comes with success in some form or other. Every youngster ought to be entitled to attend a successful school and in any case, it is much more rewarding for adults to work in a successful school.

Our definition of success is where in a school:

- all talk is of 'our' achievement and everyone is determined to improve on their own and shared achievement
- all pupils are increasingly aware of their potential and that this is seen as without limit if they make the effort
- everyone feels fulfilled in what they do and contributes to the fulfilment of others
- the full range of success – sporting, academic, artistic, practical support for others, triumph over adversity – is celebrated
- all members of the school community are committed to their own continuous learning and support that of others
- everyone is aware of the schools' collective past and present success and is ambitious to contribute to that collective legacy for future generations
- nobody is in fear of physical or emotional abuse.

The school is there to facilitate these aims and to promote the fun of learning and the pleasure of achievement.

S for Support staff

When you first visit a school your reception area makes an impression. Schools realize this and ensure that those who staff the 'front desk' are welcoming and thoughtful. Exactly the same 'first impressions' are made by phone and the speed at which messages left are acknowledged. Such impressions contribute to whether or not a problem escalates or subsides, how a visiting inspector or business person enters their meeting with the head or some other senior colleague.

Beyond the front desk lies the 'outer office' – unless in small schools they are one and the same thing of course. This 'outer office' is at the centre of a web of support staff encompassing site maintenance, catering and a range of other supportive activities in the departments, houses or phases. Within and beyond the 'outer office' are people who carry out roles vital to the smooth running of a successful school.

The bursar, for example, is increasingly vital to the management of the school and needs to be *au fait* with finance, personnel and legal implications besides health and safety whilst ensuring the budget is run effectively and planned with well-balanced estimates of risk. The site manager is another vital person in the school ensuring that the school fabric is attended to whether it needs to be repaired, cleaned or extended. Nowadays, there will be a facilities manager of ICT who steers a wobbly course between the variable competence of staff on their perpetual learning curve in ICT and the inadequacies of ICT providers.

It is a far cry from when we started out on our teaching careers when we had the sense to realize that the school 'secretary' ran the school along with the 'caretaker'. Get on the wrong side of either and your career was facing difficulty!

So support staff are vital and their numbers have multiplied over the first decade of this century. It is time therefore to banish the phrase 'non-teaching' staff. It still hangs around in schools which are not sensitive to the subliminal messages of language (see C is for Common language).

Most importantly, all the messages of change, leadership, review, learning, and many of the other aspects of school improvement involve and apply to support staff as well as teachers. They too have their 'hyacinths' (see H is for Hyacinths) and it as well to encourage their use to the benefit of the school: they too enjoy the right balance of appreciative enquiry to problem solving (see A is for Appreciative enquiry). The best schools recognize that support staff are the hidden key to school success.

A
B
C
D
E
F
G
H
I
J
K
L
M
N
O
P
Q
R
S
T
U
V
W
X
Y
Z

A
B
C
D
E
F
G
H
I
J
K
L
M
N
O
P
Q
R
S
T
U
V
W
X
Y
Z

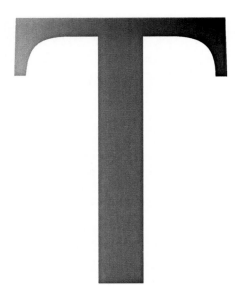

T is for Target setting

> If you would hit the mark, you must aim a little above it; every arrow that flies feels the attraction of the earth.
>
> Henry Longfellow

Target setting first surfaced as an idea in the summer of 1993 when Ted Wragg took evidence for an independent review of what was wrong with education in Birmingham. He explored the idea with many witnesses, including the teacher unions and the idea emerged of three sorts of educational targets as part of a bargain between key stakeholders. There would be:

- *targets of input* – represented by a commitment from the city council to increase the schools budget in real terms for a period of three years
- *targets of experiences provided to youngsters* (see E is for Experiences, enrichment and entitlement)
- *targets of outcome* – represented by ever higher scores in SATs and GCSE.

It was the last set of targets which were to become controversial. We used them to start a dialogue with the city's schools asking them to aim for each age group to improve on the performance of their immediate predecessor group and to consider 'realistic targets' and 'ambitious ones', assuming everything went well such as low absence, good staff, and crucially the pupils understanding what they need to do to 'improve on their previous best'.

When the Labour Government of 1997 took them up however, they used the targets 'top-down' for every Local Education Authority (LEA) to use as a benchmark for improved outcomes. Soon LEAs simply passed them on to their schools and took up monitoring in a top-down way. Headteachers, themselves increasingly under the cosh with OfSTED, league tables and 'floor targets', have been severely tested not simply to replicate the 'top-down' process.

Yet, ideally, we believe that target setting is much more subtle than that. We have set out elsewhere what we see as the need for a common language so far as pupils are concerned, drawing a distinction between 'estimates', 'predictions' and 'targets', (see F is for Fischer Family Trust).

So far as members of staff are concerned, there is a different ideal approach in primary and secondary settings.

- In the best primary schools, rather than monitoring being something done to the staff by the senior leadership team (SLT), with a focus on targets of their pupils' expected levels of progress, the staff themselves review each of their pupils' progress and, unprompted, and on a regular basis, they talk with the SLT about interventions that will help those youngsters not making the progress. In those schools as a team effort they are setting ever higher targets for their collective efforts but have the common sense not to allow that to distract them from helping each and every pupil to make optimum progress.
- In the best secondary schools the approach is necessarily slightly different. Each department is compared with what other departments achieve with the same pupils and with departments in other schools, and then targets are set for improvement. The school uses knowledge of other schools with comparable intakes to spur on its own performance, (see F is for Family of schools). Some schools have incorporated within their staff performance management system targets for improved performance of particular sets or individual pupils (see E is for Examinations).

T is for Teach First

We have included Teach First not because it has national coverage, it does not, but we believe it stands as proxy for the many routes that now exist for progress towards teacher qualification. The majority of teachers starting out will still come from a PGCE route that involves a more or less close partnership with a university education department. Then there were School Based Partnerships (SCIPS) and the Graduate Teaching Programme (GTP) which have now given way to Schools Direct. Moreover, any successful school knows the value of being involved in some way in the routes into teaching whether offering places on PGCE courses or on GTP / Schools Direct. One head told us, 'it helps ensure we are talking about teaching' and she explained how she encourages triangulation which she described as follows: 'The trainee plans a lesson and then I and the trainee's mentor teach it to different groups and then we all discuss it together.' For the best schools therefore, involvement is an ideal way to stimulate debate about teaching and learning and a means of spotting talent for appointments.

Teach First started in London in a small way in 2002 to solve a shortage of secondary teachers. It has come a long way and developed an impressive and bold mission statement: 'Our mission is to address educational disadvantage by transforming exceptional graduates into effective, inspirational teachers and leaders in all fields'.

Teach First is dedicated to building a network of teachers and leaders to work in schools in challenging circumstances so that all children and young people can get access to the best education. In the short term, this is done by recruiting exceptional graduates who would not otherwise have considered teaching. In the long term it is about creating a movement of leaders who are committed to influencing system change in education, from both inside and outside the classroom. Teach First recruits graduates – known as participants – to teach in schools for a minimum of two years and they undertake a leadership development programme. After six weeks preliminary training they work towards a PGCE, in the first year supported by university tutors and school mentors. Beginning in the second year participants also have the opportunity to work towards a Masters qualification designed to further develop their abilities to be effective leaders in schools. Following successful completion of the programme participants become Teach First Ambassadors – more than half stay in teaching and others commit to systemic changes in education through their work as governors or in other forms of employment. From 2002, Teach First graduates worked in secondary schools – firstly in London Challenge, then in other City Challenges, gradually expanding all over England. In 2008 Teach First launched a pilot to place graduates in primary schools which has now led to the expansion of primary provision across the country. The organization aims to place over 1,000 graduates annually by 2012 and by 2020 expects to have an Ambassador community of over 9,000, and within this 100 headteachers of challenging schools.

There have been several reports on measuring the impact of this initiative. The 2010 report conducted by Manchester University provided compelling evidence that Teach First participants are effective classroom practitioners, and that their presence leads to positive pupil outcomes. Selection criteria are demanding and as there is competition for places, only the best candidates are recruited. The core competencies include leadership, planning and organizing, problem-solving, interaction, resilience, self-evaluation, humility, respect and empathy.

Partnerships with schools are integral to the achievement of Teach First and many schools have now built up strong relationships over several years. Headteachers remark particularly on their enthusiasm, commitment, energy and resilience and their impact as role models to pupils as recently qualified, highly achieving graduates.

T is for Teacher credibility

Students are very perceptive about knowing which teachers can make a difference to their learning.

John Hattie

John Hattie's groundbreaking studies of what improves pupils' learning and outcomes are the most comprehensive ever completed. One of the highest ranking factors in the 2011 publication *Visible Learning for Teachers*, was teacher credibility, rated the fourth most important factor out of over 150 'interventions'. This finding, although based on extensive research, is not news in itself and many other books and research articles have referenced the 'teacher effect', not to mention thousands of personal testimonies.

The old TDA recruitment slogan, 'Nobody forgets a good teacher', sums this up nicely. However, analyzing exactly what are the characteristics of teacher credibility is a matter for further debate. There would seem to be a consensus that there are four dimensions to credibility: trustworthiness, competence, dynamism and immediacy. With reference to trustworthiness, the pupil must feel that the teacher has their best interests at heart and really cares about their success in class. Pupil surveys consistently refer to the importance of teachers being fair and consistent in terms of classroom discipline, making sure to include everybody in activities and treating all pupils the same. All these actions develop trust and if, in addition the teacher takes an interest in the pupils' development outside the classroom, then even deeper trust is built. Competence is another key dimension involving curriculum mastery delivered in a meaningful way. There are whole lists of teacher standards and OfSTED criteria covering competence and clearly good classroom management skills are key, and pupils recognize that good planning and design are as important as caring and fair treatment. The third characteristic often described as dynamism may be better described as being passionate about learning and able to present material in an exciting and engaging way including a diverse range of techniques. Pupils immediately recognize enthusiasm and the ability to energize, excite and inspire them which gives the teacher great credibility in their eyes. Fourthly is immediacy, which involves using particular techniques to reduce the distance between the teachers and their pupils, such as the use of 'we' and 'us' or different ways of motivating individuals and the class as a whole to feel special and keen to learn. Pupils learn better when the teacher is engaging and animated. It helps to grab their attention and motivate them to participate fully.

A
B
C
D
E
F
G
H
I
J
K
L
M
N
O
P
Q
R
S
T
U
V
W
X
Y
Z

Pupils know who are the best and most credible teachers in their school. They talk about teachers who are interested in them as individuals, who make learning exciting, who are good communicators, always willing to help and obviously enjoy their jobs. They also tell stories about the spontaneity, humour and mannerisms of their teachers. Above all they respond to them as passionate teachers who love learning and like them, wanting them to achieve their very best.

Further reading
See C is for Classroom interventions, T is for Teachers and teaching (and learning) and L is for Learning.

T is for Teachers and teaching (and learning)

> **It is the supreme art of the teacher to awaken joy in creative expression and knowledge.**
>
> Albert Einstein

Working in the classroom with pupils, teachers divide their time among three sorts of activity:

- the first is golden: it's when a pupil, or some of the pupils understand an idea they didn't before, learn a new skill or show an inquisitive extension of their desire to learn
- the second is consolidating pupils' learning
- the third – much less rewarding for all concerned – is 'occupying time'.

Schools and their teachers know that the more they can spend time in the first two territories, the more children learn and the school is successful.

In everyday life the best teachers are striving for improvement. They work on the axis of expectation and self-esteem set out below.

As can be seen in the diagram on the following page, high expectation on the part of the teacher and high self-esteem on the part of the pupil leads inevitably to success. The reverse – low on both parts – leads equally obviously to failure. A debate on the two blank squares however, might lead to discussion of the dangers of complacency through too low expectations – the perennial charge of OfSTED – or too high expectations, inducing in the least confident learners the possibility that they learn to fail. The trick, of course, is for the teacher to understand enough about the ingredients of raising expectation and self-esteem.

We set out below what appear to us to be both the beliefs and the habits of outstandingly successful teaching.

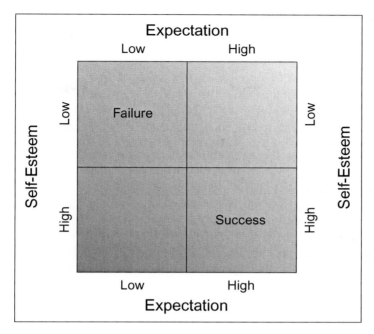

Beliefs

- Transformability rather than ability of children.
- Success for all not some.
- Intelligence is multi-faceted.
- Every child needs a worthwhile relationship with at least one adult and it may not be you.
- A child's failure to learn is a challenge to your teaching strategies not a sign of ability on the part of the child.
- A child showing great effort in learning is a positive sign of character not of a lack of ability.

Habits and behaviours

- Always improve their story techniques.
- Always polish their skill in questioning.
- Always extend their best explanations.
- Mark other colleagues' class assignments.
- Observe other colleagues teaching.
- 'Sing from the same song sheet' – up to a point.
- Treat teaching as a cooperative activity – use 'we' a lot.
- Store and share DVDs on teaching.
- Use formative and ipsative (i.e. against own previous best) assessment in their marking.
- Teach 'alongside', 'behind' and 'in front of' youngsters.
- Share leadership and management.

A

B

- Teach in the corridors.
- Share their 'hyacinths' of learning (see H is for Hyacinths).
- Accept the unpredictability of teaching.

C

D

E

F

Just looking at this list it's clear that no one teacher would pass all the criteria. That brings us to our other major point which is that every teacher, however outstanding, should surely be seeking to improve at least one aspect of their approach. This sets an example of a learning role model which youngsters can emulate as they take on from the teacher the move in formative assessment which leads from dependent to independent learning.

G

H

I

J

K

It is also worth reflecting at this stage on recent changes in the balance between teaching and learning. Phrases such as 'co-construction of the curriculum' have emerged to describe ways in which pupils can be engaged in devising their own learning. In the primary sector, 'projects' have always allowed an element of that. In secondary schools it has been less common, though 'enterprises' whether in drama or business have involved a cycle of pupils' mind mapping, planning, testing their ideas, polishing them, and then creating, displaying, performing and critiquing their own work.

L

The issue remains of how and when to move from the 'sage on the stage' to the 'guide on the side'.

M

N

Further reading
See Q is for Questions, S is for Storytelling, L is for Learning, L is for Lesson Plans, M is for Marking, T is for Teacher credibility.

O

P

 There is, in fact, no teaching without learning.

Paulo Freire

Q

R

S

T

U

V

W

X

Y

Z

Of some our teachers, we remember their foibles and mannerisms, of others, their kindness and encouragement, or their fierce devotion to standards of work that we probably did not share at the time. And of those who inspired us most, we remember what they cared about, and that they cared about us, and the person we might become. It is the quality of caring about ideas and values, this fascination with the potential for growth within people, this depth and fervour about doing things well and striving for excellence, that comes closest to what I mean in describing a 'passionate teacher'.

Robert Fried
The Passionate Teacher

A
B
C
D
E
F
G
H
I
J
K
L
M
N
O
P
Q
R
S
T
U
V
W
X
Y
Z

A
B
C
D
E
F
G
H
I
J
K
L
M
N
O
P
Q
R
S
T
U
V
W
X
Y
Z

T is for Teachers talking about teaching

One of the writers who has impressed us most is the American researcher, Judith Little, who, as long ago as the early 1980s, claimed 'Schools are successful, when the following four things happen:

1. teachers talk about teaching
2. teachers observe each other teach
3. teachers plan, organize, monitor and evaluate their teaching together
4. teachers teach each other'.

We suspect the reason why these statements are so persuasive, is because you can immediately see how each of them can be made more likely to happen.

Teachers talk about teaching

For example, the first is more likely if all school and faculty meetings are about teaching, learning, assessment and curriculum. Business is never discussed there. More likely, too, if the headteacher, at the end of a school day, visits the staffroom to talk informally about her own teaching. This shows how, by use of open discussion, she hopes to improve it. It's even more likely if staff are expected in turn to circulate interesting things they've read – about teaching, learning or their subject of course – on a regular, programmed basis.

Teachers observe each other teaching

The second objective will happen if teachers have the opportunity to observe each other in a focused way. So, involvement in initial education and training of teachers is an opportunity to facilitate inter-classroom observation. This involves three parties – senior teacher, trainee and colleague – in the planning of a lesson together, followed by unthreatening observation of each teaching the same lesson and then collectively discussing their different approaches.

Another example of how to make it happen would be to use one of the five annual INSET / training days for staff to make focused visits to comparable schools which are actually in session. A team follow-up discussion would explore what's been learned. Other ideas include:

- Setting up the chance for all staff to have their own practice privately videoed and for them to review the outcome privately.
- Having a 'see interesting practice' week once a year when teachers in pairs observe each other's practice informally.

Teachers plan together

Teachers planning, monitoring and evaluating their work together will happen if there is the expectation that every department facilitates it. This affects the nature of meetings; moderating each other's marking; and the device described above – three teachers planning a single lesson and then all teaching it. In one school we know, all these three are positively encouraged; the school organizes its timetable so that staff can bid for time to do one of these three activities as a part of their off-timetable PPA time. In this way, they can participate either on a regular basis or in one of their non-metronomic 'days' or 'weeks' that break up the metronomic repetition of the conventional timetable.

Teachers teach each other

Teachers teaching each other demands a change in approach to staff development. Professional development meetings in school time where colleagues share practice will ensure teachers teach each other. One example of teachers working together we have seen was in a school where teachers debated, agreed to produce and then created a booklet for all pupils called 'Language to think and learn'. Based on theories of multiple intelligence and the need for variety of learning approaches, the booklet set out the vocabulary for each subject and for examinations that they wanted the pupils to understand – high order conceptual language, if you like. All the staff then set about teaching the meaning of the vocabulary, week by week, to all the pupils in Year 7 (see Butterfly on page 98). A similar approach has been applied in Years 8 and 9 – the whole issue of course was reinforced by displays of the vocabulary in every room. As we have already suggested, as an obvious point, teaching ideally leads to learning. So every member of staff in that school staff has a 'Learning plan for the year'!

In another school, for each year group at the beginning of the year there are short 'study skills' or 'learning to learn' courses: at a foundation level for Year 7 with such items as 'learning to listen', progressing through mind maps to revision in Year 10 of research skills – of course, this is made so much easier as a result of access to the internet.

Finally, there is assessment, so frequently interpreted as the chore of marking. But 'marking' can be by peer group, by the pupils themselves, by computer, as well as by the teacher or indeed support staff. Outstanding lessons sometimes will contain peer assessment interludes of each other's progress and performance, and perhaps of the outstanding teacher's too. It's fair to say that it's impossible to have a really successful school without an active and rigorous assessment system that reflects good AfL principles on the one hand, yet avoids the '$^4/_{10}$ – try again' syndrome. Reports for parents and parent days reflect the teamwork of assessment and are led by the form tutor.

In an outstanding school, teachers mark each other's work and know that one of their main and precious tasks is to enable the pupils to see for themselves how to improve their own work (see M is for Marking).

Above all, teachers, teaching assistants and mentors will try to avoid 'normative' language implied in the poem from Ed Buscemi called 'The Average Child', as follows:

I don't cause teachers trouble. My grades have been OK
I listen in my classes, I'm in school every day.
My parents think I'm average, my teachers think so too
I wish I didn't know that as there's lots I'd like to do.
I'd like to build a rocket; I've a book that shows you how,
Or start a stamp collection, but there's no point in trying now.
For since I've found I'm average, I'm just smart enough you see
To know there's nothing special I should expect of me.
I'm part of that majority, that hump part of the bell
Who spends their life unnoticed in an average kind of hell.

T is for Teams and teamwork

Individual commitment to a group effort – that is what makes a team work, a school work, a society work.

Vince Lombardi

Balancing the individual and the team is a vital task in school life. So far as pupils are concerned the emphasis on tests and exams, where methods almost exclusively emphasize the individual rather than the 'individual as a member of a team', can dominate and lead to imbalance. Sport is a good way of balancing the two: Team GB celebrated exceptional success in the 2012 Olympic Games and it is appropriate to apply the concept of 'teams' to school improvement. It is clear that no organization can succeed without team goals and effective teamwork often expressed in the saying 'Together everybody achieves more'. Although there are some obvious examples of teams working in schools we sometimes find that the idea of teams is implicit and assumed rather than explicit and overt. Nor is the matter simply one for pupils, the senior leadership team is the most obvious expression of a team within a school, which ought to be bound together by a core purpose and a collegiality seeking consistency and coherence in everything they do to achieve success. In secondary schools there are a variety of other teams most commonly faculty or subject teams but also year teams and pastoral teams.

Primary schools and special schools, depending on their size, may also have year or phase teams. For very small schools there can only be one team, the school team, which makes the tasks of achieving a common purpose and consistency much easier. Some schools have deliberately introduced a competitive ethos to intensify the drive for improvement. It should be stressed that the key phase here is 'collaborative competition'; channelling healthy internal competition within a strong school culture of shared values, beliefs and attitudes which make up 'Team school'.

Some examples of collaborative competition among staff are those between faculties and subject departments in a secondary school who strive to create the best learning environments and the best student outcomes. Sometimes the students themselves are asked to be the judges of this in competitions for the 'subject of the year'. Where there is a house system, staff and students work together in healthy competition across a range of endeavours and outcomes. In primary schools the collaborative competition may be between phases such as early years, Key Stage 1 or Key Stage 2 or in larger schools between year groups. Of course, collaborative competition may expose significant in-school variation as well as intensify the drive for improvement. Its purpose is to provide a springboard for discussion and debate about effective teamwork and the capacity to improve. As far as the student body is concerned they are far more used to competition, whether as a class or a year group, and compete for rewards in terms of participation and success in school projects. A good example of this is the weekly award for the class with the best attendance either within a year group or across the whole school. There are of course, a great variety of school teams in sport and a range of other activities.

In terms of teaching and learning some teachers will introduce the concept of teams competing to achieve the best learning outcomes within a class sometimes with their own 'captains' and 'coaches' or across a year group. Under E for Examinations we have a butterfly on pupils competing together for success, where each tutor group is divided into two teams of similar ability. They compete in terms of attainment, attendance and participation in school life with published league tables mid-year and at the end of the year.

Many schools regularly discuss a more explicit adoption of teams, teamwork and collaborative competition within the organization and culture of the school to drive forward school improvement, partly to ensure that everybody subscribes absolutely to the vision, core purpose and values of the whole school.

 Team work is the ability to work together towards a common vision and the ability to divert individual accomplishments towards organizational objectives. It is the fuel that allows common people to achieve uncommon results.
Andrew Carnegie

T is for Time management

First, there's the obvious point about the much misunderstood 'time to think'. As one head, dismissively told us: 'I do my thinking all the time. It occupies every waking moment. When I want to focus the sum total of my thinking, I spend an evening writing a paper, he added, 'I am often speaking with a group of colleagues. Out of that and all of the senior leadership team reading the same article and listening to each other's views, comes my own or our collective refreshed direction or the solution to a problem'.

Secondly, if you analyze what you do each day, it can be broken down into listening, speaking, reading and writing and most forms of human activity (apart from sleeping) usually involve one or more of these.

Thirdly – and this is surely the key for the successful headteacher – you can only read and write in isolation, whereas you need other people to listen and talk. That's presumably why another successful head said to us forcefully: 'I never look at my computer – the email or whatever – between eight in the morning and half past five in the evening. Nor do I do any paperwork then either. I can do all of that before and afterwards, because I do that alone. The time the school's in session is precious. The whole community is there. And it's therefore time for the pupils, the staff, governors and other members of the wide community'. She went on to say that if she ever found herself inadvertently backing away from that guiding principle and staying in her office, she knew she was on a very slippery slope.

On the other hand, another primary head we know uses Facebook as a transformational means of communicating with parents. For her a hand-held device goes with her everywhere and she is 'posting' items regularly. Time is so precious, that some people say that learning to use time wisely and to best effect is the key skill for a headteacher to master.

Further reading
See K is for **Key expenditures of time by school leaders.**

T is for Times Educational Supplement (TES)

We cannot imagine a successful school which doesn't have a copy of the *Times Educational Supplement* (TES) in their staffroom. Indeed we know of some large schools which, conscious of the comparatively infrequent use of their staffroom buy one for each faculty area. We can see why.

The TES is over 100 years old and has been through a number of different formats. It is in a particularly rich vein as we write this book. It has adopted a magazine format and has within it not just news and opinion pieces, but also two parts especially valuable to schools: TESpro and the Resources section. The first can be collected and should be part of the staff library (see L is for Library) – and incidentally back copies are available in digital form which could be on the school's virtual learning environment – while the second will lead any teacher keen on professional development to a cornucopia of resources via www.tes.co.uk. In the last three or four years, for the first time in its history, TES has many of its opinion pieces written by practising teachers.

Of course, there are other professional journals directed to a particular phase of education, such as *SecED, Junior Education* and *Early Years Education* as well as of course subject journals and those from professional associations (unions). The daily newspapers also cover education and the *Guardian* has an online teachers' network.

We think that successful schools see the encouragement for teachers to use these resources as a way of supporting staff's professional development.

T is for Timetable

It is worth starting with a heartfelt plea for both primary and secondary colleagues that there should be two timetables: one metronomic and routine, in the sense of the three, four or five period day in secondary schools or the English, mathematics and science and so on of primary colleagues; the second should be non-metronomic and provide the opportunity for those planned activities that take up a whole morning, day or week. This second type provides enrichment and intensive immersion learning some of which will be outside the classroom, such as visits to places of interest or residentials. Too often this second non-metronomic timetable has little rationale and can appear to the outsider to be serendipitous and therefore not a serious part of a whole-school learning policy and practice.

In some secondary schools the joke is that during May the member of the senior leadership team responsible for the timetable disappears for a couple of months and re-emerges in mid July looking suspiciously bronzed, knowing a great deal about the test matches and Wimbledon and brandishing the next year's timetable as 'the only answer that will work'. With the changes in OfSTED inspection criteria and protocols it is more likely than previously that inspectors will visit a school when some non-metronomic activity is taking place, so having a thought through rationale will be crucial. For primary schools such a rationale can be linked to project or topic work, which we argue strongly ought to be renamed 'research'.

Secondary metronomic timetables can be complicated. How long should the lessons be? How many should there be in a day? What are the virtues and drawbacks of 50 minute or even 100 minute lessons? How often do students have to change locations in the school? Should there be a weekly or fortnightly timetable and if the latter, what impact does that have on the number of different teachers a Year 7 child encounters? Is there a need to 'block out' Tuesday and Thursday afternoons for post-16 cooperations between schools?

How these and other questions are answered in practice powerfully affects what is possible and the person organizing the timetable has a huge impact on the lives of the school community.

Of course the story above of the 'timetabler' is apocryphal but not so far from the truth as to be totally unbelievable. Worse are those schools where the timetable is still very provisional in September thereby causing a tetchy start to the school year. When a 'timetabler' leaves, a school's succession planning is tested to destruction.

So the first point to make about timetablers is that the person who does it and who understands how it is done is very important. Those who become headteachers who have never been the timetabler may be at a disadvantage when compared with those who have done it, simply because they don't know what can and can't be done. But the emphasis is on 'may be at a disadvantage' because of course you may have a very accommodating and flexible colleague responsible for the timetable.

It seems to us that successful schools always seem to have more than one person knowing techniques such as timetabling so that there are two creative minds involved in the task and also that there is some succession planning and a 'fail – safe' device. One school we know sees it as a task that ambitious young teachers should get involved in so that they have early appreciation of the complexities of timetabling.

Of course, who does the timetable is just one consideration. The factors and priorities taken into account before the exercise starts are crucial to the life and well-being of staff and students alike. This is one of many issues where it is sensible to make sure that schools don't behave in an isolated way but research carefully what is possible.

T is for Transition

Transition causes most people in education to sigh in a resigned way. It is our Achilles heel. We know it's not very good but seem unable to do much about it. At the age of 11 it is clearly an issue but it surfaces to some extent every summer as, even at primary level, pupils move from one class teacher to the next. The butterfly at the end of this entry illustrates how one head has done something to minimize that problem.

Primary schools are similarly concerned about entry to school and recent attention to birth to five programmes and the Early Years Foundation Stage has been an attempt to ameliorate the longstanding issues of school readiness and parental involvement.

At the age of 11 though, there is the added complication of the students passing from childhood towards the beginning of adolescence when, having ceased being children they are unsure of what sort of adults they will become. Complications crowd in. Deferred gratification is an issue; not being seen as a fool in front of your peer group is a greater problem so that the likelihood of the learner concealing their ignorance grows. Children who in Year 6 have begun to think they are failures will soon look for signs in their new school that they are right.

We suggest the following changes or examples of good practice to improve life chances for Year 6 / 7 children:

- Introduce a secondary school familiarization 'week' and start off Year 7 in July so that there is far less danger of the most vulnerable youngsters 'losing learning' during the long summer break.
- Remember that parents are the one reliable point of continuity in the process and involve them in a special 'meet your child's tutor' session where expectations are clearly spelt out and agreed.
- Ensure the primary pupil's 'best piece of work' in at least English, mathematics and science, is attached into the front of the Year 7 corresponding work folders / exercise books / e-portfolios so that their teachers can encourage them to use that as an agreed starting point for 'improving on previous personal best'. This practice, already common in some schools, encourages the good use of formative assessment.
- Find out from primary schools which of the children at transfer are 'most at risk of learning to fail' (see F for Failure) and then try to establish their interest and what they are good at, going out of your way to show personal interest in those youngsters early in Year 7. Provide one-to-one support for such youngsters in the basics.

Additionally, of course, there are schools which have agreed to start Year 7 at the end of the summer term, while others have established a 'primary room' so that partner primary schools can visit during Year 6. Exchange of teachers and older pupils working in primary schools are two other examples of practice intended to make transition a success rather than a set-back to learning.

Improving transition between year groups

Description

Each autumn, in November, teachers spend a day with their former year group. For example, the Year 2 teacher spends the day in the classroom of the Year 3 teacher who is teaching the children she taught the year before. The purpose is that the Year 2 teacher goes round and looks at the work and talks to the youngster she taught the year before, in order to improve continuity of learning and to try to make sure that the new teacher is aware of say three children whose progress is pleasantly surprising her and three children whose progress might not be all she had hoped.

A
B
C
D
E
F
G
H
I
J
K
L
M
N
O
P
Q
R
S

U
V
W
X
Y
Z

Comment on impact

The school claims that this practice has various outcomes. First, it encourages teachers to talk more to each other about 'levels of progress' and enables them to spot those children for whom the transition from one year to the next has coincided or caused a 'pause' in learning. It has also led to teachers getting children to take work to 'show' to their former teacher and to increase dialogue both about rates of progress and those children who may be most at risk of falling behind.

T is for Trust

Trust underpins and affects the quality of every relationship, every communication, every work project...it changes the quality of every present moment and alters the trajectory and outcomes of every future.

Stephen Covey

In his book *The Speed of Trust* (2006), subtitled *The One Thing That Changes Everything*, Stephen Covey sets out why building trust is so important for the success of any organization. Where levels of trust are low, staff will be working in an unproductive environment with a divided staff and low levels of energy, innovation and development. By contrast, in organizations with a high level of trust there are positive and transparent relationships, leading to increased invention and confidence and the release of energy securing progress and improvement. To put it simply, where trust goes down, speed will also go down and costs go up. When trust goes up, speed will also go up and costs comes down. Covey refers to the 'trust dividend' where the dividend you receive is like a performance multiplier, elevating and improving every dimension of your organization. We would argue that with schools, high trust significantly improves communication, collaboration, execution, innovation, engagement and relationships with all stakeholders – critically between staff, students and parents. Of course, there are different dimensions of trust at work in schools.

The first level is self-trust or personal trust which deals with the confidence we have in ourselves as staff and students to keep commitments, to be a person worthy of trust and able to inspire trust in others. The second level is the relationship with others and the consistent behaviour and qualities expected, especially by those in leadership positions such as respect, clarity, transparency, expectations, loyalty, accountability and keeping commitments. The third level is organizational trust which relates to the alignment of structures and systems and may be termed as professional trust – those who are committed to and ready to learn from one another. We know that high trust systems lead to high performance and achievement in individual schools and in partnerships. We also know that creating a climate of high trust starts with the actions and behaviour of educational leaders – quality assurance rather than quality control, which is always about checking up on people. We have talked elsewhere about delegation which is a key indicator of a high trust school, not just from the senior leadership team, but within other teams as well as to teachers, support staff and students. We have also referred to the student voice and student leadership and the importance of trusting them to carry out their role with the best interests of the school community in mind.

Partnerships with parents have to be based on trust. Where they see policies being consistently applied with regular communication and a spirit of openness, parental confidence in the school will grow rapidly but of course the reverse is also true, especially with families where their own experiences of school have not been positive. We have also referred elsewhere to a range of partnerships between schools and other agencies as a means of improving schools, which is based on the trust to create value for others and receive value from others. In terms of school improvement schools need to re-calculate their trust dividends. Are they real and quantifiable? Are they a performance multiplier? How could schools and school leaders do more to inspire trust? What is certain is that you can't have success without trust.

T is for Tutor and tutor period

 A child who has not a worthwhile relationship with at least one adult in the school is not really at school.

Edward Thring

Primary pupils will talk about their 'class teacher' and secondary students their 'tutor'. It used to be said that the most powerful influence over the success of a secondary school was how well the tutors did their job in the tutorial periods whenever they occurred, which was usually at the beginning of the school day. So strong still is the influence that you can often trace absence patterns and exam success to the effectiveness of the tutor period and the individual tutor.

How the day starts powerfully affects your attitude to what we then do and how we behave: 'meeting and greeting' influences how we all feel. In the best schools it starts on the roads and pathways towards the school's entrances and in the playground as staff exchange banter with students as they all arrive in the morning.

A typical list of the activities implied in the role include the following:

- Registering students at the start of each day, and completing a formal record of attendance for students in the form register using the key provided.

- Collecting notes of absence and ensuring all relevant staff are made aware of longer periods of absence notified in advance by parents.
- Monitoring and signing of student homework diaries on a weekly basis, and the following up of any general messages from parents. Form tutors should also 'chase' parents who are not signing diaries.
- Acting as first point of contact between the home and the school.
- Accompanying students to assemblies on assembly days and helping to prepare and coordinate a form assembly on at least one occasion each academic year.
- Delivery of an agreed PSHE course timetabled as a single period each week.
- Allocating a 'buddy' to assist in the induction of new students, and ensuring new students are given copies of the form timetable, homework timetable, and homework diary.
- Forming of positive relationships with each and every member of the form.
- Encouraging standards of excellence within the form in all aspects of school life. Encouragement of individuals within a form and the form group as a whole, to engage in activities likely to bring distinction upon themselves and the school.
- Establishment of 'ground rules' for discussion and interaction between form members – and monitoring of general student relationships.
- To write form teachers' reports on each student for school reports, to take account of each individual's record in all aspects of school life.
- To monitor behaviour of students in the form through interaction with subject teachers.
- To liaise with key stage coordinators on disciplinary issues where necessary.
- To attend regular meetings led by key stage coordinators to discuss, monitor and implement procedures to deal with pastoral issues, PSHE, rewards and sanctions and other issues.
- To assist key stage coordinators in keeping accurate student records for members of the form.

We have taken this list from a school which clearly has a particular approach both to tutoring – it is linked to PHSE – and to how they write job descriptions – in our view too detailed. Many schools will have a different approach; for example vertical tutor groups are now increasingly common.

Two final points are worth making. First, many schools now see the role of tutor as something for support staff to engage in and secondly, tutorials can be made better; the activities that work well and the subtle interpersonal messages such as how the register is taken is a subject well worth reviewing from time to time collectively. We would say that it cries out for a butterfly collection of its own (see the introduction for an explanation about butterflies).

Further reading
A comprehensive guide to the rationale for that development a vertical tutor groups can be found at www.verticaltutoring.org with helpful links to the extensive TES website.

Tutor groups

Description

A school decided that one of the major hidden disadvantages of its tutor system was the way in which it named its tutor groups. This was after the names of the teachers so 7 TS implied that the tutor was Tom Scott; 8 JH was the group belonging to Judith Harris and so on. Instead they debated with each incoming year group the names of famous people who had contributed to the world's success. So tutor groups became 7 NM for Nelson Mandela or 8 FN for Florence Nightingale.

Comment on impact

The advantages of this according to the head included the fact that debate took place to choose the famous person when children arrived and they had therefore a stake in the name. Also when a teacher left, the identity of the tutor group was continuous rather than undergoing an identity change. (It is at least arguable that there is also a subtle message about student voice here too.)

Private tutors – for all pupils

Description

Most secondary schools now arrange Easter revision classes, residentials and study skill sessions. They also have 'after school' or 'lunch hour' voluntary extra sessions in Year 11 and academic coaching for every youngster.

One school decided that 'familiarity' was a problem. Naturally, the youngsters know their teachers really well. So they cooperated with another school in a different part of the city and offered 'private tuition' to Year 11 students. The private tutors came from the other / partner school. Participating students' parents were asked to contribute £10 for eight lessons with the deal being that they would get the £10 refunded if pupils attended all the sessions. (They forfeited £3 if they missed one, £6 if they missed two and all if they missed more than that.)

The students were hugely impressed by their new 'tutors'. The head commented: 'After all, the well-off parents get private tuition anyway. Why shouldn't we arrange it for all our youngsters?' The parents liked the scheme. The school reckoned it raised performance by at least one grade over the school's predictions.

A
B
C
D
E
F
G
H
I
J
K
L
M
N
O
P
Q
R
S
T
U
V
W
X
Y
Z

Comment on impact

The financial arrangements ensured that the legal requirement to provide free education for every child was observed, while capitalizing on the idea that what people pay for is especially valued. The school was also aware that some staff were giving private tuition to pupils from other schools in their spare time anyway. So this made sure that all their pupils could benefit from the 'private effect'.

U is for Uniforms

Thirty years ago it was relatively rare for a primary school to have a uniform; it was not uncommon for a secondary school to have no uniform either, though students may have worn a coloured sweatshirt. Now it is rare even for a primary school not to have uniform. You might ask why there is an entry under uniform for a book on school improvement. It would be a good question for it may seem there is no connection between the two!

Nevertheless, in order to improve performance it is a route that many schools take. They tinker with uniforms and we provide this entry because we think it is an opportunity to involve pupils and parents. Some heads also say that school uniforms provide a point which causes arguments with students about school rules and as such is a good topic on which to insist on behaviour compliance. For the schools where we have been involved it also has provoked a good debate about the need to help youngsters from poorer backgrounds comply without adding further to their poverty. Parents who have experienced both a uniform and non-uniform approach will balance the pressures of costly fashions with those of lost or dirty items of obligatory dress.

A
B
C
D
E
F
G
H
I
J
K
L
M
N
O
P
Q
R
S
T
U
V
W
X
Y
Z

U is for University links

During the period from 2010 to 2012 a sea-change in the way English universities are run has meant that student attitudes – indeed those of their parents also – have changed. The prospect of taking on substantial personal loans in order to fund a university course has deterred some students from considering extending their education beyond the age of 18 at university. As one head told us 'I hope that all students are aware of the range of financial support that is available to those from poorer backgrounds. Like you two, I was entitled to a full grant because, like you, I came from a poor family. Students today will receive, if not the generous living grants we did, at least a sufficient amount that if, as we did, they obtain some part-time employment as well, there is no reason why they shouldn't end up with a degree, plus a fee debt that won't start to be paid back until they have reached a certain salary and then will be like a graduate tax.' We agreed with this analysis.

As a destination for school or college leavers therefore, university remains a desirable destination for many. It may be a local university or the Open University that is the right option. Some may think going to university has nothing to do with school improvement. Clearly it needs to be balanced by other worthwhile objectives for progression but every successful school knows it needs to be talking to youngsters about high aspirational destinations for when they leave school.

Raising student aspirations in this direction, especially for first generation students, remains a priority. The best of the 'Aiming higher' programmes, despite the withdrawal of funds, are being sustained partly because university funding has required them to demonstrate the progress they are making with access for students from poorer backgrounds and from areas, schools and colleges which serve those students.

We think, however, that much more can be done and we set out as follows initiatives taken by schools which appear to have been beneficial so far as university links are concerned:

- Enlist undergraduate voluntary help for extra-curricular clubs, one-to-one tutoring and coaching. Many universities have organizations to arrange the necessary details including CRB checks and so on. In Oxford, the two universities combine in doing this through something called 'The Hub'.
- Persuade the university closest to your secondary school to offer honorary membership of the appropriate university faculty (geography, mathematics and so on) to the school head of department entitling them to attend seminars. This has been started in Oxford and if it can be successful there, it can be anywhere. It is good for recruitment and for CPD.
- Get the partner higher education department to offer 'fellowships' to subject

leaders, either primary or secondary, as appropriate for a fixed period to entitle attendance at seminars in education.

- Offer part funding to any staff wishing to do a Masters and get the local university to teach it partly on site after school.
- Offer a place on the governing body to the university as a representative of community interest.
- Get a researcher from the university to be a school researcher in residence. (see R is for Research).

A
B
C
D
E
F
G
H
I
J
K
L
M
N
O
P
Q
R
S
T
U
V
W
X
Y
Z

A
B
C
D
E
F
G
H
I
J
K
L
M
N
O
P
Q
R
S
T
U
V
W
X
Y
Z

V is for Values

> **It is unlikely that you will be able to inspire, excite and motivate unless you can show who you are and what you stand for.**
> Robert Goffee

It is a truism to say that successful schools have a high degree of shared values. These shared values might include:

- Being committed to success for all members of the community, rather than success for some at the expense of others. That's why norm-referencing is such a dangerous fellow-traveller for schools, where we have a moral duty to treat children as they might become, rather than as they infuriatingly are.
- Seeing intelligence not as 'given', 'predictable' or 'general', but as 'multifaceted' and infinitely capable of development. This is a really tricky one, not least because it's counter-intuitive to all the practices of our own earlier years and those of previous generations. But most people recognize intuitively so many of the non-academic intelligences; not just the art and craft, physical, visual and musical, but also the emerging interest in growing and developing what we now call 'emotional intelligence'. Also, in particular, the capacity to understand oneself and other people and act accordingly.

- Trying to be inclusive rather than exclusive as a school community.
- Practising formative and ipsative assessment – that is measuring the pupils' understanding of the next step in their own learning and ensuring they act on it, while trying to improve on their own previous best.
- Ensuring that young people realize that education is a 'lifelong' not a 'once and for all' activity.

These values derive loosely from, and certainly need to be put alongside, the moral precepts that we all associate with the religions and classical philosophers. They will inform the whole community's actions, particularly those who lead and have the most influence on the school community, namely the headteacher, staff and older pupils. They know they have to live with the knowledge that there has to be a consistent thread between 'what they say', 'what they do' and 'who they are'.

To these constantly upheld values, the school attaches its straightforward 'mission statement': what they stand for and are trying to do.

A mission statement might say 'Our school is a place where:

- all members of the school community talk of 'our' achievement and everyone is anxious to improve on previous best collectively as well as individually
- all pupils are increasingly aware of their potential and that achievement is without limit if they make the effort
- everyone respects each other, feels fulfilled in what they do and contributes to the fulfilment of others
- the full range of success – sporting, academic, artistic, practical support for others, triumph over adversity – is celebrated
- all members of the school community are committed to their own continuous learning and support that of others
- everyone is aware of the school's collective past and present success and is ambitious to contribute for the benefit of future generations to that legacy
- we facilitate these aims and promote the fun of learning and the pleasure of achievement.'

The separate parts of these mission statements are reinforced at assemblies, at awards ceremonies and parents' meetings and in tutorials. They may find expression in a list of next priorities in development plans.

In days past, schools had their Latin school motto, today some schools still have mottos to express and reinforce, simply and pithily, what the school stands for. One we both like is: 'Think for yourself and act for others'.

Further reading
See C is for Culture of schools.

V is for Virtual Learning Environment (VLE)

The speed at which our e-environment is moving is best illustrated by looking at our then (2008) up-to-date entry about Facebook in our book *What makes a good school now?*:

> *Facebook; a social networking site that uses corporate email addresses, particularly university emails, to verify users as members of already existing social networks and then becomes an extension of that network.*

In the same book there was no mention of Twitter and countless other developments accessible through the worldwide web. Indeed 20 years ago a mobile phone weighed, and was, the size of a half brick. Now very few secondary students haven't got regular access to them and many other hand-held devices and every school will have a policy and approved practices for their use.

Most schools will now have access to an e-learning platform which means that:

- All pupils can access their homework, lesson plans, videoed 'best explanations' of 'difficult to understand' concepts, computer assisted learning programmes, school reports, timetables and individual coaching advice. They text and can be texted by their teachers.
- All staff can access the same list plus faculty / departmental and school management information, professional development programmes and networks, RAG (red, amber, green) list of pupils' progress on a regular basis and a wealth of other useful information about pupils and curriculum.
- All senior leaders in the school can access all the above and a range of management information relating to budget, performance of staff and pupils and comparable information about other schools.
- All parents can access information about their own children's attendance, marks, reports and homework.
- Governors can access those parts of the above they have decided is appropriate to them.

Every member of the school community has their personal space on this integrated system. It can be accessed remotely and at any time. So great are the digital changes that anything we write or a school does will be changed regularly.

One feature we think is constant is what a Demos leaflet (*Their Space: Education for the Digital Divide* 2007) has described as eight myths which any school must address.

The first six are labelled the 'moral panic' propositions:

- The internet is too dangerous for children.
- Junk culture is poisoning young people and taking over their lives.
- No learning happens and digital technologies are a waste of time.
- There is an epidemic of internet plagiarism in schools.
- Young people are disengaged and disconnected.
- We're seeing the rise of a generation of passive consumers.

They counterpoise these with what they describe as two myths which they call 'digital faith':

- All gaming is good.
- All children are cyberkids.

Every school has to debate these from time to time as the digital developments challenge the status quo. We think on every occasion the chance to bring parents and the students themselves into resolving the issues shouldn't be overlooked.

V is for Vision and vision statements

 A school without a vision is a vacuum inviting intrusion.
Roland Barth

At staff meetings and in staff development days, the skilful leaders speculate and then formulate a 'vision statement'. If the school has a vision statement, it will be framed in a description of what the school will be like in five or so years into the future. It will be linked to what people are doing now and what they will do in the future to reach the improved state of affairs envisaged. It can, and sometimes does, take the form of a video with accompanying text. Usually the fruitful areas for change lie in adapting and making the best use of the e-learning technologies, but will also encompass changes in the local and global world. For instance, recently, schools, not just in London, have made full use of the Olympics to make collective groups of pupils feel 'special' and individuals aim to beat their 'personal bests', not simply in sport but in all aspects of their school work. Now the Olympics are over, many schools have '2020 vision statements' – as well as reminding each year group that they are going to be the 2020 special generation.

The vision statement will be revisited from time to time, updated regularly by a school improvement group charged with coming up with ideas which are aimed to create continuous improvement in all aspects of school life. The school improvement group will comprise a cross section of all staff at all levels: it may seek the views of pupils and parents if they are not already part of the group. Members of the group will have one thing in common: they will be 'energy

A
B
C
D
E
F
G
H
I
J
K
L
M
N
O
P
Q
R
S
T
U

W
X
Y
Z

creators' not 'energy consumers'. They will be 'what if' seekers after silver linings, who ask 'how we could', rather than tired cynics, who see clouds, regard everything as half empty and say 'why we can't'.

Finally, the school is a place where stories abound and should be told by leaders at all levels. They are good stories – there's no better storyteller than a good teacher – and the stories focus on both the past and the future, which, after all, is the school's business.

> The very essence of leadership is that you have a vision. It's got to be a vision that you articulate clearly and forcefully on every occasion. You can't blow an uncertain trumpet.
>
> Theodore Hesburgh

> Vision is the ability to see what is unseen, realise what has yet to be, and act upon one's beliefs in the face of uncertainty.
>
> Carl Rogers and Jerome Freiberg

School vision and leadership as learnt from the story of Noah's Ark

- Think and plan ahead; it wasn't raining previously.
- Don't miss the boat.
- Remember that we are all in the same boat.
- Keep your head above the water and avoid the temptation to walk on water.
- Don't let the tigers eat the lambs.
- Beware of the woodpeckers.
- Look out for doves carrying olive leaves.
- Celebrate rainbows.
- Build your future on higher ground.

A
B
C
D
E
F
G
H
I
J
K
L
M
N
O
P
Q
R
S
T
U
V
W
X
Y
Z

W is for World class

Secretaries of State and Education Ministers of all political parties are fond of using the expression 'world class' as a benchmark to measure success against international competitors. The Organisation for Economic Cooperation and Development Programmes for International Student Assessment surveys are used as a league table to exhort the school system to greater efforts. In 2012, the judgement of politicians is that the UK is standing still while others race past. Other regions and nations are regularly cited as having achieved high standards as well as making opportunity more equal – from Alberta to Singapore, Finland to Hong Kong and South Korea.

McKinsey and Company have produced two publications *How the World's Best Performing Systems Come Out on Top* (2007) and *How the World's Most Improved School Systems Keep Getting Better* (2010). While their examples have their own unique and individual approach to education in very different contexts, it is claimed that they all share certain common features: improving teacher quality, granting greater autonomy to the front line, modernising the curriculum, making schools more accountable to their communities, harnessing detailed performance data and encouraging professional collaboration. Much of the debate is about school systems rather than individual schools and such is the rhetoric that school leaders have often disengaged from this comparison, but many have been keen to compare their success as individual schools. Through such organizations as the National College and the British Council schools have sought to visit and learn from other schools in the world sharing ideas and experience. Throughout the European Union there are a number of programmes and partnerships for schools and students to share their learning and expertise; So how does a school benchmark its success as being 'world class' and is this a useful construct? Some schools judged to be 'outstanding' by OfSTED have directly engaged with the term and have come up with the following language to describe world class schooling:

- A compelling and inclusive moral purpose.
- Instilling a strong global dimension into the learning experiences of all children and young people.
- A capacity to engage with a range of school partners across the world.
- Success against the most stretched of benchmarks nationally and internationally.
- A culture of innovation and creativity.
- Enquiry minded and research engaged.
- Inspirational leadership.
- Exceptionality of teacher practice and quality.
- Remarkable achievements and striking impact.
- A passion for excellence.

Further reading
Alistair Smith, *High Performers* and Andy Buck, *What Makes a Great School?*

 We are what we repeatedly do. Excellence, then, is not an act, but a habit.

Aristotle

X is for eXtra-curricular activities

When schools are debating, and sometimes lamenting the pressure forced onto them by the test and exam system within which they operate, they often reassure themselves by looking at the range of extra-curricular opportunities they provide for their pupils. It is of course the case that the timetabled curriculum comprises at most 20% of the student's waking time and while schools rightly see that as precious, they are aware of the chance to supplement it through extra-curricular activities.

In our journeys round schools we have picked up the following points:

- *All* staff – not just teachers – can and will want to contribute to sharing of a passion, if they know that passion has given them huge enjoyment. It is worth therefore establishing at interview what all new appointees can contribute to the programme.
- From time to time, through performance management, it is possible to find a member of staff's 'hyacinth' and see whether he / she can be encouraged to bring it into school life.
- Friends of the school may also wish to run a fixed term set of courses / clubs for interested youngsters.
- If a university is nearby, undergraduates may be willing to run an after-school

activity. We have come across a real enrichment of a school's extra-curricular programme through this method.

- Primary schools welcome visits from former pupils and we have come across more than one secondary school where they have encouraged sixth formers as part of a 'community action' programme to firmly commit and carry out a club activity in their former primary school.
- The schools with the most active programme have a named member of staff responsible for encouraging and evaluating the programme.

X is for X Factor

Remember that...some people make things happen, some people watch things happen, some people wonder what happened.
Anon

All schools have an 'X Factor' in terms of their unique and distinctive contribution to education provision. In some schools it is unrecognized, in others it is simply a potential but in others it is proven. However, there are quite a lot of schools who struggle to describe their X Factor and it is a good exercise for school leaders to discuss and debate this idea. Some leadership teams have begun to think of their 'DNA' in terms of decision rights, information, motivation and structures. In terms of decision rights the X Factor could be: high levels of trust between everybody in the school community, based on shared values where culture and ethos are embedded in the deeper level of basis assumptions and beliefs and unconsciously are the 'glue' that holds everyone together. In terms of information the X Factor could be related to: enquiry-mindedness, knowledge transfer, innovation and creativity between everybody in the learning community. Motivators can be complex but the X Factor is often to be found in a very high level of alignment to a common purpose, reinforced constantly through a shared language of aspiration, expectations and ambition. With reference to structures the X Factor could be the creation of an optimistic, lively, energizing, working environment with opportunities for growth and change.

As visitors to several thousands of schools over a long period of time we often find that the X Factor is best described in the high quality relationships that exist between children, young people and adults with mutual respect and kindness in a very positive climate for learning, where considerable attention has been paid to the whole-school environment. Simply put the X Factor question is: What makes you unique and distinctive as a school? It is a question upon which all schools should reflect.

X is for X: wrong

And wrong it is to mark pupils' work in a way that reduces assessment to simple ticks and crosses – indeed it is the very antithesis of assessment for learning!

Further reading
See M is for Marking and A is for Assessment for Learning.

A
B
C
D
E
F
G
H
I
J
K
L
M
N
O
P
Q
R
S
T
U
V
W
X
Y
Z

A
B
C
D
E
F
G
H
I
J
K
L
M
N
O
P
Q
R
S
T
U
V
W
X
Y
Z

Y is for Year heads

Although there is a movement for secondary schools to re-create the house system, or experiment with 'schools within schools' and have vertical tutor groups, in many schools it is still the norm to have one person who has direct responsibility for all the pupils in a particular year group. Of course, this would not be the case for a one form entry primary school where there would more likely be a head of a key stage. Despite many changes in the organization of secondary schools we still find the notion of one person being accountable for a year is very prevalent. What has changed is the range of accountabilities. Heads of year posts used to be almost entirely pastoral posts, working with class tutors and concerned with pupil well-being and particularly behaviour and attendance. Where that is still the case secondary schools have sometimes appointed staff on the basis of a range of appropriate skills, not necessarily those having teaching qualifications. More commonly the role has changed to include considerable attention to progress and standards of achievement. Some heads of year are now called 'Progress champions', 'Pupil progress leaders' or 'Learning and progress coordinators' and they are expected to know just as much about academic progress as the well-being of their students. They are also expected, if they are heads of Year 7, to link effectively with literacy, numeracy and SEN post holders in primary schools and all are expected to liaise with colleagues in subject departments.

As year heads so often are responsible for taking assemblies of their particular year they have huge potential influence on behaviour, culture and outcomes. Indeed achievement can be powerfully influenced by heads of year: this is a dynamic and changing role and at its best adds great value to the leadership of a school and the outcomes for the students.

Further reading
See T is for Tutor and tutor period and P is for Pastoral.

Y is for Yes we can

 They can because they think they can.
Virgil

Barack Obama's great slogan in his 2008 campaign for the Presidency of the USA 'Yes we can!' constantly asserted to the American people that they could embrace change to create a better society. School leaders and teachers at all levels are also challenged to win a mandate for change and then put this into operation. We have referred elsewhere in this book to the power of optimism as a force multiplier and the importance of cultivating positive mindsets to help everybody work better and achieve more. This in turn provides the energy to drive forward an exciting and enterprising school. We have observed first hand many school leaders building confidence, competence and self-esteem into their institutions – students and staff alike. Similarly, we have observed many teachers inspiring and motivating their students to great success often against the odds. They do this through developing high levels of self-esteem which is the key to motivation, perseverance and resilience. We know that without personal and institutional self-belief, confidence and determination, schools are unlikely to improve so every conversation, every lesson, every assembly, every school event has to reinforce this.

Further reading
See *The Six Pillars of Self-Esteem* by Nathaniel Branden.

 Nothing great was ever achieved without enthusiasm.
Ralph Waldo Emerson

 Whether you think you can or think you can't you're right.
Henry Ford

A
B
C
D
E
F
G
H
I
J
K
L
M
N
O
P
Q
R
S
T
U
V
W
X
Y
Z

A
B
C
D
E
F
G
H
I
J
K
L
M
N
O
P
Q
R
S
T
U
V
W
X
Y
Z

Y is for YouTube

Many teachers now use clips from YouTube as part of their lesson plans or as tasks for pupils to refer to for homework. Perhaps the most frequently visited by staff and pupils alike is the Ken Robinson clip: 'Do Schools Kill Creativity?' which very effectively gets to the heart of what schooling and education are all about. One school we know says it scours YouTube for any clips of well-known writers and speakers to use for sessions in meetings and on Inset days.

Further reading
See V is for Virtual Learning Environment (VLE).

Z is for Zone

 Leadership is all about turning fear into confidence, creating clarity from confusion and mobilising people in pursuit of a better future.

Matt Church

'Zone' has two meanings in an educational context; the one is straightforward and physical and the other more elusive as a psychological concept.

To deal with the second meaning first, 'being in the 'zone' whether as a school leader, teacher or learner, refers to a psychological frame of mind. To grow and evolve we need to be constantly experimenting and pushing ourselves. The psychologist, Vygotsky, first gave this idea a name: 'the zone of proximal development'. By this he meant the gap between what we can do without help and what we can action with help. It is closely related to formative assessment and is the zone at the edge of our confidence, where we need to find out more about what we are capable of. Sometimes schools refer to 'success zones' where people within the school have taken powerful steps to grow themselves and lead others. Learners may refer to themselves as being in the 'zone' which means that they are in a state of deep engagement with authentic and focused attention.

A
B
C
D
E
F
G
H
I
J
K
L
M
N
O
P
Q
R
S
T
U
V
W
X
Y
Z

The second meaning is more prosaic. There are often references to 'action zones', as in the government initiative of a decade ago which designated parts of the country as particular 'education action zones' in order to drive up achievement. In a school, the term 'action zone' signifies a priority of attention to a particular set of actions or to improving a particular area of the school's provision.

Z is for Zenith

 The path to school improvement is always under construction.
David Woods

Zenith is defined in the dictionaries as 'the greatest height' or the 'culminating point'. Even though it shouldn't come last alphabetically this is an appropriate place to finish the book as we believe everyone can improve on their previous best performance and achieve the greatest success by drawing upon the strategies outlined in previous entries. It is also appropriate because schools often use the metaphor of climbing a mountain to describe their journey of school improvement. For some, the first step is to establish a secure base camp as the foundation for success. For others, it is beginning the ascent, climbing steadily and establishing further camps. There are also some who are approaching the summit but realize that this is elusive because once they claim to have conquered this the next steps are downhill. We are better to travel as pilgrims, like John Winthrop – Bunyan's famous character – with our eyes firmly fixed on the 'Shining City upon the Hill' – the zenith of all our endeavours.

 If you do not raise your eyes you will think that you are at the highest point.
Antonio Porchia

A
B
C
D
E
F
G
H
I
J
K
L
M
N
O
P
Q
R
S
T
U
V
W
X
Y
Z

Never doubt that a small group of thoughtful, committed people can change the world. Indeed, it is the only thing that ever has.

Margaret Mead

The world has moved along, not only by the mighty shoves of its heroes, but also by the aggregation of the tiny pushes of each honest worker.

Helen Keller

REFERENCES AND SELECTED BIBLIOGRAPHY

Abbot, J. (1994) *Learning Makes Sense – Recreating Education for a Changing Future*, Letchworth: Education 2000.

Ayers, W. (1993) *To Teach: The Journey of a Teacher*, New York and London: Teacher's College Press.

Barber, M. and Mourshed, M. (2007) 'How the World's Best Performing Systems Come Out on Top', Mckinsey and Company.

Barber, M., Chijoke, C. and Mourshed, M. (2010) 'How the World's Most Important Improved School Systems Keep Getting Better', Mckinsey and Company.

Barber, M. (1996) *The Learning Game: Arguments for an Education Revolution*, London: Weidenfeld & Nicholson.

Barber, M., Donnelly, K. and Rivzi, S. (2012) 'Oceans of Innovation', IPPR.

Barth, R. S. (1990) *Improving Schools from Within*, San Francisco: CA.Jossey-Bass.

Bastiani, J. (2003) *Involving Parents, Raising Achievement*, Nottingham: DfES Publications.

Beadle, P. (2010) *How to Teach*, Carmarthen: Crown House Publishing.

Bentley, T. (1998) *Learning Beyond the Classroom*, Abingdon: Routledge.

Berwick, G. (2010) *Engaging in Excellence:* Vols 1 and 2, Bromley: Olevi.

Black, P. (2003) *Assessment for Learning: Putting it into Practice*, Oxford: OUP.

Black, P. and Wiliam, D. (1996) *Inside the Black Box: Raising Standards Through Classroom Assessment*, London: NFER-Nelson.

Black, P. and Wiliam D. (2002) *Working Inside the Black Box: Assessment for Learning in the Classroom*, London: NFER-Nelson.

Boaler, J. (2009), *The Elephant in the Classroom: Helping Children Learn and Love Maths*, London: Souvenir Press Ltd.

Branden, N. (2007) *The Six Pillars of Self-Esteem*, London: Random House.

Brighouse, T. (1991) *What Makes a Good School?* Stafford: Network Continuum.

Brighouse, T. (2006) *Essential Pieces: The Jigsaw of a Successful School*, Abingdon: Research Machines Publications.

Brighouse, T. (2007) *How Successful Headteachers Survive and Thrive*, Abingdon: Research Machines Publications.

Brighouse, T. and Davies, B. (Eds) (2008) *Passionate Leadership in Education*, London: Sage.

Brighouse, T. and Fullisk, L. (2007) *Education in a Global City – Essays from London.* London: Institute of Education, University of London.

Brighouse, T. and Woods, D. (2005) *Butterflies for School Improvement*, Nottingham: DfES Publications, (London Challenge).

Brighouse, T. and Woods, D. (1999) *How to Improve Your School*, London: Routledge.

Brighouse, T. and Woods, D. (2006) *Inspirations – A Collection of Commentaries to Promote School Improvement*, London: Continuum.

Brighouse, T. and Woods, D. (1997) *School Improvement Butterflies* Birmingham: Questions Publications.

Brighouse, T. and Woods, D. (2008) *What Makes a Good School Now?* London: Continuum.

Bubb, S. (2005) *Helping Teachers Develop*, London: Sage.

Bubb, S. and Earley, P. (2010), *Helping Staff Develop in Schools*, London: Sage.

Bubb, S. and Earley, P. (2007), *Leading and Managing Continuous Professional Development*, 2nd ed, London: Paul Chapman.

Buck, A. (2007) *Making Schools Work*, London: Greenwich Exchange.

Buck, A. (2008) *What Makes a Great School?* London: London Leadership Strategy and National College.

Burke, C. and Grosvenor, I. (2003) *The School I'd Like*, New York: RoutledgeFalmer.

Cain, S. (2012) *Quiet, The Power of Introverts*, London: Viking.

Chapman, C., Armstrong, P., Harris, A., Muijs D., Reynolds, D., and Sammons, P. (Eds) (2012) *School Effectiveness and Improvement Research Policy and Practice – Challenging the Orthodoxy*, London: Routledge

Claxton, G. (2002) *Building Learning Power: Helping Young People Become Better Learners*, Bristol: T.L.O. Ltd.

Claxton, G. and Lucas, B. (2010) *New Kinds of Smart*, Maidenhead: Open University Press.

Clegg, A. (1980) *About our Schools*, Oxford: Blackwell.

Coates, M. (Ed) (2010) *Shaping a New Education Landscape*, London: Continuum.

Collins, J. (2001) *Good to Great*, London: Random House.

Covey, S. (2006) *The Speed of Trust*, London: Simon and Schuster.

Cox, E. Bachkirova, T. and Clutterbuck, D. A. (2010) *The Complete Handbook of Coaching*, London: Sage.

DCSF, (2009) 'Breaking the Link between Disadvantage and Low Attainment, Everyone's Business', Nottingham: DCSF Publication.

DCSF, (2008) 'The Extra Mile: How Schools Succeed in Raising Aspirations in Deprived Communities', Nottingham: DCSF Publication.

DCSF, (2008) 'The Impact on Parental Involvement on Children's Education' Nottingham: DCSF Publication.

DCSF, (2008) 'Vision for London, 2008-2011', Nottingham: DCSF Publication.

Desforges, C. with Abouchaar, A. (2003) 'The Impact of Parental Involvement, Parental Support and Family Education on Pupil Achievement and Adjustment: A literature review', DfES Research Report 433.

DfE (2012) 'Teachers' Standards', DfE Publication.

DfE (2010) 'The Importance of Teaching- The Schools White Paper' Norwich: TSO.

DfES (2006) '2020 Vision: Report of the Teaching and Learning Review Group', Nottingham: DfES Publication.

DfES (2006) 'Making Good Progress: How can we help every pupil to make good progress at school?', Nottingham: DfES Publication.

DfES (2007) 'Making Great Progress, Schools with Outstanding Rates of Progression in Key Stage 2', Nottingham: DfES Publication.

DfES (2005) 'Learning Behaviour: Report of the Practitioner's Group on School Behaviour and Discipline', Nottingham: DfES Publication.

DfES (2004) 'Putting the World into World-Class Education', Nottingham: DfES Publication.

Dudley, P. (2011) *Lesson Study: a handbook*, www.lessonstudy.co.uk.

Dweck, C. (2006) *Mindset, The New Psychology of Success*, London: Random House.

Earley, P. and Porritt, V. (Eds) (2009) *Effective Practices in Continuous Professional Development: Lessons from Schools*, London: Institute of Education, University of London.

Eliot, A. (2007) *State Schools Since the 1950s: The Good News*, Stoke-on-Trent: Trentham Books.

Emery, H. (2011) 'A Strategy for Pedagogical Development', DfE publication.

Eurydice (2011), 'Mathematics education in Europe: Common challenges and national policies', Brussels: Education, Audiovisual and Culture Executive Agency.

Fisher, K. OECD, (2005) 'Research into Identifying Effective Learning Environments', Paris: OECD.

Fried, R. L. (1995) *The Passionate Teacher*, Boston: Beacon Press.

Fullan, M. (2010) *All Systems Go*, California: Corwin Press and Sage.

Fullan, M. (2003) *Change Forces with a Vengeance*, London: RoutledgeFalmer.

Fullan, M. (2005) *Leadership and Sustainability*, London: Sage.

Fullan, M. (2001) *Leading in a Culture of Change*, San Francisco: Jossey-Bass.

Fullan, M. (2004) *The Moral Imperative of School Leadership*, London: Sage.

Fullan, M. (1991) *The New Meaning of Educational Change*, London: Cassell.

Fullan, M. (2008) *The Six Secrets of Change*, San Francisco: Jossey-Bass.

Gann, N. (1998) *Improving School Governance*, Abingdon: RoutledgeFalmer.

Gardner, H. (1995) *Leading Minds: Anatomy of Leadership*, New York: Basic Books.

Gardner, H. (2006) *The Education and Development of the Mind – Selected Works*, Abingdon: Routledge.

Gardner, H. (1991) *The Unschooled Mind: How Children Think and How Schools Should Teach*, New York: Basic Books.

Gilbert, I. (2002) *Essential Motivation in the Classroom*, Abingdon: Routledge.

Gladwell, M. (2005) *Blink: The Power of Thinking Without Thinking*, London: Allen Lane.

Gladwell, M. (2008) *Outliers: The Story of Success*, London: Allen Lane.

Gladwell, M. (2000) *The Tipping Point: How Little Things Can Make a Difference*, London: Little Brown.

Gleeson, D. and Husbands, C. (2001) *The Performing School*, New York: RoutledgeFalmer.

Goffee, R. and Jones, G. (2006) *Why Should Anybody Be Led by You?* Boston: Harvard Business Review Press.

Goleman, D. (1996) *Emotional Intelligence*, London: Bloomsbury.

Goleman, D. (2002) *The New Leaders: Transforming the Art of School Leadership*, London: Sphere.

Gray, S. P. and Streshley, W.A. (Eds), (2008) *From Good Schools to Great Schools*, Caliornia: Corwin Press.

Grey, D. (2005) *Grey's Essential Miscellany for Teachers*, London: Continuum.

Green, H. and Hannon, C. (2007) *Their Space: Education for the Digital Divide*, London: Demos.

Handy, C. B. (1994) *The Empty Raincoat: Making Sense of the Future*, London: Hutchinson.

Handy, C. B. (1997) *The Hungry Spirit*, London: Hutchinson.

Hargreaves, A. and Dennis, S. (2009) *The Fourth Way*, California: Corwin Press.

Hargreaves, A. and Fink, D. (2006), *Sustainable Leadership*, San Francisco: Jossey Bass.

Hargreaves, A. and Fullan, M. (1998) *What's Worth Fighting for in Education?* Maidenhead: Open University Press/McGraw-Hill.

Hargreaves, A. and Fullan, M. (1992) *What's Worth Fighting For in Your School?* Maidenhead: Open University Press/McGraw-Hill.

Hargreaves, D. H. (2006) 'A New Shape for Schooling?', London: SSAT.

Hargreaves, D. H. (2010) 'Creating a Self-Improving School System', Nottingham: NCSL: Nottingham.

Hargreaves, D. H. (1998) *Creative Professionalsim*, London: Demos.

Hargreaves, D. H. (2005) 'Personalised Learning', 4 and 5, London: SSAT.

Hargreaves, D. H. (2003) 'Working Laterally: How Innovation Networks Make an Education Epidemic', Nottingham: DfES Publication.

Hargreaves, D. H. and Hopkins, D. (1991) *The Empowered School*, London: Cassell.

Harris, A. (2008) *Distributed School Leadership*, Abingdon: Routledge.

Hart, S., Dixon, A., Drummond, A. J. and McIntyre, D. (2004) *Learning without Limits*, Maidenhead: Open University Press/McGraw-Hill.

Hattie, J. (2008) *Visible Learning: A Synthesis of Over 800 Meta-analyses Relating to Achievement*, Abingdon: Routledge.

Hattie, J. (2011) *Visible Learning for Teachers*, Abingdon Routledge.

Higham, R., Hopkins, D. and Matthews, P. (2009) *System Leadership in Practice*, Oxford: OUP.

Hill, R. (2008) *Achieving More Together – Adding Value Through Partnership*, Leicester: ASCL/RM Publications.

Hill, R. (2011) 'The Importance of Teaching and the Role of System Leadership', Nottingham: NCSL.

Hill, R. and Matthews, P. (2010) *Schools Leading Schools II – The Growing Impact of National Leaders of Education*, Nottingham: NCSL.

Hopkins, D. (2007) *Every School a Great School*, Maidenhead: Open University Press.

Hopkins, D. (2001) *School Improvement for Real*, Abingdon: RoutledgeFalmer.

Hopkins, D., Reynolds, D. and Gray, J. (2005) *School Improvement –Lessons from research, Nottingham:* DfES Publication.

Hutchings, M., Greenwood, C., Hollingsworth, S., Rose, A., with Minty, S. and Glass, K. (2012) 'Evaluation of the City Challenge Programme', DfE report, London: London Metropolitan University.

Jonson, B. (2003) *Ten Thoughts About Time: A philosophical enquiry*, London: Constable.

Joyce, B., Calhoun, E. and Hopkins, D. (1999) *The New Structure of School Improvement*, Maidenhead: Open University Press.

Kao, J. J. (1996) *Jamming: The Art and Discipline of Business Creativity*, London: Harper Collins.

Leadbeater, C. (2005) 'The Shape of Things to Come', Nottingham: DfE Publications.

Levin, B. (2009) *How to Change 5000 Schools*, Boston: Harvard Educational Press.

Little, J. W. (1981) 'The Power of Organisational Settings', Washington, DC:

National Institute of Education.

Lucas, B. (2009) *Evolution: How to Thrive in Crazy Times*, Carmarthen: Crown House Publishing.

MacBeath, J. (1999) *Schools Must Speak for Themselves*, London: Routledge.

MacGilchrist, B., Myers K. and Reed, J. (2004) *The Intelligent School* (2ⁿᵈ Edn), London: Sage.

Maden, M. (ed.) (2001) *Success against the Odds, Five Years On*, New York: RoutledgeFalmer,.

Maden, M. and Hillman, J. (Eds.), (1996) *Success against the Odds*, Paul Hamlyn Foundation, London: Routledge.

Macfarlane, R and Woods, D.C (2011) (Eds.) *Glimpses of Greatness*, London: London Leadership Strategy and National College

Macfarlane, R. and Woods, D. C. (Eds.), (2010) *Going for Great*, London: Leadership Strategy and National College.

Macfarlane, R and Woods, D.C (Eds.), (2012) *Growing Greatness*, London: London Leadership Strategy and National College.

Matthews, P. (2009) 'How do School Leaders Successfully Lead Learning?' Nottingham: NCSL.

McCourt, F. (2005) *Teacher Man*, London: Fourth Estate.

Moore, A. (2012) *Teaching and Learning – Pedagogy, Curriculum and Culture*, Abingdon: Routledge.

Mortimore, P., Sammons, P., Stoll, L., Lewis, D. and Ecob, R. (1998) *School Matters*, Berkeley, CA: University of California Press.

NCSL (2010) 'Executive Heads', Nottingham: NCSL.

NCSL (2007) 'Leadership Succession: An Overview', Nottingham: NCSL.

NCSL (2008) 'Review of the Landscape: Leadership and Leadership Development', Nottingham: NCSL.

NCSL (2009) 'School Leadership Today', Nottingham: NCSL.

OfSTED (2009) 'Barriers to Literacy', London: OfSTED.

OfSTED (2006) 'Best Practice in Self-Evaluation', London: OfSTED.

OfSTED (2011) 'Excellence in English: What we can learn from 12 outstanding schools', London: OfSTED.

OfSTED HMCI Annual reports 2009-2010, 2010-2011, 2011-2012, London: OfSTED.

OfSTED (2000) 'Improving City Schools', London: OfSTED.

OfSTED (2010) 'London Challenge Report', London: OfSTED.

OfSTED (2012) 'Moving English Forward: Action to Raise Standards in English', London: OfSTED.

OfSTED (2007) 'Parents, Carers and Schools', London: OfSTED.

OfSTED (2005) 'Remodelling the School Workforce', London: OfSTED.

OfSTED (2011) 'School Governance', London: OfSTED.

OfSTED (2010) 'Twenty Outstanding Primary Schools – Excelling against the odds', London: OfSTED.

OfSTED (2009) 'Twelve Outstanding Secondary Schools – Excelling Against the Odds', London: OfSTED.

OfSTED (2010) 'Twelve Outstanding Special Schools – Excelling Through Inclusion', London: OfSTED.

O'Sullivan, H. and West-Burnham, J. (2011) *Leading and Managing Schools*, London: Sage.

Paul Hamlyn Foundation, (2012) 'Learning Futures', London: Paul Hamlyn Foundation and The innovation Unit.

Petty, G. (2009) *Teaching Today – A Practical Guide*, Cheltenham: Nelson Thornes.

PriceWaterHouseCoopers, (2007) *Independent Study into School Leadership*, DfES Publications, Nottingham

Riley, K. A. (1998) *Whose School is it Anyway?* London: Falmer Press.

Robinson, K. (2002) *Out of Our Minds: Learning to be Creative*, Oxford: Capstone.

Seligman, M. (2002), *Learned Optimism: How to Change Your Mind and Life*, USA: Vintage Books.

Senge, P. M. (1990) *The Fifth Discipline: The Art and Practice of the Learning Organisation*, New York: Doubleday.

Sennett, F. (2004) *400 Quotable Quotes from the World's Leading Educators*, California: Corwin Press.

Sergiovanni, T. J. (2001) *Leadership: What's in it for Schools?* London: RoutledgeFalmer.

Sergiovanni, T. (2005), *Strengthening the Heart-Beat*, San Francisco: Jossey Bass.

Silver, H. (1994) *Good Schools, Effective Schools*, London: Cassell.

Smith, A. (2011) *High Performers, The Secret of Successful Schools*, Carmarthen: Crown House Publishing.

Smith, D. and Benson, D. (2010-2012), Ark Academy Case Studies, London: Ark Academy.

Smith, J. (2000) *The Learning Game: A Teacher's Inspirational Story*, London: Little Brown.

Stoll, L., Fink., D and Earl, L. (2003) *It's About Learning (and It's About Time)*, London: RoutledgeFalmer.

Stoll, L. and Seashore, L. K. (2007) *Professional Learning Communities: divergence, depth and dilemmas*, Maidenhead: McGraw-Hill International.

Syed, M. (2010) *Bounce – The Myth of Talent and the Power of Practice*, London: Fourth Estate.

Taylor, C. and Ryan, C. (2005) *Excellence in Education The Making of Great Schools*, London: David Fulton.

Teach First (2010) 'Ethos and Culture in Schools in Challenging Circumstances', London: Teach First Publications.

Teach First (2007) 'Lessons from the Front', London: Teach First Publications.

Tunnadine, T. (2011) 'System Leadership Through Extended Leadership Roles', Nottingham: NCSL.

Van Maurik, J. (2001) *Writers on Leadership*, London: Penguin Business.

West-Burnham, J. and Coates, M. (2005) *Personalizing Learning: Transforming Education for Every Child*, Stafford: Network Educational Press.

West-Burnham, J. and O'Sullivan, H. (2011), *Leading and Managing Schools*, London: Sage.

Whelan, F. (2009) *Lesson Learned: How Good Policies Produce Better Schools*, Fenton Whelan.

White, R. C. (2000) *The School of Tomorrow*, Maidenhead: Open University Press.

Woods, D. C. and Cribb, M. (Eds) (2001) *Effective LEAs and School Improvement*, London: RoutledgeFalmer.

Woods, D. C. and John, S. (2010) 'Lessons Learned from London', London: London Leadership Strategy and National College.

Woods, P. (1993) *Critical Events in Teaching and Learning*, Abingdon: RoutledgeFalmer.

Wragg, E. C. (2005) *The Art and Science of Teaching and Learning: The Selected Works of Ted Wragg*, London: Routledge.

INDEX